This book is dedicated to my family and the families I met in the field, for all their support, encouragement, and willingness to be engaged by the questions of an anthropologist.

Where Are You From?

Where Are You From?

Middle-Class Migrants in the Modern World

Dhooleka S. Raj

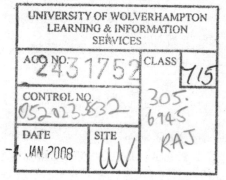

UNIVERSITY OF CALIFORNIA PRESS

Berkeley / Los Angeles / London

The first epigraph on p. vii is taken from Carol Greenhouse and Davyyd Greenwood, Introduction to *Democracy and Ethnography*. Albany, N.Y.: University of New York Press, 1998.

The second epigraph on p. vii is taken from Homi Bhabha, *Nation and Narration*. London: Routledge, 1990.

The third epigraph on p. vii is taken from Terry Eagleton, *The Idea of Culture*. Oxford: Blackwell, 2000.

University of California Press
Berkeley and Los Angeles, California

University of California Press, Ltd.
London, England

© 2003 by the Regents of the University of California

Library of Congress Cataloging-in-Publication Data

Raj, Dhooleka Sarhadi, 1969–.
     Where are you from? : Middle-class migrants in the modern world / Dhooleka S. Raj.

        p. cm.

    Includes bibliographical references and index.

        ISBN 0–520–23382–4 (acid-free paper) — ISBN 0–520–23383–2 (pbk. : acid-free paper)

        1. Punjabis (South Asian people)—England—London. 2. South Asia—Emigration and immigration. 3. London (England)—Ethnic relations. 4. South Asians—England—London. 5. Middle class—England—London. 6. Immigrants—England—London.
        7. Hindus—England—London. I. Title.

DA676.9.S6 R34   2002

305.6'9450421—dc21   2002009721

Manufactured in the United States of America
12   11   10   09   08   07   06   05   04   03
10   9   8   7   6   5   4   3   2   1

The paper used in this publication is both acid-free and totally chlorine-free (TCF). It meets the minimum requirements of ANSI / NISO Z39.48–1992 (R 1997) (*Permanence of Paper*).⊖

Identity, difference, and culture are always heavily charged with histories of asymmetrical power relations, aspirations, and vulnerabilities.

Carol Greenhouse and Davydd Greenwood,
Democracy and Ethnography

The colonial presence is always ambivalent, split between its appearance as original and authoritative and its articulation as repetition and difference.

Homi Bhabha, Nation and Narration

It becomes difficult to say whether we are living in a world in which everything is dramatically different or increasingly identical.

Terry Eagleton, The Idea of Culture

Contents

Acknowledgments

The friendships formed with the families I studied have surpassed the research scope of the fieldwork phase. My husband and I are happy to now include many of them in our transnational connections. I have learned from them more about the ups and downs of life and have enjoyed their friendship beyond what I can even attempt to represent with these words. My life course began to resonate with the families I studied. Like many of the migrants when they first established themselves in Britain, I was newly married and adapting to a new life stage, social role, and society. Of course, my migration came at a very different historical time and under a different context. Nevertheless, I shared with the parental generation the experience of dislocation and movement. Like many people who were at first unsure how long they were going to be in Britain, I had moved there only "temporarily" to get an education. I ended up living in Britain for almost seven years. With the children, I shared the sense of being a child of a migrant and growing up as a minority. The many points of familiarity with my own experiences, as well as the differences, helped me to think about the links between us in a way that moved beyond thinking about what constitutes ethnic group identity. I came to see the differences and variations of the global South Asian ethnic experience. I thank the families for their support and interest in this work.

The fieldwork project and research relied on material support as well. I would like to appreciatively acknowledge the support at various points in this project from the Overseas Research Student Award (CVCP,

London); the Cambridge Commonwealth Trust (University of Cambridge); the Sir James Lougheed Award of Distinction (Canada); the Social Sciences & Humanities Research Council Doctoral Fellowship (Canada); the IODE War Memorial Doctoral Scholarship Award (Canada); the Richards Fund (Department of Social Anthropology, University of Cambridge); the Lord Frederick Cavendish Studentship (Lucy Cavendish College, University of Cambridge); the Smuts Memorial Fund (University of Cambridge); the Sutasoma Trust Hardship Fund (the Sutasoma Charitable Trust, Cambridge); and the George Bidder Grant (Lucy Cavendish College, Cambridge). These various bodies allowed me to pursue my lifelong dream of getting a Ph.D., funded the research project and allowed me to travel to present my work at various conferences and forums. All of this was crucial to produce the first draft of this book. For the space, time, and sanctity to rework my early material as well as assistance in beginning a new research project that grew out of this work — to addresses the lives of Hindu Punjabis in India — I want to thank The Managers of The Smuts Fund and the Center of South Asian Studies for awarding me the Smuts Hinduja Fellowship, University of Cambridge, the Social Sciences and Humanities Research Council of Canada, and Lucy Cavendish College. I am grateful to Harvard University's Radcliffe Institute for Advanced Study for the fellowship and room of my own, which allowed me to put the finishing touches on the manuscript.

Although it is a solitary pursuit, writing is seldom a solitary project. In the process of becoming an anthropologist I have incurred many intellectual debts as well as developed wonderful friendships, all of which have helped to shape my project of thinking creatively about ethnic identity in the modern world. I thank the two Press reviewers for their helpful comments. I would like to thank Naomi Schneider of University of California Press for her unfailing support, suggestions, and for an all-around good-natured and timely engagement with my work as I wrote from Japan, England, and the United States. From the early stages of this project, various people have facilitated bringing it to fruition by reading parts of the manuscript; engaging in lively discussions; helping to complete the necessary research tasks, such as photocopying, archiving, and computer support; as well as providing useful advice. My sincere thanks go to Anna Abulafia, Alan Macfarlane, Arjun Appadurai, Marcus Banks, Roger Ballard, Jennifer Banner, Chris Bayly, Susan Bayly, Amy Ciliberto, Leslie Cintron, Samantha Chan, Kathleen Coll, Joyce Davis, Jeevan Deol, Annabelle Dixon, John Eade, James Ferguson, Ilana Gershon, Ester

Goody, Kevin Greenbank, Louise Houghton, Caroline Humphery, Craig Jamieson, Gordon Johnson, James Laidlaw, Purnima Mankekar, Valentina Napolitana, Norbert Peabody, Pauline Perry, Ato Quayson, Anita Robboy, Margaret Rodman, Andrea Stockl, Marilyn Strathern, Francesca Sawaya, Veronica Schild, Lok Siu, Anne Sudbay, the South Asian Studies Research Forum (United Kingdom), Alissa Trotz, Steven Vertovec, Helen Watson, Pnina Werbner, and Laura Wright. I gratefully acknowledge permission from Lord Swarj Paul and the Honorable Dr. L. M. Singhvi to quote them here. Thank you to Nandini Goud for granting permission to reproduce her work as the cover image; sincere appreciation to Dinesh Vizarani and Yamini Telkar of Saffronart.com and to Anupam Munsiff for assistance in securing permission.

In particular I would like to thank my supervisors over the years who worked most closely with me and helped give me a strong sense of anthropology and critical inquiry: Roderick Wilson at the University of Alberta; Malcolm Blincow at York University; and Susan Benson and Susan Bayly at the University of Cambridge. My dream of becoming a scholar was fueled by their constructive and critical engagement with my work and their kind words of encouragement.

My training in anthropology began long before my official enrollment in anthropology courses. My mother's insistence on an openness to all people and her strong spiritual beliefs, which included an openness to all forms of religious worship, and her horror at the violence that transpires in the name of religion gave me a sense of how differences between people were a matter of changing perspectives. My father's critical admonitions and observations of people's prejudices, his gentle but firm commitment to humanism, as well as his need to travel constantly and to engage openly with the world at large, shaped my own ideas about culture, community, and identity. My brother's experiences and experimentations with difference — through his skateboarding phase, in conversations with our grandparents, and his companionship — provided me with a lived sense of how difference could be variously articulated. The Kahlon, Kapur, and Seth families' perspectives have also shaped my own thinking about cultural difference in many ways. These foundations were strengthened when I was first married. My husband's family claimed the global in ways that I had never experienced — as part of their work for the Indian Foreign Service — and yet they steadfastly claimed India. My late mother-in-law, whose passing because of cancer was a deeply personal loss, was often a source of inspiration for me, especially in her openness and curiosity about all people. In our conversations she was always ready to challenge and help me clarify my ideas of Punjabi identity. She was also astute in her comments when she visited us in England and spoke to "my informants." I dedicate Chapter 7, "Being British, Becoming a Person of Indian Origin," to her memory. While getting to know the rest of my husband's family, I have learned a lot about their experiences with culture and difference in the United States and India. Vijay, Anil, and Arun, and families, I thank you all for your encouragement.

When I was just beginning this project I met my husband in the United Kingdom. From that moment forward, he has proven to be a source of inspiration, as well as unfailingly engaged with my work on culture, ethnicity, and identity. We share a curiosity for the world and an intense wanderlust, which has taken us to live in Tokyo, Sydney, London, and Washington, D.C., and to visit Western Europe, Asia, South East Asia, and Canada. A global nomad since he was an infant, he has told me that he and his friends at school were known as "fourth-culture kids." His playful response to the question "Where are you from?" continues to amuse and delight me — when we were in Japan he would reply: "I am an American; I was born in Turkey, grew up in the U.S., Uganda, and Russia, was schooled in the foothills of the Himalayas, am married to a Canadian, work for a British company, live in Tokyo." For all those complications and clarifications, this book is a testament to his steadfast support to help me see this project to completion.

Preface

Every summer, from the time I was four until I was about sixteen years old, I dressed, danced, dined, and fashioned ethnicity, quite literally, on stage. Among other performances, my friends and I participated in Heritage Days, one of the largest outdoor festivals in the world. It is held the first weekend in August, back home in Edmonton, Western Canada. Heritage Days was a family event. In its very early days, my father was Master of Ceremonics on stage for the India pavilion, and my mother helped backstage. At various points, friends and family helped bring together the India pavilion.

A few years after I had last been on stage, I was a research assistant at the University of Alberta, Department of Anthropology. The project we worked on looked at ethnicity, and I accompanied the professor to meet Horst Schmidt, whose brain child was Heritage Days. He told us that he was suspicious of multiculturalism's connotations and proposed instead something that everyone could relate to, so that everyone could be proud of contributing to Canada. His work helped to achieve a specific sense of multiculturalism, one that emphasized commonalities in difference that made a strong nation. Only later did I realize that this official holiday with a very specific meaning of multicultural and heritage happened only in Alberta, Canada. Heritage Days — I had no idea just how local this sense of the global was.

Heritage Days, as staged in Alberta, includes everyone. It is an overt celebration of heritage. Of course, it was 3-D multiculturalism: Dining, Dancing, and Dressing. During it all, the forth "D" of multiculturalism —

Difference — was ironically ubiquitous and yet somehow unmarked, because of the stress on the nation-state. The English served tea and scones; the Welsh had the town with the longest name in front of their pavilion. At the Scottish stall, one could eat haggis, and the Irish put on an amazing pre-Riverdance performance. Italy served great food; Poland and Ukraine had more good food and dance; Pakistan served chicken curry and rice; and Greece and Germany . . . well, you get the picture. The French and the native Canadians also had stalls. The fair included representation of all people who lived in Western Canada, and everyone made their heritage public. I don't want to give the impression that there were no scuffles or politics, but once every year, people got together in Hawerlak Park, the large expanse of river valley green near downtown Edmonton, to celebrate what they brought to the Canadian nation. They do so to this day.

It was only after I left home for graduate school, first in Toronto and then in England, that I realized how uniquely "difference" is experienced in different places. I found that multiculturalism and heritage did not have the same resonance as they had when and where I grew up. My anthropological training gave me certain tools to decipher the complexities of everyday lives: culture, ethnicity, community, difference, the nation-state. At the University of Alberta, I acquired a base in cultural anthropology to think about culture and its organizing principles. York University expanded this and challenged me to think critically about the modalities of culture, identity, and ethnicity, particularly with the tensions between using a material and symbolic lens. During my doctoral training, I took these issues farther while exploring their intricacies through sustained fieldwork and dialogue with those who offered their own perspectives based on their own work on race and ethnicity, political anthropology, and South Asia.

In Toronto I learned that multiculturalism was a gloss for various non-white issues, and in England this was much the same, but the United Kingdom had its own specific history of racial violence and colonial legacies. In my travels and while living in Sydney, Delhi, and Tokyo, I became fascinated with the various ways that my own difference was marked and how others broached their cultural curiosity with or awareness of me. At times difference is marked in a way that is overtly offensive, like when people ask, "Do you speak English?" Other times, people forgive cultural faux pas and differences because "the foreigner," " the gaijin," or "the firengi" is assumed not to know. At other times difference is not clear-cut and people "pass." I have been mistaken for an Italian and a

Greek. During the Gulf War and post-September 11 various people have wondered aloud if I was from the Middle East, and they have asked, "Are you Muslim?" On November 4, 2000, at the Kennedy Center in Washington, D.C., a woman seated beside me spontaneously started speaking to me in Spanish, as a few had done before. This type of "passing" was short-lived, particularly since I cannot speak Spanish and didn't have any of the other referents. This book is a personal, political, and anthropological engagement to understand how people differently construct ethnicity, identity, difference, and belonging.

CHAPTER I

Questions of Ethnicity

In 1985, at the height of Margaret Thatcher's reign in the United Kingdom, Norman Tebbitt, a conservative member of Parliament, publicly queried South Asian loyalty to the British nation, because these minorities did not cheer for the English teams in international cricket games against India and Pakistan.[1] The infamous "cricket test" of allegiance for South Asians continues to have social and political significance. In May 2001, the headlines again questioned why Asians were not supporting England in cricket. There was, however, a twist. Two major British newspapers, *The Guardian* and *The Observer,* quoted England's cricket-team captain, Nasser Hussain, who had publicly stated, "I really cannot understand why those born here, or who came here at a very young age like me, cannot support or follow England."[2] Public rallying cries such as these serve as a broader political commentary on the seeming incapacity and unwillingness of Asian minorities to become loyal to Britain.[3] Tebbitt's and Hussain's question of belonging presumes that South Asian cultural integration to British society can be measured and assessed in a specific manner and that Asian minorities arrived in Britain with preformed allegiances to a South Asian homeland that passes through the generations.

In essence, Tebitt and Hussain were implicitly posing the question "When will you belong?" During fieldwork with middle-class Hindu Punjabi families in London, England, I learned that this question and a second, more explicit question of ethnicity — "Where are you from?" — are perpetually asked of migrants and their children.[4] These quintessential questions of identity are one way to invite a conversation about self and other. Asking "Where are you from?" can be a friendly gesture to learn more about and get to know a person. It certainly seems to have become socially acceptable and can be heard in everyday conversations, especially when people first meet. But this seemingly innocent question can also be experienced as a disruption. It is a question of ethnicity and difference, especially when the identity connections between people and places are destabilized, become problematic, or are entirely undone.[5] What happens when people move? Or their ancestors moved? For those who migrate, move, or are born after the fact of movement, whether the children of refugees, migrants, diplomats, military, or expatriates, the question can be insidious and problematic.[6] The unstated assumption behind the question is that one is a sojourner; one is not from here, or can only claim to be here temporarily. The words of one young Hindu Punjabi man demonstrate the derogatory connotations of this question. He stated, "I go back to India, and I'm a stranger, and I accept that. But I'm still a stranger here too."[7] These words provide insight into how South Asian minorities in Britain experience alterity in both locations they could potentially claim. In other words, when my interlocutors are asked this question in Britain, they are expected to reply, "India"; on the other hand, when asked the same question in India, they reply, "Britain."

In asking and responding to questions of ethnicity such as "Where are you from?" and "When will you belong?" people share their understandings of culture and difference. These two queries reveal that people are trapped in a conceptual straightjacket when thinking about ethnic minorities, such as London's Hindu Punjabis. Three issues dominate: first, there is a general sense that the migrants bring *a* culture from *an Indian* homeland; second, their ethnic culture is a transitory phenomenon; and third, the minorities will acculturate and assimilate. Each assumption hinges on a specific understanding of culture that can be exchanged with community, ethnicity, and, implicitly, nationhood. The eclipse of the inherent negotiations and contestations renders ethnic identity a tidy cultural package, a template, with certain sets of meanings, behaviors, beliefs, and boundaries — some are "marked" precisely because they highlight the boundary and others remain "unmarked" (Appadurai 1996). Multicultural nation-states, scholars, and even ethnic individuals circulate this nostalgic sense of culture that creates a perception, ubiquitous in ethnic identity politics, whereby the ethnic individual is permanently, albeit complexly, tied to a point of origin. The underlying assumption is that ethnic minority cultures simultaneously stay the same *and* experience intense changes. As a result, the everyday forms of difference experienced by minorities are increasingly culturalized, establishing a general nostalgia for culture.[8]

Asian minorities have also culturalized their difference and assume imagined autochthonous Indian and British cultures. Parents would share with me their concerns about their children's language skills in Punjabi or Hindi, their sense of changing religious identity, or pride in their child's grasp of Hinduism. At other times, they would be anxious about the marriages of their children. The children also held specific understandings of culture as related to community, ethnicity, and identity. For instance, Deepak, a young man who migrated to Britain from India when he was three years old, asked me, "Where are you from?" We had just sat down to do an interview, and the question was asked at the moment when we had little information about each other. I was unsure how to reply; there are moments in the field when it is difficult to know exactly what is being asked, or what is likely to be answered. When I sought clarification, Deepak elaborated, "Oh I was just trying to figure out if you are Punjabi or Gujarati." Deepak's friendly way of framing ethnicity was intended to elicit a sense of premigration group identity. Thus, I learned one of the ways in which ethnic minorities are often bound up in the closures involved in producing the nostalgia of culture.

The equation of culture, identity, community, and ethnicity circumscribes the ways people can think about diversity into "homogenous heterogeneity" (Gershon 2001). The following statements capture this nicely and show two ways people are thinking about and experiencing diversity in modern Britain: "I want to see the word 'Asian' dropped out; we need to be British," said Lord Swraj Paul during a Network East BBC2 interview after being granted life peerage in the House of Lords in the United Kingdom.[9] Robin Cook, British Foreign Secretary, in a widely-quoted speech to the Social Market Foundation, observed, "Chicken tikka masala is now Britain's true national dish, not only because it is the most popular but because it is a perfect illustration of the way Britain absorbs and adapts external influences. Tikka is an Indian dish. The masala sauce was added to satisfy the desire of the British people to have their meat served with gravy" (April 19, 2001; quoted in *The Guardian*). Both statements are friendly gestures across the putative cultural divides created by migrations. Thus, Lord Paul's declaration is more than a play on words, it is also a power play, which highlights the contextual construction of identity and alterity for migrant communities. In explicitly dismissing "Asian," he attempts to exchange terms of ethnic group identity for national belong-ing.[10] Lord Paul's quote is one instance of a *central* rupture in "the guerilla warfare of the interstices" (Lavie and Swedenburg 1996: 13).[11] Lord Paul claims a British identity, challenges an automatic assumption of Asian iden-tity, and rejects a hyphenated identity.[12] In contrast, the Foreign Secretary's statement is about a changing sense of Britain and a different type of power play: it invokes interstices and multiculturalism (later in the speech quite explicitly). Cook's words reveal another aspect of the "guerilla warfare" — that regarding who has the power to define the terms of ethnicity and who will be absorbed and need to adapt. This way of thinking about diversity relies on a changed sense of what it means to be British; however, ethnic-ity is fetishized anew, as a desire controlled by the British. Juxtaposing Lord Paul's quote with that of the British Foreign Secretary exposes how ethnic and national identities are conceived of as being exchanged, as choices and products. Lord Paul's and the Foreign Secretary's reflections on diversity are premised on distinct ideas of the self and the other.[13]

Reading difference as a "contingent relationship," the two quotations are crucial commentary on British diversity. "'Difference,' however, is not intrinsically oppositional but insistently plural; 'difference' affirms a con-tingent relationship rather than a bounded set of characteristics." In each statement, difference is taken to be "a matter of individuals' a priori mem-bership in collective groups . . . [and there are grave] inadequacies of such automatic, a priori ethnicizings of difference" (Greenhouse and Greenwood 1998: 11, 13). The ways that the "a priori ethnicizing of difference" could play out in people's everyday lives was made clear to me early in my fieldwork. Manoj and I were walking through the streets of central London in search of a bank machine, and I was excited and sur-prised to see all the Canadian flags near Trafalgar Square. My friend said, "You really are Canadian. You see, I am not British, but you really are Canadian." I was struck by Manoj's inability to claim a British identity for himself — England was the country of his birth, the place where he had always lived. He was a British citizen and carried a British passport. And yet he pointed out to me the distinct ways we could, as children of migrants, differently experience identity and belonging. He was ruptur-ing the culture box. Somehow, when faced with my mild assertion of Canadian pride, he offered an insight into the implications of asking the question, "Where are you from?" In his view, while I was *from* Canada, he was not *from* Britain in the same way. In distinguishing the ways we belonged to our respective nation-states, he revealed the dangers involved in the automatic "ethnicizing" of difference.

My friend's observations on national identity, Lord Paul's attempt to eschew the Asian label, and Cook's observations on tikka masala are all statements about the power to define oneself in diversity. Each assumes a cultural divide that can be observed in how Asians can claim a British identity, or how Britain has absorbed and adapted minorities. With everything premised on the nostalgia for culture, it is difficult to work through the complexities of diversity. Diversity is created in social inter-actions between people and a nexus of power relationships. In debates of multiculturalism, group rights, and the role of the state, there is a focus on ethnic individuals' promotion of culture. Focusing on the ways diver-sity is a response to ethnic minorities highlights a culture clash between groups and elides the complex ways that culture and difference are lived in day-to-day life. Moreover, that focus eclipses the role of the state as it ignores how the law and other social institutions can actually help to cre-ate difference (Minow 1990; cf. Menski 1987; Poulter 1990). Identity pol-itics in Britain, and in other nations that espouse multiculturalism (in all its variant interpretations, see Harris 2001), are dictated by a mandate of accountability in which governments and other agencies reinforce and assume a notion of stable cultural identities.

Britain is not alone. Many other nation-states confront similar issues of how to imagine coexistence.[14] Social cohesion, tolerance, and diversity are all ways to conceive of difference in multicultural nation-states. The dilemma of difference is the "risk of recreating difference by either notic-ing it or ignoring it" (Minow 1990: 40). The nostalgia for culture re-cre-ates a perpetual trap in which the only possible model of diversity imag-inable is assimilation. Assimilation is assessed in two dominant measurements of cultural change premised on the nostalgia for culture — intergenerational culture clash and integration pressure. These reveal that the paradigm of diversity is based on a cultural adaptation of the ethnic minority. But, as Manoj's observations reveal, the Asian person is the one who needs to adapt, and yet, no matter what they do, they cannot claim to be British. This model of diversity perpetually re-creates the nostalgia for Indian and English cultures and establishes a fault line between them, which makes reconciliation impossible. The ethnic group is continually made into the "other" and a counterfoil to national identity that renders diversity a de facto problem for the nation-state.

My own nostalgia for culture was challenged early in my fieldwork. Manoj, the young man quoted above, who regularly asked me difficult questions about my work, inquired, "Why do you say 'Punjabi Hindu'?" My fieldwork had just begun and I could not give him a response. I asked him, "What do you prefer to call yourself?" He replied, "We are Hindu Punjabi." Later, I learned that British Asian youths used "HP" as a short-hand reference. "HP" is a striking term of identity. In the late nineteenth century the British census officials asked about Hindu identity in the Punjab (Ibbetson 1883) and marked the religious and geographical boundaries of identity. The same questions of identity and representation are asked in contemporary Britain. "HP" is a specific response that is a product of the British-born generation. This ascription is possible, because the slippage between "community," "culture," and "ethnicity" in nominal identities such as "Punjabi," "Hindu," "Asian," or "HP" is un-marked. Unless the various terms of identity are questioned, Punjab is rendered a faraway and exotic land, an essentially timeless land, important only insofar as it becomes an ethnic cultural adjective.

In identifying and calling for a counterpoint to the nostalgia for cul-ture, I take issue with the framework that equates culture cum ethnicity cum community for understanding Asian migrant families. By exploring the ways that Hindu Punjabi migrant parents and their British-born chil-dren *differently* create their ethnicity and experience being marginal, I challenge "the culture box" and the ways ethnic sociocultural group identity formation over time is taken to be a straightforward reproduction of "culture." I had complex choices of learning people's inscriptive and ascriptive identities. Identity has qualities that give it form, substance, and, most importantly, meaning in everyday life. People speak about themselves or others, or fill out government forms and job applications in ways that give identity an existence seemingly independent of contex-tualized social action. In Stuart Hall's famous formulation, identity *is* about "being" and as such has a sui generis quality for individuals.[15] It connects people and offers stability for groups. However, by pointing out the collapsing categories involved in producing the nostalgia of culture I want to resist using identity as a basis for diversity.

As I was learning about migrants and their children's lives in Britain, people revealed to me that their *culture* is constantly changing, that their *community* is formed processually, and that individuals negotiate *ethnicity;* yet, they could claim a stable ethnic cultural identity.[16] Putting a spotlight on negotiation indicates the inflection of time and process into anthropo-logical understanding of identity.[17] I use "identification" to understand the ways people negotiate various sociocultural categories of identity in rela-tion to themselves, their families, and their friends. "Identification" is "a processual active term, derived from a verb. . . . [It] lacks the reifying con-notations of 'identity'. It invites us to specify the agents that do the identi-fying. And it does not presuppose that such identifying (even by powerful agents, such as the state) will necessarily result in the internal sameness, the distinctiveness, the bounded group-ness that political entrepreneurs may seek to achieve. Identification — of oneself and of others — is intrinsic to social life" (Brubaker and Cooper 2000: 14). By focusing on identification, I expose how the institution of "being and becoming" Hindu Punjabi is about choices people make within the world they inhabit (see below).

In other words, I use time, space, and the identification process as axes for interpretation to examine the ways difference is ethnicized.[18] I want to understand "the experience of what it means to be 'in the middle of difference'" (Bhabha 1998a: 130). The chapters that follow concentrate on the negotiations of various potential HP identifications to rethink the meaning of contemporary ethnicity and its relation to a national project of multiculturalism premised on cultural templates. The penultimate focus, using a tripartite lens that separates out identity, ethnicity, and community from culture, is a call to conceptualize *difference* as something that is neither static nor absolute, but rather requires constant interrogation as a process of transnationalism.[19] Rereading the nostalgia for culture has many implications for the ways nation-states, scholars, and the general public frame diversity. I want to eliminate the need constantly to build bridges across putative cultural divides or continually to administer "cricket tests" of ethnic belonging. Diversity is created by everyday social interactions; it is not simply the result of the existence of a numerical minority. To rethink diversity, we first need to rework dominant understandings of ethnicity. In particular, this book focuses on the negotiations between parents and children and recognizes the various differences involved in creating a sociocultural group formation. In unpacking the terms of identity, I question how the nostalgia for culture makes Indian versus British a meaningful way to think about diversity. As such, this book is a detailed case study for how people are thinking through culture, difference, ethnicity, identity, and community. This examination is the first step in a much larger project of reframing diversity in a transnational world (see, for example, Appadurai 1996; Axel, 2002; Gershon 2001; Rushdie 1991; Sassen 1999; Shukla 2001; Siu forthcoming; Vertovec 1999).

Nostalgia for Culture, Community Studies, and the Insider

In the narration of homeward-oriented communities, the anthropological explorations of ethnicity in the United Kingdom and the sociological tradition of classic immigration studies in the United States are bridged by a generic story. The storyline is based on community studies. In the United Kingdom, there is one obvious lineage for these ideas: the Manchester school's work on ethnicity in Africa held particular sway on the development of British anthropology's concern with ethnic studies. Mitchell, Epstein, Cohen, and Gluckman worked in sub-Saharan Africa and highlighted massive change in ethnic identity because of urbanization (see Cohen 1974). These leading theorists worked with rural to urban migrants and emphasized the dualism of the two systems as the migrant perched precariously in between the two discrete social systems (see Ferguson 1999: 87–89). Scholars examining Asians in the United Kingdom, some based in Manchester, sought to engage with the Manchester school and particularly Gluckman's views (P. Werbner 1990b).[20] This specific commitment shaped an intellectual and historical tradition for studying ethnicity, which some argue has created "[t]he unfashionable image that the study of ethnic minorities has in the context of British social anthropology" (Gell 1994: 356; see also Rapport 2000; and reply from Ballard et al. 2000).[21] As a result, accounts of Asian ethnicity in Britain need to "look sufficiently like studies of the exotic" (Gell 1994: 357) in order to be worth their anthropological salt.

The engagement of British anthropology with South Asian minorities resulted in a series of well-researched explorations of minority cultures. Cultural maintenance and assimilation were analyzed with an emphasis on primordial factors, a concentration on instrumentality, or a combination of both.[22] For example, researchers examined kinship, social networks, and *biradari* (clan) relationships (Anwar 1979; R. Ballard 1989; Jeffrey 1976; Shaw 1988; P. Werbner 1987, 1990a, 1990b) or issues of cultural clash (Ahmed 1978; Anwar 1976; Ballard 1979; Taylor 1976). Often these explorations were made in the context of specific religious, language, and caste "communities" that are formed by primordial "givens" and maintained by "instrumental" concerns.[23] The ethnic community studies tradition perseveres, for example, *Desh Pardesh* "draws together eleven specially written ethnographic accounts exploring current processes of social, religious and cultural *adaptation* within a *specific,* and usually *highly localized,* British South Asian community" (R. Ballard 1994a: 3, emphasis mine). In Britain and America, ethnic minorities continue to be studied as communities that create culturally specific webs woven from remnants of their past, premigrant lives.[24] Their web of meaning is often either in a state of maintenance or intense destabilizing change.

Unlike the trajectory of research in America, the community studies tradition continues to dominate research on South Asians in Britain in which social scientists imagine ethnicity to be a tidy web that, at the most, has messy nodal points.[25] To be sure, there have been some challenges to this approach from those who have attempted to nuance Asian and Black identity in Britain in terms of race, politics, and music (Alexander 2000; Back 1993; Brah 1996; Eade 1994, 1996; Kalra 2000; Sharma, Hutnyk, and Sharma 1996; Hutnyk and Sharma 2000). Some began to move away from thinking only of the community and developed ideas about British Asian identity as a result of thinking about work and exclusion (Saiffullah-Khan 1977, 1979; Wallman 1979; Eade 1989, 1994, 1996; and Westwood 1984). Critical sociologists of race have developed more politicized and less culturalized understandings in their studies of Caribbean migrants in the United Kingdom (although these are often tightly bound to the figure of the working-class migrant). Indeed, researchers studying South Asian ethnic minorities in Britain have put a spotlight on ethnicity in Britain (Banks 1996; Baumann 1996; Brah 1996; Gillespie 1995; Sharma, Hutnyk, and Sharma 1996; see also the debates between Benson 1996; Eade 1996; and Werbner 1996a; Gell 1994, 1996; and P. Werbner 1995).[26] Nevertheless community seems to be collapsible into culture, ethnicity, and identity, premised on an "a priori ethnicizing of difference" (Greenhouse 1998: 13). Many anthropologists challenge our understanding of ethnic and racial minorities with respect to community (Baumann 1996; Gregory 1999); identity (Gillespie 1995; Alexander 2000); peoplehood (Axel 2001; Shukla 2001); citizenship (Rosaldo 1999; Ong 1999); religious groups (Toulis 1994; Vertovec 1992, 1996, 2000); homeland orientation (Siu forthcoming); the nation-state (Handler 1985; B. Williams 1989); and transnationalism (Glick-Schiller, Basch, and Blanc 1996). Arjun Appadurai's concept of the "ethnoscape" suggests the possibility and allows the conceptual work necessary to understand the facts of "changing social, territorial, and cultural reproduction of group identity" (1990: 191). Ethnoscape rejects thinking about ethnic minorities in terms of a closed system, which reproduces fixed essentialized communities. Nevertheless, ethnic minorities continue to be thought of as living in "an *unending sojourn* across the boundaries of different nation-states" (Schuster and Solomos 2001: 5, emphasis mine). How can social scientists move beyond the nostalgia of culture framework?

The eminent magazine *Anthropology Today* published a letter that is an example of researchers' conceptualization of British ethnic minorities. This letter, written by scholars of British ethnic minorities, responds to an article calling for a new anthropology of Britain (Rapport 2000). Rapport had critiqued research on British ethnic minorities, and in their response the scholars seek to engage Rapport and other anthropologists in a debate:

Nigel Rapport's account of the "new" anthropology of Britain (A.T. April 2000, p. 20) highlights a scholarly apartheid, a racialized divide between those who study the meaningful lives of white Britishers, mainly villagers, and those studying the (apparently) unmeaningful lives of the excluded and the silenced, the marginalized and the unmentionable: Britain's ethnic immigrant settlers and ethnic minorities. The account can only be described as a travesty of British society and of anthropology today. Perhaps it is time to wake up to the fact that not only is Britain a multicultural, multiracial plural society, a place of inner cities and deprived neighborhoods beyond rural pastoralia and romantic individualism, but that British anthropologists have been studying that society for the past thirty years and more, ever since the post-war migration to Britain began.[27]

The scholars strongly challenge the image of Britain as an imagined autochthonous nation in the letter, taking anthropologists to task for presenting a biased vision of British society and indicating the wealth of research on ethnic minorities that has been done to date. However, by inserting ethnics in terms of an unproblematic difference — referring to "the excluded, the silenced, the marginalized and the unmentionable" — they circumscribe ethnicity to an absolute difference. This is made clear in taking "rural pastoralia and romantic individualism" to be the counterfoils to "inner cities and deprived neighborhoods" that make Britain "multicultural and multiracial."

The letter also reveals the sense of exclusion researchers of ethnic minorities face in Britain. The scholars note they have been conducting research in Britain for more than thirty years. And yet, instead of informing the literature on Britain, ethnic minority research is often conceptualized as an outpost of an area study, where the primary location is elsewhere. That is, the study of ethnic minorities is a branch of the sending society rather than inherently about Britain. As Benson argues, "Asian ethnic minorities have indeed been seen by anthropologists as a kind of solution to the disappearance or increasing inaccessibility of anthropology's traditional barbarians, the tribes and small-scale societies of the non-western world" (Benson 1996: 47). Asian "ethnic minorities" are treated as anthropology's traditional subject matter, related to anthropology's search "at home" for a subject that could substitute for fieldwork abroad. Previous work on South Asians in Britain has often treated the ethnic minority as relatively isolated within the host society, best understood in terms of its internal traditions, institutions, and values.

The culture cum community cum ethnicity formulation was articulated most strikingly when I was moving in anthropological circles. Inherently, I was seen to have conducted research as an insider, as a Hindu and as a Punjabi. Many anthropologists before me have argued against the simple dichotomy of insiders and outsiders (Abu-Lughod 1988; Altorki and El-Solh 1988; Kumar 1992; Mankekear 1999; Nakhleh 1979; Narayan 1989). These scholars carefully exposed one of the crucial assumptions of otherness that continues to pervade scholarship in muted form, yet I faced the same assumptions.[28] Whereas the insider is comfortable, the outsider is often seen to undergo culture shock in functioning in a new language and learning new cultural rules (Jackson 1987; D. J. Jones 1970; Nakhleh 1979; Strathern 1987).[29] However, as many have argued, the whole insider-outsider model is false; "All too often the insider/outsider question is posed too simplistically as a dichotomy between subjectivity and objectivity" (Shami 1988: 115). The advantages and disadvantages of being an outsider or an insider are carefully weighed, insiders wielding the ease of cultural knowledge and outsiders carrying the sword of objectivity, each jousting for a better position.

Glossed as insider research, my work contributed to doing fieldwork "at home." With increasing numbers of people doing fieldwork "at home," anthropologists have revisited the debates on whether insiders or outsiders are preferential positions.[30] The difference between understanding myself as an insider or an outsider relates to my central thesis of questioning the dialectic of transnational ethnic subject positionality suspended between two extremes. Sometimes, "home" was understood in an abstract sense — not my home per se but "the West" or an area not "traditional" for social anthropology. The demarcation is described as "a Cartesian separation between observer and observed" (Morsy 1988: 75). These types of separation are aimed at attaining objective distance yet sympathetic understanding of people, but, as Mankekar argues, we need to "militate against the conventional anthropological project of the discovery of otherness through the ethnographic encounter" (Mankekar 1999: 35).[31] The ways in which anthropologists understand culture and community and difference and identity in those that they study, and the general assumption of constancy and continuity between these terms, will render me an insider, although I am studying South Asians in London. The definitions of "insider-outsider" are connected to the ways in which the South Asian diaspora is imagined, predicated on a spatiotemporal constant.[32]

During fieldwork, I learned that these people were not forever caught in any ethnic "webs of meaning" built from religion, language, or mar-

riage. Although not evoked explicitly, the image of "the web" is a powerful one; the role of fieldwork is to uncover the bonds of culture, and the
researcher examines cultural identity as an independent interwoven cultural whole. Indeed, the people I studied presented themselves as having
ethnic traits that gave closure to their ethnic culture. And yet when I
attempted to understand the parents' lives alongside that of their children,
to grasp "transnationalism from the ground," I realized that I needed to
ask how they lived community, ethnicity, and identity in a transnational
frame. Thus, my interlocutors also revealed to me how their markers of
identity are continuously changing, how the meaning of being a Punjabi,
a Hindu, an Asian, or a Briton changed depending on context. As webs
intertwined and constantly, although elusively, shifted, I learned that
there is no closure or fixity to such webs, and presenting a "thick description" of a "web of meaning" for Hindu Punjabis became impossible.

There were multiple bases for connections and disjunctures between
myself and those I worked with, and I found there were no real insiders
or outsiders.[33] There is no "home" or "insider" research with my work in
London, because it is not my home and because *being of* the diaspora does
not involve cultural reproduction but only "the sharing of difference"
(Ghosh 1989: 78). Difference and connections mediate my ongoing work
with Hindu Punjabis. With their children, I shared the experience of
growing up a postcolonial in the Commonwealth and having parents
who were migrants to a different land. These similarities were further bolstered by specific understandings of Hindu Punjabi identity, but I came
to realize differences even in the ways the children and I have experienced
and learned about being and becoming Punjabi, Hindu, Black, Asian,
Canadian, and British. I want to exchange the insider-outsider idiom,
which posits a false distinction and assumes a specific understanding of
culture, ethnicity, and identity as constituted as a prior whole across an
uninterrupted diasporic terrain.[34] Instead, in an attempt to understand a
"subject matter . . . that only provisionally hold together" (Shukla 2001),
I adopt an understanding of the various messy connections and overlapping disjunctures that allow for the existence of differences and ruptures.
In the field, I learned the many negotiations of identity, ethnicity, and
community that allowed for moments of connection across various
spaces of difference. To combat the insider and outsider idiom, my reactions to the field are woven into this ethnography. I hope to share my
own interpretive dilemmas and choices by interweaving a narrative of discovery with a narrative of finding. The contrasting and sometimes jarring
switches between the two narratives highlight contrasts in my authorial

stance and my fieldwork experience. By owning up to the interlocution between the fieldworker and the fieldwork, I use the writing style itself to explore how I learned about people's lives and make the *authorial I* obvious. Many opt to separate these two registers completely. In such a framework, the fieldwork as a process of discovery develops into a written register of authority. My intention is to always be aware of the discovery, and of my own reactions, in the attempt to show how knowledge of a group can be produced without reiterating the nostalgia for culture and the spaces of difference that creates clear-cut insiders and outsiders. Their lives forced me to question the ways in which the community studies tradition continued to inform conceptualizations of the minority experience and to dispute the obsession to ask why and how immigrants lose culture when they move from a homeland.[35] Instead of asking what their culture is, I ask how minority knowledge and collective agency produce a transnational terrain.

"This, My People": Who, What, Where, When, and How

For any anthropologist, the most immediate duty of fieldwork is to find people, a task that becomes quite difficult when dealing with a dispersed population in a large urban center like London.[36] I had been going to various "Asian" events around London, and the well-known process of fieldwork serendipity led me to my initial meetings with Punjabi Hindus.[37] I had heard about a bookshop that stocked "Asian books" near the British Museum. I sought it out, hoping that there might be a message board with information on "cultural events" that would lead me to people. I looked for the store on a typical dreary London day, entered, and told the owner a bit about my project. Immediately he started speaking to me in Punjabi and was animated in his conversation. He played a sample of Zakir Hussain's tabla on a small stereo, as we discovered our mutual interests.[38] I had found someone who was strongly opinionated about Punjabi culture. He began regaling me with the basics: "Krishna [the diety] was a playboy but the only ones ready to admit it are Punjabis . . . . *Bhangra* is a youth dance craze. These youth [the young British Asians creating 'fusion' music] forget the origins in drinking *bhang* [a mixture of hemp, sugar, and almonds], which makes people dance in a certain way." Unexpectedly, to illustrate his point, he threw his arms into the air and moved his shoulders up and down to the absent bhangra beat. The conversation continued spontaneously, covering all sorts of topics, which he dictated. Just as I was thinking myself entirely fortunate to have met someone who was so willing to share his ideas and opinions with me, he charged, "Why are you studying Punjabi culture?" His demeanor and attitude had suddenly changed, and I was a bit taken aback. I suddenly felt the vulnerabilities of the beginning of this new project, which were only exacerbated because I had not yet even found the people that I was trying to study. I asked what he meant by his statement.

> "At the essence," he stressed, "Punjabis are consumers, there is nothing to study." To prove his point he added, "If you went to a temple the women would be discussing their saris or the price of gold and the men on the other side would be talking about business and how much they had paid for their Mercedes Benz." (FIELDNOTE ENTRY, SEPTEMBER 1994)

As first meetings go, it was both invigorating and jarring—was he referring to their middle-class status? Was he reinscribing the idea that ethnicity is erased by material gains? Was he simply a pedantic put off by these base concerns? I was in his bookshop for almost two hours, listening to his exposition on Punjabi culture, which at times valorized and at other times demonized the people I wanted to study. It was nice to have an engaging interlocutor; he seemed willing to speak to me, when he wasn't giving his opinions to his customers, sometimes chasing them out of his store with his sharp tongue. At the same time, I was acutely aware that I did not want to commit some sort of anthropological faux pas by saying, "Hey you're the first Hindu Punjabi I've met, know any more?" or "So where is that temple with all the stereotypical Hindu Punjabis concerned with gold and cars?" In a bit of a bind—not wanting to leave, enjoying his company and his challenge to prove my choice of topic, but also quickly realizing that I should not overstay my first visit—I decided to buy a book. His recommendations included Gita Mehta's *Karma Cola,* which I purchased. The transaction completed, I promised to return. When I got home and read the book's subtitle, "Marketing the Mystic East," I wondered if he was having a go at me or giving me a subtle warning. We had a few more meetings over the course of my fieldwork, one of them an in-depth interview, but I never did meet any other Hindu Punjabis through him. Such was the life of the urban researcher: it was difficult to meet dispersed middle-class people, but when I did, it was a small triumph. The challenges of not having anyone to interview were soon overcome. By the end of my fieldwork, I had many "Aunties" reminding me that I had not yet taken their interviews and "Uncles" who would ask me when my book would be published.[39]

My fieldwork experience was mediated by those whom I met as well as by the politics of London as a multicultural, cosmopolitan, global, immigration metropolis. Naming London (population more than six million) as a field site includes and excludes many spaces and events that constitute the urban landscape. Researching in an urban terrain raises a number of questions. What does doing fieldwork in London consist of? Where does the field begin? Is fieldwork in a place? In a space? Does "being" in London constitute the "doing" of fieldwork? Or do Asians, specifically Hindu Punjabis, need to be present? The urban landscape is isolating, fragmented, potentially creative, and distinctive. It has been researched by those interested in theorizing the urban and postcolonial (Eade 2000) or in juxtaposition to a perceived rural (Bashram 1978; Bott 1957; Hannerz 1980; Little 1974; Raban 1974). The London Underground Rail announcement "Mind the gap!" provides one metaphor, which, for me, encompassed various aspects of being in the city. The statement cautions commuters to be wary of the gap between the train and the platform. The phrase is also appropriate as an analogy for urban fieldwork; it can be applied to the physical as well as symbolic distances between people that characterize the urban setting. As anthropologists, we first "mind" and then bridge these gaps of everyday life. The inaugural gap faced by all anthropologists is first contact.[40] This defining feature of anthropology is a methodological obstacle for the urban researcher. Recognition of the difficulties of urban participant observation, however, is not new; as Benson relates, "The inner city environment is a daunting one for an inexperienced anthropologist committed to the canons of participant observation" (1981: 151).[41] With my research, the ideal of *continuous* participant observation would not be possible when working with a dispersed population in a multicultural city such as London.

The main difficulty in working with dispersed Hindu Punjabis, a numerical minority within the Asian population, is that they are easily hidden or subsumed by urban life.[42] I had no family connections with anyone in London, and therefore no easy access to network through existing social ties. Although I tried to be systematic, my attempts were frustrated by the fact that the landscape of the city allows people to appear and disappear so readily. I explored many places to meet Hindu Punjabis, including some of London's 203 places of Hindu worship, social centers, and youth clubs.[43] However, most dispersed Hindu Punjabis whom I initially met did not have any formal group membership based on their "Punjabi-ness," which has been one of the usual entry points for urban anthropologists (such as religious organizations, social clubs, or some *caste*-based groups such as the Gujarati caste or religious same society). These factors resulted in a field strategy of meeting as many Asians and Hindus as possible.[44]

First Contact — Learning to Mind the Gap!

I arrived at King's Cross station from Cambridge in the fifty-two minutes promised by British Rail. Outside, a long queue of black taxicabs produced the distinct smell of diesel on a warm August day. Almost everyone was there to travel — about to embark on a journey, or had just returned. No one was smiling. Although there was noise and general train station hustle and bustle, no one seemed to talk to one another, no one even looked at one another. The first urban fieldwork rule was learned that day: do not initiate eye contact. But without eye contact, how would I meet people?

This is a bit dramatic for first contact story; I am trying to capture the romance of going to the field. In actuality, this is the account of an early visit to London. But for fieldwork, I arrived by car. I was moving all of my possessions out of my college room into my new home, my new home as a young bride. I had just been married and relocation to field setting was, for me, simultaneously a relocation into a new social role. (FIELDNOTE ENTRY, AUGUST 31, 1994)

I needed to find Punjabi Hindus — where to look? Perhaps Janmashtami *celebrations at Bhaktivedanta Manor, Letchmore Heath (the largest gathering of Hindus in Europe) would attract some Punjabis.[45] My husband accompanied me and both of us commented on the high level of organization. Volunteers quickly directed cars into on-site parking spaces in the field. No one was being loud; for a large festival of approximately 30, 000 people, it seemed so quiet. We walked across the field, which belonged to the temple, towards the Manor and into a tent full of devotees. They asked us for our signatures on a petition that read — KEEP OUR TEMPLE OPEN — addressed to government MPs and the Minister of the Environment [then, John Gummer]. I later found out this was an illegal gathering.[46]*

During the two hours queuing for darshan I was surrounded by people speaking a language that I later recognized as Gujarati. I did not hear anyone speaking Punjabi around me, or Hindi. Where were the Punjabis? I met not one at the largest and most auspicious festival of Hindus in Europe. (FIELDNOTE ENTRY, SEPTEMBER 15, 1994)

Nishma and I met at a multicultural radio station where she worked. It was not a planned meeting but when I told her of my research, she was immediately receptive and sympathetic. The anthropological act of loitering with intent (or participant observation) took me to many settings with her and her friends. For example, we went to a party in Brixton, out for coffee in Leicester Square, ate bagels in Brick Lane (in the East End) and just "hung out" at her place.

One weekend we went to a Dusshera mela *which she deemed important for my research. She explained to me that it has been celebrated on a large scale for a number of years and she and her family had attended annually. We were to meet up with her parents at the North London park but could not find them in the rush; she used her mobile telephone to ring one of her cousins who was inside (also on a "mobile") and he met us at the main gates. The park was full of rides for children, various tempting food stalls, and those selling religious and other items. All around people spoke Punjabi, Hindi, and English. I had finally found "my people."*

Fenced off from spectators, at a safe planning permission distance, in anticipation of being burned there was a huge Ravan *effigy, it seemed to be more than 40 feet tall. To the right of the effigy was a stage where the Ramlila was being performed. After the evil* Ravan *effigy was burned, we went to her place for masala tea and to digest all the deep fried food we had just consumed. It was the first time I met her parents. Almost immediately, a transnational connection was established between their family and mine via Canada. Nishma's father's cousin in Canada turned out to be my parent's family friend. Her father immediately marked a different relationship towards me with the words: "You are family now; please consider this your home."* (FIELDNOTE ENTRY, OCTOBER 7, 1994)

These jarred and disjointed ethno-vignettes reveal my first contact with the Hindu Punjabis of my research and demonstrate how I began to negotiate the "gaps" of urban life. After many other meetings and contacts, research became regular and gained momentum so that participant observation became possible.

Participant observation with dispersed Hindu Punjabis, once located, was further hindered by their full-time work schedules, which initially limited participant observation research to evenings and weekends.[47] My work spanned the entire Greater London area and included parties, Asian theatre events, bhangra gigs, Asian comedy nights, meals, temples, weddings, Leicester Square cafés, parties in Brixton, and evenings at home with families in front of their "telly." The final research was constituted through a process of empirical bricolage, including general Asian events (religious and nonreligious), meetings with Hindu Punjabis (which did not necessarily exclude general Asian events, but were events when I was mostly around Hindu Punjabis), religious non-Hindu events (for example, Guru Nanak's birthday, which I attended with an HP family), dinner parties, social teas, informal meetings, and interviews.[48] The ethnographic moments when they did come together as a group resulted in a variety of different fieldwork situations: planned, spontaneous, daytime, evening, family-oriented, festival, as well as political. Information was gathered during conversations with young HPs as we drove across London, while going to parties where HPs mixed with "Blacks" and "whites," and when meeting someone who owned his own business. Fieldwork was intense and at times involved engaging with many individuals in several locations during the course of a day. In this way, I attempted to get a full sense of the many ways in which people experienced being Hindu Punjabi in London.

Once located, my concerns turned to how to present myself as a researcher. There were a number of reasons that my own status was an initial issue. The most relevant was the fact that the people with whom I was doing research expected questionnaires, a formal interview, and other definite actions reflecting their understandings of the research enterprise. These people were familiar with research, albeit perhaps not anthropological. At a first meeting, one interlocutor began to question my methods and how I was doing qualitative research, as she had also used this methodology in her own medical research projects. Her vision of qualitative work was one based on interviews. Participant observation, or "loitering with intent," as I have come to call it, was not how any of the people I met conceived of research. In order to gain access and to solicit further information, therefore, I conducted semistructured interviews. I began interviewing six months after beginning fieldwork, and twenty-one interviews were conducted with migrants and eleven with children of migrants.[49] The interviews were taped and were on average sixty to ninety minutes in duration (the shortest was forty minutes and the longest was four hours), some taking place over many visits. I conducted interviews with some families with whom I had already begun participant observation. With others, the interview allowed me to further explain my research and introduce my informants to the anthropological process of participant observation.

After gaining further access to some families, our initial meetings, without the guise of the interview, were terribly awkward. Fieldwork can last from twelve months to many years in duration, and the role of a researcher continuously changes over the research period. I quickly realized the need to change my role from a "researcher" to someone they could relate to easily. The children were generally around my age or younger, and I was glad to begin friendships with them. The parents, however, were much older, and my being their child's friend was no guarantee for interaction. Thus, the role that afforded me some empathy, access, and opportunities for participant observation with the parents was that of a recently arrived migrant. The first time that I discovered that sharing my own changes could potentially be useful in my research was while in the kitchen with Nishma's mother (the family with whom I had a larger Canadian connection). Initially, Aunty did not talk much but when she did, she always had interesting observations and comments. One day, she was making chappatis for dinner. Nishma and I were in the kitchen helping. I told Aunty how much I had missed my mother's cooking and had found the responsibility for daily cooking difficult, especially since I had not cooked in my parental home. She began to tell me about her life when she arrived as a new bride in Britain. She laughed about having to take the bus just to get chappati flour from a specialty store to make dinner and then not being able to buy too much because she was only cooking for two: "In the beginning, there was only one shop in Euston and we used to go and buy at the Patak's shop. And as your Uncle was working all the time seven days so I used to go on the buses to get all the grocery. Just a little bag of atta. And now you get it everywhere, anything, you need it, it is there ASDA, TESCO, Sainsbury's, it is all there now." At that moment, I realized her willingness to speak was related to her empathy for being recently married and in a new environment. In conversations with other women, I would share my own experiences of being newly married, ask for cooking recipes, and request their tips for cooking shortcuts suited for the urban middle-class working woman.

The parental generation had familiarity in dealing with being a new migrant, since they had undergone that experience. After settling, they learned the requirements of everyday life and made adjustments to life in Britain, which included additions and deletions to recipes and rituals. They were aware of their own cultural changes and were quick to take on the role of a teacher or cultural broker for later migrants.[50] Parents were well versed in the role; it used their hospitality skills, their knowledge, as well as respecting their status as "knowing elders" whom one consults for advice. Of course, there were differences. I would indicate these in my invocation of the status with the words "I can't imagine what life was like for those arriving thirty years ago." The migrants replied with narratives of their lives, often of tales from their arrival and initial settlement in Britain. This strategy, extremely successful with the parents, sometimes alienated me from their children. They were much more familiar with research methods, as well as qualitative research, so different strategies were required. I explained that I wanted "to hang out with them," and although some of the relationships ended after the interview, others continued.

Eventually I abandoned a conscious presentation of myself. If we were at a social gathering at a temple or a party and someone asked who I was, one of the Aunties would reply, "*Ai sadi beti ban-gai*" [She has become our daughter]. Others used variations of the phrase such as "*beti samajh lo*" [think of her as a daughter] or "*beti jis tarah hi hai*" [she's like a daughter (to us)] — using the kinship term "*beti*" to indicate our connection and type of relationship.[51] Reciprocally, I referred to them as "Uncle" and "Aunty," and these referents are used throughout this text. Although these kinship terms are used, there should be no misunderstanding of familial relationship: there are no kinship bonds to the people I studied; these are fictive kinship terms of respect and connection. The invocation of the status of a daughter or my use of fictive kin terms seemed to indicate a new role for me, yet the fact that I was doing research was never far behind. People would joke about me scribbling things down into my notepad or asking questions.

Over time, friendships formed, there were annual follow-up visits until 2000, and to this day I continue to be in touch with the main families I studied. The reference "interlocutors" is odd for me. Although some people were research "subjects" in the sense that they allowed me to do my research, others shared in the process of discovery about identity. Now most of the core families are family friends. We shared transnational connection because of my research, and with the youths, I shared the connections of being a minority and a child of migrants, since my parents were part of the "brain-drain" migration to Canada. The children and I differed in various understandings of the terms, but we shared the fact that we were not Indian, and yet we had overlapping experiences in our homes. Since then, I have come to realize that various transnational connections are also lived as diasporic differences. At the time though, I was a bit puzzled by our similarities and differences, and we had mutual questions about each other's lives.

The moments and spaces when Hindu Punjabis rupture and re-create the nostalgia for culture, specifically their processes of making "HP" a viable label, are the focus of this book. Through each chapter I work toward recognizing that although transnationalism involves large-scale processes of the movement of capital, technology, and resources, it is also made and unmade in the dynamics of intimate spaces and moments of everyday life. In particular, I unpack the various names by which these people can be known to show how each is produced through processes of identification and the politics of representation. I track how the negotiations for the institution of Hindu Punjabi identity works out in specific conditions, in which the people I write about discover themselves to be Hindu, Punjabi, Asian, Black, and British.[52] Each term of identification is undone in the subsequent chapters by addressing "community," "culture," and "identity," using people's own ideas about who they are.[53] In all, I wish to offer an exploration of the contexts in which these emerge as choices and anything but choices of identification. I highlight how people become and mark that space between the boundaries of being insiders and outsiders in various situations to show the moments of negotiation and how these identities operate singly in some encounters and multiply, ambiguously and simultaneously, in others. The chapters are organized around the chronology of settlement: first becoming an outsider and then what it means to be Punjabi Hindu and to negotiate alliances around that identity as well as being Asian and Black, Indian and British.[54]

In the next chapter, "Being Vilayati, Becoming Asian," I introduce the core Hindu Punjabi families and a few principal individuals in the wider context of their immigration. I argue that the trope of a migration story constructs a tidy Asian identity, predicated on thinking about migrants outside space and time. The focus on migration limits ethnic minorities to be forever in dialogue with a homeland. Instead, using historical context, I offer that the spaces of difference involve the disruption of culture cum ethnicity cum community to create people who are marked as "outsiders" both from the places they leave and those to which they travel. In doing so, I begin the book by questioning the ways difference is structured in terms of an absolute insider-outsider position predicated on specific understandings of space and time.

Highlighting the 1947 Partition of British India, Chapter 3 examines the historical contingencies of Punjabi identity. In "'I Am From Nowhere': Partition and *Being* Punjabi," I reveal Partition as a defining moment for Hindu Punjabis in London. The chapter examines the resonance of Partition in the specific understandings of community and culture that have come to have salience for London's Hindu Punjabis. The moment of Partition sets in motion my concern with processual identity; I therefore examine the role of their dislocation for demarcating identity. By doing so, I reveal how prior movement determined the possible identification for being Punjabi, a process that continued to be fraught with specific meanings after migration to Britain. "Punjabi" is a reference to a geographical place, but for Hindu Punjabis that geographical place has been rescripted to where they have their social relationships in Delhi, rather than the place marked on the map as "Punjab."

In Chapter 4, "Becoming a Hindu Community" I examine how cultural change is central to religious communities and how community exists only in moments. Modern understandings of Hindus are traced through the original British India census question. The young people of my research, as well as their parents define themselves as "Hindus." What does being a Hindu mean? Exploring changes in how this question has been understood demonstrates how "identity" can change while remaining nominally constant. Thus, the question "What is a Hindu?" which is inextricably linked to the historical implications of the British Raj, also reveals twentieth-century understandings of the "Hindu community." I highlight how Hinduism changes while claiming to be a consistent identity marker using three different sites of enquiry — the temple, worship, and the act of learning to belong to the Hindu community. In looking at difference, I disrupt the ethnicity cum community cum culture cum identity identification. Including the temporal realities of being a part of the community disrupts the omnipresent aspect of "being Hindu" and reveals how they have become British Hindus, a minority religion implicated by a specific experience of difference.

Marriage is a critical aspect of maintaining collective identity by providing continuity of identity between generations; it ensures that ethnic identity is maintained for the future. It is also a flashpoint of how difference is inscribed, especially regarding the choice of a life partner. In Chapter 5, "The Search for a Suitable Boy" I explore the subtle ways in which the nostalgia for culture is challenged, and how the sense of collective identity shifts because of the interpretations of some of the young women and their parents. Marriage is one way people talk about being transnational. I look at marriage as a potential space of difference where issues of cultural knowledge and agency play *out in,* not *on,* the transnational terrain. Marriage solidifies identity through alliance but there are fluid and contested ideas of exogamy and endogamy. In negotiating marriage the parents and children reveal how their actions are simultaneously moments of transnational identification.

In the early chapters I look at how culture-community-ethnicity is taken to be negotiated and seamless, whereas in Chapter 6, "Becoming British Asian: Intergenerational Negotiations of Racism," I explore how boundaries, or "external definitions" of identity and community, affect identifications. In that chapter, I write ethnographically about racism to understand two nominal categories: "Asian" and "Black." Racism, too, is taken to be a shifting and negotiated aspect of their lives. I contrast the experiences of the parental generation with that of their children to examine how they reflect the politics inherent in the rise of the so-called new racism. By looking at the ways they are Black and Asian, I bring forth a nuanced understanding of agency and race in which difference gets highlighted as the primary signifier and culture, community, and ethnicity equate and are subsumed under markers of difference based on the solidification around being a visible minority.

The final ethnographic chapter, "Being British, Becoming a Person of Indian Origin," sketches out how identity is negotiated in terms of national belonging. Whereas the first chapter emphasized how Hindu Punjabis became outsiders, here I examine how they become insiders and are able to claim Britain and India as homelands. Specifically, I look at the moment when these "Asian" migrants become "Britons": when they leave Britain. The migrants have initiated a neomyth of return to their "homeland." The parents frame India as a homeland, but what that actually means has changed over time. I examine how the coalition of understandings about nationhood and belonging renders parents and their children forever immigrant in England. As India is actively imagining itself as a homeland, I show how the equation of culture cum community cum ethnicity cum identity is being (re)formulated to include national belonging. By taking the moment of being British when they leave Britain and visit India alongside their becoming "Non-Resident Indians" and "People of Indian Origin," I reveal how they produce transnational identities through their decisions to retire.

Chapter 8, "'Where Are You *Originally* From?' Multiculturalism, Citizenship, and Transnational Differences," considers how nation-states can influence people's identification. Official policies of multiculturalism can create a dangerous tautology of assumed exclusion. In this chapter I explore specifically the national policies premised on an understanding of cultural difference that arises from the dissonance of a minority whose nostalgia for culture is assumed to be from elsewhere. Taking one innocent example of how the nation-state influences the scope and breath of how coexistence can be imagined (see Minow 1990), I unpack a well-intentioned citizenship report and show how difference, premised on the nostalgia for culture, is going to be taught as part of curriculum on citizenship education for school-aged children. The chapter examines how difference as an ideology in Britain is perpetuated because diversity is understood in some official policy circles as the need for *tolerance* of minorities. Thus, I also seek to question the ways multiculturalism has become a global principle that enshrines differences by being sympathetic to minorities, without specific entitlements, and yet reinscribes particular notions of otherness that are tied to the national imaginary of coexistence among citizens. In doing so I extend the discussion to thinking about how nation-states inherently determine how migrant transnational identification can take place in everyday life.

This book addresses how transnational identities take shape in the modern world, by focusing on the ethnographic case of Britain's Hindu Punjabi families. My interlocutors revealed their identities to be Asian, Black, Punjabi, Hindu, Indian, and British. In the detailed case study, I reveal how each potential categorization comes to have meaning for individuals and is established and experienced as a salient identity in Britain. The ethnographic chapters consider how people actively produce their identifications in spaces of difference. In the final two chapters I examine this further by considering changes in Indian and British national policies that implicate the lives of ethnic minorities. I am arguing for a nuanced understanding of globalization as a lived experience. Such an understanding must involve both identifying the social and cultural parameters of change involved in a movement of people, while being wary of reinscribing a notion that cultural identity is tied to a place. In other words, in light of the negotiations inherent to the spaces of difference that create and change identifications, South Asian minorities can no longer be taken to be extensions from a cultural prior.

In revealing the various contestations involved in creating a meaningful overarching "cultural identity," I question how anthropologists, society in general, and nation-state policies have culturalized the many forms of differences that migrants experience, thus petrifying what is in fact a complex, changing, and thoroughly transnational field for the production and negotiation of difference. Region, religion, race, and nationality are all stuffed into a "culture box," whereby culture is the primary reference for the ethnic minority. With everything in a "culture box," differences merge into one another, and I illustrate how this occurs in a range of settings — from religious observances to marriage practices, to questions of citizenship, to experiences of the new racism. The specific terms that make their identification possible are constantly being negotiated across various differences, and yet migrants and their children are imagined in similar ways by the nation-state where they live and by the ones they left behind. Rather than understanding my object of enquiry, that is, South Asians in Britain, in terms of ethnicity as a "whole culture" transplanted to Britain, which changes form because of pressures of assimilation, integration, or incorporation, or which remains the same because of the usefulness of tradition and cultural ties, I argue that the social scientists' toolkit of culture, community, and ethnicity gets muddled if attention is paid to issues of difference, representation, and power. The play of these elements and constant redefinition of South Asian culture in diverse locales *creates* transnational connections (cf. Clifford 1994: 306). I examine the ways transnationalism occurs in the intimate spaces of everyday life and how it is experienced and created by inflecting time and space into ideas of community, identity, and ethnicity to question the ways scholars and others constitute "culture." It is difficult to call for examining the precise exploration of a nostalgia for culture when so many senior anthropologists are abandoning the analytical salience of culture, identity, and community (see Strathern 1995a, 1995b; Kelly and Kaplan 2001; Handler 1994). Yet if we take seriously the need to understand the production of indigenous knowledge, then culture, identity, and community are necessarily and inevitably part of the terminologies of analysis needed to understand migrant lives. Hall and others have declared identity to be a process; less well understood is what it means to live identity processually. Using transnational tools of power, representation, and difference allows anthropologists to research ethnic minorities in the globalized world without prescribing a conceptual straitjacket that explains transnational migrant lives predestined to wavering between home-host cultures. This toolkit fundamentally alters social scientists' notions of the subject of research. The immigrants and their children are not aberrations of the modern world and hangers on to tradition; rather, they are deeply implicated and interpellated by transnationalism. My goal is to add to that debate by exploring the ways that culture, ethnicity, identity, and community are variously used, refined, and revised by migrants and nation-states within a specific context of the transnational terrain.

CHAPTER 2

Being Vilayati, Becoming Asian

Keeping up with the Kapurs, the Chawlas, the Kalias,
and the Aggarwals in London

At one time, Vilayat was England, but [now] it could be anywhere
[in the Western Hemisphere] that was not India.

Interview with Karnal Bhandhari, teenage migrant who moved
to Britain from Africa because of the Amin exodus

Ethnic identity terms are sometimes crude, other times nuanced. In Britain, the people I studied were known as "Asians," an ethnic referent for all those having origins in the Subcontinent. The term arose from a distinctly postcolonial British sensibility about the postwar migrants who landed on its shores from South Asia. In comparison take the Punjabi term "Vilayat," which refers to a place that has come to mean "outside" India. A person who went to Vilayat became a Vilayati, someone from the outside. As Karnal Bhandhari makes clear, "Vilayat" at one time meant England, and those Indian migrants who had lived in England and returned to India during the colonial period and afterward were known as "Vilayati" — "Vilayat" — returned. The Punjabi term "Vilayati" is rarely a self-referent, unlike "Desi," a term used by those in the diaspora to refer to the community originating in South Asia. By becoming Vilayati, the migrants' movement to Britain marked them as being from outside "home."[1] These terms give a sense of the ways that migrants simultaneously became outsiders to India and Britain.

26

Ironically, then, they were seen as "outsiders," when they became migrants to the United Kingdom. At the same time, they were marked as outsiders from the places they left behind. Migration was the first step in turning these people into "double outsiders": Asian and Vilayati. For each the sense of difference was predicated on a changed notion of belonging to a home(land), and they were perpetually and simultaneously marked as being from outside of the nation. Yet take the other term now in common parlance, "Desi." This term is used by the first and second generation to refer to those who have origins in Desh, literally meaning "land," but taken to pertain to the South Asian Subcontinent. It is a Hindi and Urdu word, which in British India was used as an adjective to refer to items grown or made in India (such as butter, almonds, and so forth) as opposed to Europe or England. This seemingly straightforward term of belonging to the land of India needs to be unpacked in light of the migration history of South Asians to the United Kingdom. One particular migration story, widely accepted, reveals how South Asians settled in the United Kingdom based on a four-phase schemata. A crucial part of this story is that the migration of women and children create the Asian community in Britain. At one level, the act of migration made the Hindu Punjabis outsiders, which was in turn the first act in creating Asians who are imagined to be connected to a homeland in specific ways.

During the course of my fieldwork three events took place that crystallized the implications for Asian identity in Britain in which the Asian was characterized in the British national press: the struggles over the right to public worship at Bhaktivedanta Manor; the death of Tarsem Singh Pureval (editor of the Punjabi-language *Des Pardes* magazine) by suspected members of the Khalistan movement; and the murder of Quudus Ali by National Front Skinheads in East London. In each of the national stories, the sense of being from the outside, of being Asian, was repeatedly splashed across the papers.

In this chapter I examine the migration story to challenge how Asian migrants are thought to be in a constant dialogue with a home culture. Instead, by showing how they are marked as outside because of their migration, I want to undo the confluences of ethnicity, community, and culture as tied to place. This reframing implicates how South Asians are imagined as an anthropological subject. To show that their migration marks them only in terms of being outsiders to the "pull" nation, that is, to concentrate only on the ways in which they are Asian and a minority, overlooks the temporal and spatial constructions of identity and difference at the global level. By looking at the complicated ways they experience the disjuncture of transnational migration, I challenge how we think about cultural change as the product of movement between two unconnected places. Instead, they are constantly marked as being double outsiders, a category that negates the ways they are simultaneously inside and creating India and Britain and shows them to be without any absolute claims to a nation. But in using the term Desi, I indicate their claim to a transnational ethos.

My research in London allowed me to eventually meet almost two hundred Hindu Punjabis who had migrated during the postwar period, most arriving during the 1950s–1960s peak of postwar development. I left my own family home in Canada for Vilayat to pursue a doctorate degree from the University of Cambridge. I conducted the fieldwork on which this book is based between August 1994 and October 1995, and then made annual visits until 2000. I worked with a core of thirty families. Each was similar in that the parents were nearing retirement, had established middle-class status (see below), and were, in terms of caste status, *Kshatriya* (*Khattrī*), *Bania*, or Brahman.[2] Before coming to England, I had never heard the terms Vilayat or Asian as marker for South Asians. I was instead more familiar with "East Indian," which is primarily used in Canada to differentiate South Asian migrants from Canada's First Nations indigenous people. My move to cross the academic terrain had personal implications: I learned about the junctures that constituted home and outside for a migrant.

I worked most intensively with four main families living in North London and Essex (the sprawling suburbia in the eastern reach of London)—the Kalias, the Kapurs, the Aggarwals, and the Chawlas. These four families were the most generous with their time and the most patient. During the course of fieldwork, I spent a lot of time with them in the evenings and on weekends, on overnight visits, and, if they were free, during the daytime as well. Sometimes I met the adult children first and then the parents; other times it was vice versa. Each Uncle and Aunty has his or her own migration history and experience of living in England during this period. Their stories form part of the larger picture of the impression of Hindu Punjabi identity in London, but it is important not to lose sight of their individual stories. I want to introduce each of the families and a few key individuals separately.

The Kalias

Nishma Kalia was a woman I met at an ethnic radio station. She was an aspiring media diva, billing herself as the queen of gossip. I was waiting to meet the main DJ for the morning and drive-home shows to conduct an interview, but he was still on the air. Just after Nishma's shift, I entered. She was in the front waiting area and asked me whom I had come to see. She was on her way to an Asian comedy show with a couple of friends; they were waiting for another friend to arrive. In the meantime, we all chatted for a while in the reception area.

Eventually I met Nishma's parents and extended family, which over the course of research and beyond has included her aunts, uncles, cousins, and maternal grandmother, who variously live in London, Canada, and India. When he was in his early twenties, Mr. Kalia had moved to Uganda, Africa, to work and came to England before the Amin crisis. At first, he worked in a factory while attending college and eventually worked for the Greater London Council as an engineer. He returned to India in the late 1960s in search of a bride. Mrs. Kalia hailed from Delhi, though she had in fact lived all over India, but her parents were settled in Delhi. They had come from the part of Punjab that was annexed to Pakistan, but she never liked talking about that too much.[3] She was a primary-school teacher, registered with a temporary teaching agency that had sent her to work in all areas of London. They had moved around London, but eventually settled near Alexandria Palace, in a wonderful Victorian terraced house. Both Mr. and Mrs. Kalia were looking forward to Nishma's marriage and their own retirement, so that they could travel and be free to do their own things. We always seemed to return to these topics in our conversations. Mr. Kalia was especially skilled at bringing these up; he made clear that getting Nishma settled and married was his last duty as a father. After that he could enjoy his old age.

The Kapurs

I informed Mr. and Mrs. Kalia that I needed to meet more people and wanted to go to a Hindu temple, so they invited me to join them for a Diwali celebration. I met their friends, the Kapurs, at the Kapur home. Mrs. Kapur lived with her twenty-something daughter, Arti, in North-East London. Arti was one of four daughters, the only one yet unmarried and thus the only one still living with her mother. Arti worked in the Docklands. Two daughters lived in Texas and one just outside of London. Mrs. Kapur's husband had passed away about five years earlier of heart complications. She had worked in factories her whole life and her husband was an engineer. Arti and Nishma had grown up together, but had grown apart. Mrs. Kapur and the Kalias nevertheless remained friends.

Arti and I struck up a friendship that involved innumerable conversations about everything from fashion to marriage — a subject that seemed to crop up constantly. Occasionally she would stay nights at our flat, since she worked nearby. So we got a chance to meet quite often. Once, she claimed that she was on a journey to find herself before she got married, a journey that at one point boldly involved an "adventure holiday" to sub-Saharan Africa.

The Aggarwals

Once the Kalias and the Kapurs introduced me to the temple where there were a lot of Hindu Punjabis, I asked one of the executive officers, Mr. Bhasin, if he would help me meet people. I told him about my research. His own migration, he said, occurred in the 1970s. When we next met at the temple, he supplied a list of some members of the temple who might be helpful. Mr. Bhasin's own name was noticeably absent, and he made it clear to me that he thought the "pillars of the community," usually migrants who had arrived in the 1950s and 1960s, could provide me with much more information. The list included the Aggarwals, because, as he explained, they had been pivotal in establishing the temple, they were very active, and they knew a lot of people. Mrs. Aggarwal and I first "met" over the phone. I introduced myself as a researcher who had received her name from Mr. Bhasin. Unknown to me at the time, temple politics were rife and she was highly suspicious of my phone call, asking me a number of questions. It was an awkward introduction; however, after I satisfied her initial queries, she granted me an interview. She specified that we would only have half an hour and repeated this a number of times in our short conversation; she made it clear to me that she was an extremely busy woman. Luckily the interview took place at her home, with my tape recorder on her kitchen table. Once she met me and again grilled me about my intentions and university affiliations, she seemed placated by my responses and my presentation of a business card. Keeping my eye on the kitchen clock, at the half hour I thanked her and said that I did not want to take up any more of her time but would be happy if we could continue the discussion at another meeting. She insisted that I stay and made a cup of tea. Our first meeting lasted two and a half hours. In time I learned that Mr. Aggarwal had come to England to study and, like many others, thought that he would return to India with his wife and daughter after five years. Five turned into thirty-five, and now the Aggarwals have two grown children, a son who is an accountant and a daughter who is a medical doctor.

At the time of my research the Aggarwal children were both globe-trotting: Arun took off six months and Sapna one year to see the world. As a result of their absence, my husband and I got to spend a lot of time with the Aggarwals, helping to fill in their temporarily empty "nest." My fieldwork coincided with Mrs. Aggarwal's planning of Sapna's wedding. Since Sapna was away, I often accompanied Mrs. Aggarwal to a number of posh London venues and helped her, often simply by keeping her company and providing an additional opinion. Since conducting fieldwork, I have come to know their adult children as well. Arun is now working for an American company, living in Massachusetts, and married to Pamela, a woman he met while traveling. Sapna traveled around the world, to Sydney and India and around Asia. She married her boyfriend, Michael, an Englishman, and they have two babies. They now live in London, just five minutes from her parents, having lived in Japan before returning to London.

The Chawlas

My meeting with the Chawlas is another example of fieldwork serendipity. Their names were on Mr. Bhasin's list from the temple; however, I met their son, Sanjeev, the weekend before I was going to call Mr. Chawla. We were both at an Asian event, a comedy and bhangra dance gig. We joined common friends for a light meal in a hotel restaurant near Russell Square, and I sat near Sanjeev and Soniya (his girlfriend who became his wife) and told them about my project. They kindly agreed to be interviewed. At the time, I did not realize that Sanjeev was the Chawlas' son. After meeting him in his home on the following Friday night for an interview, he introduced me to his parents. He was going out clubbing that evening, but his parents were going to be at home. I took their interview right then and there. Sanjeev had an older sister who was married and living in India. She was born in the United Kingdom, and it seemed that Mrs. Chawla harbored some resentment that she was so far away. Sanjeev worked with his father in their family business.

After returning to my home that evening, I noted their details and connected his family name and telephone number with that given by Mr. Bhasin from the temple. I was surprised and relieved that they were members of the same family and that I had interviewed them together! This may seem a trivial occurrence, but to this day I consider small events like this a godsend for the fieldworker who is attempting to transverse the urban terrain (a time-consuming and sometimes very frustrating experience). As it turned out, they lived near to the Aggarwals; in fact they were family friends and the parents had served on the temple committee at various times. Those active at the temple seemed to know many families or at least know of them. Over time, they had a rotary of phone numbers of people dispersed around London. When they organized events, mail flyers and telephone calls were used to bring them together.

Mr. Ram Sharma

I met Mr. Ram in his workplace. He owned a corner shop in Ilford and was able to take time while at work to do our first interview. When customers came in to buy cigarettes or a group of school girls bought packets of gum, I would hit the pause button on my tape-recorder so he could continue his daily work. It was one of the hardest interviews I had; we only spoke for about forty interrupted minutes. One word befits his attitude toward me: hostile. He made it clear that my presence was an imposition and that he had better things to do with his time. As soon as I sensed this from him, I suggested that I could come back at a better time. He said that it was fine to continue. Nevertheless, the interview promptly ended when guests arrived, a couple whom he led through the back door of the shop, which I came to realize was the entry to his home.

He lived in the classic English main street arrangements, the kind on the TV shows, "up top the shop." He had three children, whom I never did meet because they all were young adults who lived apart from their parents. The son was a pharmacist, the daughter a dentist, and the youngest son was away at Cambridge studying law. I asked if I could meet his wife to ask her about her immigration. He responded, "I have told you everything; there is no need." Later, I suggested that I would be interested in meeting his children; I was also met with silence. Just as I was leaving he offered me a drink or a soda, in fact he insisted on it as if playing the good host. Initially, I was devastated that the interview had gone so terribly wrong, and I wondered if I could have done anything differently to put him more at ease. The only sense that I had that his view of the whole meeting was different was when I would run into him at parties and at the temple. On such occasions, he would come up to me to chat, asking me how my book was coming along, being friendly with my husband, and telling others that he helped me out.

Mrs. Rani Sanon

Mrs. Sanon was married to a medical doctor and lived in an affluent middle-class neighborhood in West London. She was a teacher and was one of the three women I met during my research who had migrated as single woman. She met her future husband, who studied medicine with her brother, while she was studying economics. Often parents hesitated to speak to me about racism, but Mrs. Sanon was candid. Her experiences teaching learning-disabled children also gave her a sense of structural constraints in the system and of how multiculturalism was playing out on the ground. For a time, she was a multicultural coordinator for the school. She definitely had opinions about diversity.

They had two daughters, one in secondary school and the other at university. For family vacations they traveled every summer to Europe, and that year they were making plans for Italy. After our first interview I ran into her at the temple and at parties, but she never said too much more to me. She said that I was welcome back for a second interview, but I never pursued it. By that time I had met a number of people and was not "interviewing" but immersed in participant observation by spending time with people at home or, if possible, at their workplaces. Nevertheless, our conversations continued unexpectedly in social places, such as Sapna Aggarwal's wedding. She spoke to me about recent changes in her life and how her second daughter was starting university.

Mr. Prem Bhasin

Mr. Bhasin, no relation to the Mr. Bhasin who provided the temple list, lived in a classic terrace and the souvenir trinkets of a well-traveled person surrounded us when I entered his living room for the first interview. He was retired and recently widowed, and because of this was able to meet with me at many different times and become more involved in my own research project, suggesting people to meet, seeing me and my husband at the temple where he was active, and at one point encouraging us to become members so that we could vote in the temple executive (to make it easier for us, he supplied us with a list of names). This happened just after a major temple-related function and his house was full of *mithai*. He offered me a plate brimming with desserts with a cup of tea. At our many meetings he also offered varied aspects of his life story, his migration, how he settled in Britain, and his recent loss.

He had one daughter who lived in Manhattan, New York. In fact, during our first meeting she called from the United States to chat to him, and he was planning a short visit to New York. In his last job before retirement as a senior manager he had traveled all over Europe. The first time I went to the temple with the Kapurs and the Kalias was just after my interview with him. I waved hello in the crowded room packed with six hundred people, well beyond capacity. Mrs. Kapur was surprised and wanted to know how I knew him. When I said that I interviewed him, she seemed more willing to speak to me about her own life story. He was one of the well-respected pillars of society who had helped establish the temple, but he never did tell me too much about that, because that was his volunteer service and he was much more interested in telling me his life story.

Mr. Karnal Bhandari

Mr. Bhandari was one of the youngest of the migrants I interviewed. He migrated as a teenager during the Amin crisis in Africa and had moved out of Uganda to London in the early 1970s. His parents had come to Africa from the Punjab, and he was very curious about their migration as well as his own. He had a master's degree and was extremely well read and well connected in the Asian art scene. He was involved in incorporating Asian and Indian themes, including migration stories and issues, into various artistic projects. Thankfully, he was also very interested in my work. Our interviews were more like ongoing conversations full of fabulous tangents. Karnal was married with two children; unfortunately during my fieldwork his wife became quite ill, and I never had a chance to meet his family.

Trope of the Successful Migrant

All of the people I studied could be seen as living the trope of the successful migrant. They were successful professionals, their children attended good schools — in some cases private schools — and they were able to afford nice houses in respectable neighborhoods. As they established their lives in Britain, they had witnessed many changes in what it meant to be a migrant in Britain. For example, in 1996 Dr. Swraj Paul's elevation to the peerage as Lord Paul was one of the most visible events marking the achievements and struggles of postwar South Asian migrants to Britain. It revealed the ways that ethnic minorities are deeply implicated in British history and identity. His inclusion into the United Kingdom's second chamber of Parliament received wide media attention and put a spotlight on the life of a prominent Hindu Punjabi migrant. The first and only time that I met Dr. Paul was at his corporate headquarters in central London, when I interviewed him to learn about his own migration to Britain. Our meeting was brief, and he seemed to share a well-rehearsed story of migration bolstered by an offer of company literature that could fill in the specific details. In fact, the particularities of Dr. Paul's migration story were made public in the press following his £1 million donation to the London Zoo. Born in Punjab, he arrived to the United Kingdom in 1966 seeking leukemia treatment for his daughter, Ambika. She had visited the children's zoo with her father between hospital visits. After his daughter's death, he and his wife "decided to shape things anew and make our home in Britain. [Feeling] that this change and the fresh pastures would give meaningful challenges."[4] His story, combined with others, helped me to formulate the dynamic process of ethnic identification for Hindu Punjabis.

Although Lord Paul's migration and life story are unique, statistically, he is a part of the post-WWII middle-class South Asian migration to Britain. Little is known of these migrants and their lives, despite the fact that "various surveys and studies reveal that there is a significant proportion of Britain's Asian population who occupy professional, administrative and white-collar positions in the labor market, as well as setting up businesses to supply goods and services" (Daye 1994: 9).[5] To fill this research void, I undertook an urban ethnography of middle-class Hindu Punjabis. These people are dispersed and do not live in areas of high ethnic concentration. At the time of my fieldwork, most of the people I worked with lived in the suburban areas of Greater London. Formerly, several had lived in working-class districts that continue to be among the poorest areas in Britain.

Part of their story follows the trope of the classic immigrant success story, which could be misread as the "the model minority." Scholars understand the achievement of middle-class stability to alter ethnic identity. The putative abandonment of ethnic identity by the middle class is central to scholars' understandings of minority aspirations (see, for instance, Rattansi 2000: 125).[6] Such a position makes the ethnic middle class culturally and socially uninteresting because they are assumed to have discarded ethnic culture or alternatively play as pawn in a larger socially engineered structural chess game of exclusion (cf. Prashad 2000).

As a result, there is little formulation of the interstices of British class and Asian ethnic identity. The modalities of identity are infused with power dynamics and are not tidily separated — class is not separated from ethnicity, gender, or sexual orientation (see Frankenberg and Mani 1996; King 1988). I do not wish to present an exegesis of the implications of class in the modern world, but would like to add ethnographic observations of the South Asian middle-class in Britain to Ong's assertion that "less attention has been given to human agency and the cultural practices of the powerful, as well as how they have been shaped and given meaning by translocal relationships" (Ong 1999: 30).[7]

Class remains an implicit modality of identification for the people I studied, expressed through commodities, housing, travel, and many other preferences of occupation, leisure, and lifestyle. As middle-class Hindu Punjabis, they form a minority within the larger Asian minority in Britain. Since the 1980s, the demographic trend among the British Indian minority has been a large-scale production of white-collar professionals, noted by Ballard and Kalra (1994) to be roughly double the rate of white British citizens moving out of manual labor. My focus is on how, as a minority within a minority, the Hindu Punjabi middle class experienced changes in their ethnic identification. Partially this is a story of their sense of changed economic position. They constitute the Asian middle class, an ill-defined group that has various associations, professions, and histories that reflect their middle-class status.[8] The organization of their class identity is perhaps best captured in their assumptions of embracing a tale of the emigrant success story, that Indians and Asians such as themselves have enjoyed financial success and to a lesser extent political participation. However, this story has played out in very specific and distinct ways, quite unlike that of the South Asian migrants to America (for recent works on the conceptualization of the "Indian American," see Prashad 2000; Rangaswamy 2000; Shukla 2001). The main difference is that while in the United States the majority of migrants were from middle-class backgrounds, which produced a story of the model minority (a story vehemently critiqued by Prashad 2000), the majority of migrants to Britain from the Subcontinent were from rural working-class backgrounds. It is in distinction to these groups that many of those I studied organize themselves. Thus, while the people I studied did not organize themselves around their class identity, their specific sense of class identity as successful immigrants has entirely shaped their ethnic identification. The people whose lives and words inform these pages are educated professionals often working as teachers, accountants, doctors, or are self-employed. In addition, many are retired or nearing retirement. The "parental" or "migrant" generation arrived in the United Kingdom between 1949 and 1969 (the majority between 1956 and 1965). They arrived directly from India, a few from Punjab, but most from Delhi, as well as via East Africa (before the Amin exodus). Their children, and they usually have two, are now young adult professionals, jokingly known as "Puppies" (Punjabi Yuppies), who had, or were pursuing, secondary degrees to become doctors, dentists, accountants, or white-collar professionals. Leaving aside the trope of the classic immigrant success story, one in which immigrants and their children are full of achievement, I explore how their own sense of their ethnic identity has changed because of being Vilayati and Asian.

Vilayat — The Place

The parental generation, the migrants, arrived in Britain after the Second World War. Their lives since arriving in the United Kingdom reflect the tremendous change in British society that followed the war. After WWII, Britain focused on the reconstruction of the nation through comprehensive programs for housing and health, full employment and industrial regeneration. To sustain and control growth (and avoid the haphazard ways in which the period following World War I lead to instability), there was a massive reform of the economy during which time major industries became publicly owned (such as gas, telecommunications, coal, railways, road transport, civil aviation, the Bank of England, and electricity). Almost simultaneously after the war, Britain faced the end of empire. India gained independence in 1947, partially owing to the participation of India in the war, with Indian empire soldiers fighting battles in Europe and North Africa on behalf of the British. "The granting of self-government to India . . . in 1947 . . . was the key moment in the transfer of power. It was an unambiguous statement of Britain's military and financial inability and above all lack of will, to retain possession of distant lands by force" (Morgan 1999: 640). Leaving aside the claim for the British lack of will, from the perspective of the newly formed Indian nation, independence was the result of political struggle, which led to the triumph of self-governance. Of course, the vestiges of empire continue to this day. In 1997 Britain "returned" its prosperous colony of Hong Kong to China, in spring 2000 Australia held a referendum regarding the constitutional monarchy, and to this day the Governor General continues to be the Queen's representative in Canada. Her portrait is even found on all Canadian currency. These examples reveal the continuance of the imperial Commonwealth, albeit in muted ceremonial form. Nevertheless, the postwar period is taken to be synonymous with the "end of empire" for Britain. The decline of the empire, combined with the intense focus on the internal economy, made the United Kingdom distinctively introspective.

Rapid economic developments characterized the postwar period. The former laboring classes moved upward to greater affluence and stability thereby creating an urgent need for a steady flow of workers. In methodical fashion, Britain turned to her former colonies and actively recruited in the Caribbean, the West Indies, and South Asia (India, Pakistan, Bangladesh, and Sri Lanka). The mixed economy of postwar growth, bolstered by former colonial migration and balanced with social welfare, survived until the late 1960s. The early 1970s were marked by the soaring value of the pound sterling, frequent balance of payment crises, inflation, growing unemployment, and the energy crisis (which affected most of the Western nations). Thus, the brief period of postwar affluence was followed by rapid economic decline, a period with lasting effects on the social fabric of the nation. Almost as quickly as Britain wanted and needed workers, it wanted them out. It is no coincidence that the politician Enoch Powell's anti-immigration stance flourished in the rapidly declining urban industrial areas in the Midlands and London's Docklands.[9] Powell is infamous for his "inflammatory rhetoric of a maverick right-wing Cassandra" (Morgan 1999: 647), based on his decrying of the consequences of immigration with references to the River Tiber foaming with blood. These events epitomized the racial tensions of the period in which the once coveted and much-needed migrant worker became the scapegoat for Britain's sudden decline.

The official response was in the form of two successively restrictive immigration policies, the Commonwealth Immigration Acts of 1968 and 1972. These simultaneously focused the nation on their ongoing connection with other parts of the world and how events elsewhere could affect the nation. This was particularly true of the British response to the Amin crisis in Uganda and the resulting 1972 Immigration Act, which reflected the mood of a nation that intended to remain severely insular and focus on its internal problems. The grandfather clause of the 1972 Commonwealth Immigrant Act ensured that only those individuals whose grandparents were British nationals could enter the Isles. In effect, this disbarred nonwhite British citizens who hailed from South Asia and had been living in Africa for up to three generations. Many of these peo-

ple successfully applied to America and Canada for immigration (in retrospect this act was an economic loss for the United Kingdom). Since the
1960s Britain has had an increasingly restricted immigration policy, thereby creating one of the most protected boundaries in Europe. Immigration serves as a symbol for the decay of the nation.[10] It was unsuccessful,
but continued to be heard until the early 1990s. The 1970s industrial
decline combined with high inflation fueled Britain's insular response and
created a period of intense social unrest marked by union strikes, "race
riots," and National Front fascist attacks in "ethnic areas," as well as a deterioration in the institutions of tradition (including the monarchy).

The Thatcherite years that followed attempted to halt the economic
decline with severe government cutbacks. The policy agenda of this time
has been described as "the most right-wing that Britain had known in the
twentieth century" (Morgan 1999: 656). Britain continues to suffer the
social consequences of this rough ride of intensively conservative rule,
which stabilized the economy through the deregulation and privatization
of the major industries and decreased funding for health care, education,
and the "arts." The seeming insignificance of international affairs in the
British public continued until the Falkland crisis in the 1980s brought
Great Britain and her dilapidated empire into sharp focus. By the early
1990s, there seemed to be some reticent stability and openness to the outside world, characterized by the debates on the involvement in the Gulf
War and the contemplation of European integration, though these were
plagued with Euro-phobia. In the 1990s "disparities in wealth, income,
health and lifestyle had grown ever-wider" (Morgan 1999: 666) and a general feeling of despair prevailed. However, there also seemed to be rising
like a phoenix another contradictory sense of Britain. "Britain was increasingly prosperous and most of its citizens content with their lot. Ethnic
minorities had made progress after the racial disturbances of the Thatcher
years" (Morgan 1999: 667). The ethnic minorities that had supposedly
made progress included the Hindu Punjabis who arrived in London after
the war and lived during this last thirty to forty years in a nation characterized by intensive decline and insularity, which has only been alleviated
in recent years to relative stability. Concomitantly, this was a period during which some postwar migrants established themselves as solidly middle class in Britain.

The Kapurs, Kalias, Chawlas, and Aggarwals, along with the other
families I worked with, fall within the chronological period of postwar
migration. Their lives are intermingled with recent British history because
they arrived in the United Kingdom in the late 1950s and early 1960s.

During this period they formed part of the "economic" migration to Britain. Of course with increasingly restrictive immigration policies during the last forty years, the only true economic migrants to Britain are "white, male, American or European, and are coming here 'on business'. They are rarely stopped by Customs officers" (Marr 2000: 138). In contrast, many Asians who arrived during the very early period of postwar migration did not arrive here "on business"; they had been actively encouraged to migrate and were recruited to fill in for the workers moving up in the postwar boom economy.

However, middle-class Hindu Punjabi migration narratives do not conform precisely to the widely accepted four-phase model of South Asian migration to Britain. The model divides people into clustered archetypes. First pioneers arrived (students, seamen, and salesmen), then sojourners (single male migrants who thought they would return). The third phase is marked by the migration of women and children and is called "Asian community establishment." The final phase is the only one that does not involve migration but concentrates on the British-born generation and community shifts (C. Ballard 1979; Helweg 1989; P. Werbner 1987). For my interlocutors, all types of immigration seemed to occur simultaneously. I met with two couples in which the husband and wife had migrated independently, met in England, and then married (the ceremonies took place in India). These cases were exceptional. In all, during the initial period of the early 1960s, the male may have come first but he was married and there was no dominant model.[11]

The many different types of migration included single men, married men (without their wives), couples, and entire families.[12] Thus, it was not easy to isolate or describe a grand "family reunification" stage for the Hindu Punjabis involved in my study since migration histories were both temporally and experientially so diverse. For example, among my informants, there was not a sharply distinguishable gap between male and female migration phases. The Hindu Punjabi men of my research who arrived as single male migrants during the 1950s and early 1960s as part of the "working groups" returned to India to marry within five years (of arriving in Britain) and returned to Britain immediately with their wives or sponsored their wives to join them. This group's migration narratives can be seen as conforming to the second and third phases of migration whereby the majority male population began to change as individuals brought their wives to the United Kingdom. At the same time, however, others migrated after marriage, with the intention that their wives would join them in Britain (after securing housing and employment, or after beginning an educational course). They came to study, to get medical training, or to see what the prospects might be. In other cases, couples migrated together, just after marriage. This joint migration was most common when both husband and wife were doctors. When a couple migrated together, usually one spouse had obtained a firm job placement before migration. In a few instances, people who had already started families migrated, with the men being sent to England and the wife and infant following. Thus, in some of the families of my research, although both children had been brought up in Britain (two children per family was the norm), the first child may have been born in India. These were the most common scenarios for migration.

This widely accepted four-phase scheme is based on the majority trend of rural South Asian migration to urban Britain. Most families in my study, Brahmans, Khattri, or Banias, had come from urban life in India. They were very different in that respect from the Jullunder Doab Sikh Jat, Mirpuri Muslim, or Bangladeshi Syletti Muslim migrations discussed in the British ethnicity literature, which primarily involved rural families and peasant landowning castes. In contrast, only two Hindu Punjabi men of my larger core group of thirty families originated in the rural "migration region" of the Jullunder Doab. All others in my core sample were urban dwellers before migrating to Britain. A few of the "single" migrant men arrived directly from Punjab or via a short stay in East Africa, but most of the male migrants came from Delhi.[13] Likewise, many of those who migrated as families or couples did not come directly from the Punjab region. Some of the older, already retired, migrants were born in "West Punjab" (now Pakistan) and had lived briefly in East Punjab after 1947.[14] However they had generally migrated to Britain from outside of the Punjab, usually from an urban center (such as Delhi, Bombay, or even Meerut). Only one individual, my Punjabi language teacher's husband, now quite elderly and retired, had arrived before the Partition from what became Pakistan. Also, similar to the "twice migrants" of Parminder Bhachu's study, these people were of "good" social standing, with some wealth and university education. Unlike the East African Sikhs, these Hindu Punjabis were in one sense "direct migrants" (moving from India to Britain); yet because of their family experiences as Partition refugees many possessed the "making community" skills Bhachu argues that direct migrants lack (Bhachu 1985).

The four-phase model of Asian migration has inadvertently produced a gendered historical migration chronicle: it emphasizes male histories in which women are dependants. In my research, three women of the two hundred people I met had migrated independently of men. One woman of Gujarati background was born in East Africa and had migrated to England to complete a diploma in nursing. Her Hindu Punjabi "boyfriend" from Uganda (now husband) subsequently migrated to England to be close to her. Another was a doctor who came to the United Kingdom in the 1950s to gain an MBBS qualification; she initially intended to move back to India, but then settled permanently and married a doctor who was a family friend. In the third instance, a woman arrived in 1970 to study for a master's degree. She had been teaching in a college in India and met her husband in Britain through her brother (the two men were training together in medicine). These women, however, proved to be exceptions. Women's migration usually depended on their spouses or their fathers. Much of the work on British Asians does not explore gender; as Banks confirms, "the role of gender in constructing and transforming ethnic identities is still an ill-researched topic, and much of the earlier literature on ethnicity is effectively gender blind" (1996: 102).[15] However, the role of women in making "community" by their migration is widely recognized (indeed this is the main premise of the third phase). But gender is also a central factor in the different migrations to Britain. The standard account that claims men arrived as "pioneers" or "settlers" and then "sent for" women is an overgeneralization. Men often had connections with people in Britain defined through women. Of course, women arrived as "daughters" as well as wives.

Migration is not only urban-rural and gender dependent but also "time" dependent. The timing of migration and the migrants' experience was determined by the changing legislation of immigration mandates (reflecting "the mood of the nation"). Immigration is part of the technology of the state underpinning the construction of national identities. Immigration throughout British history is a contentious political issue. "During the last of Winston Churchill's administrations, in 1953, the Home Office working party which was seeking to keep 'coloureds' out produced a nakedly racist report. . . . Searching for ways of keeping out coloured migrants while, in the words of the official report, 'avoiding the appearance of doing so' led to the first Commonwealth Immigration Act in 1962 and the growth of a large apparatus of controls intended to keep Britain white" (Marr 2000: 151–52). The restrictive controls were meant to control the flow of people into Britain and had direct effects on the type of people and their settlement patterns in Britain. The Immigration Acts that affected the migrants I worked with were: the British Nationality Act (1948) when there were no restrictions on entering Britain for

Commonwealth members; the Commonwealth Immigrants Act (1962), which made entry conditional on a work voucher; and the 1968 Act, aimed at further restricting immigrants due to fears arising from East African political uncertainty (which also affected migrants arriving directly from India). The wider group of two hundred migrants among whom I did my research arrived between 1947 and 1981, although the majority of those in my core sample arrived in the 1960s.

Individuals' reflections on their differing migration experiences stressed broader immigration policy only through changing bureaucratic requirements; they emphasized the hurdles for procuring the "papers" needed for immigration, especially an Indian passport. Thus, for example, vouchers sent by friends (school or family friends) in the late 1960s were not seen as especially difficult to procure after the decision to migrate was taken. Men recounted what they needed to do and "who they knew," which helped them to migrate to Britain. Their stories were about what needed to be done. In cases when women arrived independently or separately from the men, their stories, by contrast, were stories of waiting: they stressed the time delay between applying for immigration and actually arriving in Britain. Women's time delays were in an obvious sense related to their specific migration period and the concomitant policy, but this was not how such delays were expressed. Women would not explicitly connect their own experiences of delay between applying for migration and their actual arrival to British state policy. Rather, delays were seen as an inevitable part of migration. This sense of inevitability with respect to immigration permeated my fieldwork. For example, I met a woman at a dinner party whose newly wed daughter-in-law was to arrive in Britain from Bombay. When I offered sympathies at the delay and the difficulties of waiting for bureaucracy to catch up with their lives, she replied, "Well, the government has to do this to weed out those abuses of the system. Really, we don't mind; as we are a legitimate case, we know that it will eventually happen. It is good that they do this; it is necessary." She went on to speak about her own quick arrival after her marriage in the early 1960s (she waited only three months). An acquaintance sitting nearby who was listening to our conversation was surprised and joined in with her own tale: "Really? It took me almost two years after my marriage to arrive here" (she had come after the 1968 Act).

Thus bureaucracy for most women was relevant only in the sense of having to prove their marital status, especially since many arrived in Britain with their husbands; however, for the men negotiating bureaucracy was a primary part of their migration stories. One Uncle claimed that the immigration process itself was easy, once they had overcome the main difficulty of "having the passport made" in India.[16] Many men spoke of their "approach," in other words a personal contact, in the passport offices. Passports and visas were seen not as rights but as desirable commodities, necessary to improve quality of life and to allow "further prospects." As bureaucratic instruments, passports and visas opened proverbial doors. Thus, after getting their Indian passports with full rights to enter the United Kingdom, these immigrants then took up British citizenship for various reasons: ease of travel to Europe or America and to show commitment to Britain. Indian passports were kept by a few in order to secure land in India, because, until recently, India did not allow foreign nationals to own land. When one family member kept an Indian passport, usually it was the woman. Both those who migrated from Africa and those who had family friends from Africa also mentioned keeping Indian passports because of Idi Amin's Uganda exodus. Many were conscious of potentially being exiled from Britain, even if they had accumulated wealth and had been established in the country for many generations. This relates to all the rhetoric of repatriation that plagued the 1970s.

Initially many of Hindu Punjabi migrants lived in areas of London with a large proportion of other immigrants, including those from the Subcontinent. People mentioned Aldywch, Mile End, East and West Ham, or Forest Gate.[17] But, at the time of my fieldwork, none of the families I researched lived in areas known for their large South Asian populations. Rather, they had moved into middle-class residential areas mostly to the north and east of central London, living in these locations for approximately thirteen years (mean average), though some had been living in these areas for the last twenty years (thus some of their children were raised in "all-white" neighborhoods). This stability contrasts with the time of arrival when most families, or individuals, moved at least three or four times and some had moved up to seven times in the first ten years.

They emphasized their distinctiveness from other Asians. They repeatedly told me, for example, that they did not live in areas of ethnic residential concentration like the majority of other Asians. There was, in fact, a conscious attempt not to live in such areas, or to move away from those areas quickly and "go where the money would take us." Two distinct patterns of settlement are evident. For some of my informants, initial residence was determined by living near an existing contact who lived in Greater London. Many of the people I knew arrived in Britain "knowing" someone, but not someone whom they had known before the decision to migrate was taken. Few people had more than limited family in Britain, and often these were distant kin or individuals unknown because of family quarrels. Often men and women would activate a link with individuals whom they had heard had settled in the United Kingdom. One man initially lived with a schoolmate's uncle, a connection activated only after he decided to migrate. There was thus no close connection between "chain migration" patterns and geographical concentration, as there is for other migrant groups from India. It was more common, however, for the migrants to first live in areas where there was a substantial minority community already established, renting accommodation in East Ham, West Ham (now Newham E7), or Forest Gate. Not one of the families I worked with or met had ever settled or lived in Southall. But the repeated goal was "you leave where you are for a better place and you keep going up and up, within your means to a bigger house, more amenities, more facilities, better," as one Uncle told me in an interview.

Similarly, job changing was common in this early period: four changes were average, often beginning "on the shop floor" in a factory.[18] However, at the time of my research, my informants were teachers, accountants, doctors, or owned their own businesses. Most arrived in the United Kingdom with professional Indian qualifications, such as an undergraduate degree, and the women often had done teacher training. However, these degrees were usually not recognized in Britain, and after immigration they would have to study for comparable British qualifications. Men were proud to recount the early period when they studied part-time and worked full-time in a factory. Some families told their children of the initial difficulties, others were silent about it. In either case, the children have all learned of the necessity of a good-paying job. They joke about having at least one doctor or accountant in the family, while pursuing their own academic interests (law and economics seemed popular). The children of these middle-class migrants (between the ages of eighteen and thirty-three) were college or university educated (some had gone to private schools). A few had gone to college, acquired a vocational diploma, and were now involved in a family business, working in a semiprofessional capacity (usually sales) or, exceptionally, in developing their own business. Some "children" were recently married, or looking for a marriage partner (see Chapter 5). If single and working they most likely lived at home; if studying, they lived near the university. A few relocated away from their families because of their jobs (but usually remained in the United Kingdom).

The truism bears repeating that those who are migrating are often from families that have the means and connections to send their members abroad. As Roger Ballard states:

Long distance migrants are rarely drawn from the poorest families, and for good reason. Migration is above all an *entrepreneurial* activity, in which success usually depends on making substantial initial investment. . . . Overseas migrants are therefore usually drawn from families of middling status, whose members are neither sufficiently prosperous to be wholly content with their lot, nor so poor as to be unable to afford the migrant's ticket, passport and visa. (R. Ballard 1994b: 9–10)

This characteristic definitely applies to those whom I studied. I would argue that they in fact perceived their "middling status" as relative deprivation, partially caused by conditions in postindependence, post-Partition India. That their families were well connected is obvious from the shared tales of procuring passports. Moreover, their good connections and relatively privileged status was something repeated to others and constantly evoked in social situations ("my father is . . . ," "my uncle knows . . . ," "my brother lives in . . . ," and so on). Yet many migrated to Britain in pursuit of employment and education: these attempts at betterment reflect their belief that they could achieve beyond what was possible for them in India. To search for prospects, looking "for something better," was a theme in my interactions with parents. "Something better" revolved around education, jobs, or a philosophical curiosity to see the world, experience life, and be successful by proving that "you could be your own man." Thus, the motives for migration were not so obviously clear cut as for the rural migrants who came to work in urban industrial Britain. These Hindu Punjabis were coming from an urban background, searching for betterment, but with means and education, achievement, and connections within India. Previous research has hidden both Hindu Punjabis and middle-class Asians; whether my informants were typical of these groups in general is difficult to ascertain, as comparative data is not available.[19] Nevertheless, based on existing literature their experiences of migration, settling into Britain, and the concerns for and of their children in many respects seems to be "typical" of Hindu Punjabis and British middle class Asian families.[20]

In my interviews I first took life histories from the migrants, and a gendered difference emerged when they told me about their lives in Britain. As mentioned above, men spoke about all the things that they had to do to as related to their immigration to Britain. Women often emphasized "hardship" in their life stories. Aunty Aggarwal spoke to me about her daughter's extravagance and lack of understanding of "the real value of money" (her daughter was a doctor). Aunty often recounted the money-management skills she learned during their initial Spartan existence when she would wash all the clothes by hand in cold water and would not heat water or the bedsit until absolutely necessary because of the high costs. Her change in financial status, as apparent from the Bentley, Jaguar, and Mercedes to be found in the driveway, has not erased these memories. The hardship stories emphasize both a generational transition as well as a class transition. These "hardship tales" run parallel to "the successful migrant stories" often related by men. Both revolve around "life when we first arrived" and were directly evoked for their children so that they could learn "everything in life that we have done for you, or with you in mind." This phrase, or some variation of it, was related to the children and then retold by children to each other in joking fashion. It reveals the enormous pressures toward aspirations, goals, and achievements placed by the migrant generation on their children. The phrase framed migration experiences by creating a specific narrative of migration that is passed on to the second generation. It is a narrative, which though essential and repeated, is not directly related to the specific details of their migrations. The children of these Hindu Punjabi families rarely know all of their parent's migration story, indeed many know very little of it (most children could not tell me what year their parents arrived in Britain). The narrative is important, however, in creating a sense of family sacrifice, work ethic, and guilt and debt to parents. The children feel a sense of obligation, of duty, and the "habitus" of Hindu Punjabi culture, which includes a feeling that they must make an effort to succeed and indeed surpass their parents' achievements.

Conceptualizing the Vilayati — Space, Time, and Difference

Scholars have conceptualized the migration of the postcolonial subject to Britain in terms of a newness of meetings. A number of studies on South Asians have focused on the connections between the overseas population and "the motherland" as well as on cultural change: working "at *both* ends of the migration chain" (Watson 1977: 2; see also Jeffrey 1976; E. Kelly 1990; Saifullah-Khan 1977). Scholars have produced an abundance of "Little India" or "*Chota* Punjab" type studies in the United Kingdom whereby the disarticulation of South Asian-ness or the connections with homeland are the chief concerns seconded by the concern to "crystallize the conflicts between migrant and host societies" (Shukla 2001: 563). These works studied "culture" through a comparison between British Asians and "their counterparts" whom they left behind in South Asia. Yet the research involves specific spatiotemporal assumptions about the who, where, and what of research subjects. In such frameworks, Britain's South Asian migrant communities are outposts of tradition, keepers of tradition, or losing tradition. This is not to state that the Subcontinent is not important, but that the manner through which it is assumed to provide a de facto connection has limited the ways we can understand migration and cultural change.

Research rendering the South Asian diaspora as "home and away" or "home away from home" confounds space and time. Studies that include a return to the Subcontinent to understand the diaspora confound time by going to South Asia and "working at *both* ends of the migration chain" to understand migrants' culture where a twenty- or even forty-year gap exists. Punjab in 1975 was made to stand for the Punjab migrants who may have left fifteen or twenty years earlier. These comparisons rested on specific notions about South Asia as a producer of closed communities that reproduced themselves in many settings. The appeal of this view lies in the emphasis on displacement as a trope, which disaggregates culture from territory. "Diasporic discourse in this context is strong on displacement, detachment, uprooting, and dispersion — on disarticulation. It is appealing precisely because it so easily lends itself to a strategic disaggregation of territory, people, race, language, culture, religion, history and sovereignty" (Kirshenblatt-Gimblett 1994: 339). Present-day South Asia has had rapid economic, social, and political changes that have radically altered the society from which the migrants came. The "homeland" is not a repository of information that can shed light on British Asians. The act of immigration itself made them Vilayati — they are from the outside and this specific formulation forced me to think about the links between them and their putative homeland (I return to this in Chapter 7). The children of migrants who travel to India only to discover that their values and customs are of an India from twenty-odd years ago are perhaps the best markers of cultural change, that is, cultural change in India. Youth have spoken about their cousins or relatives' musings about the "traditionalism" of their Vilayati kin. The British youth, especially the girls, speak about their shock when they visit family in Delhi or Bombay and they see girls wearing miniskirts and shorts.

In the past, the South Asian diaspora could not be imagined otherwise

because of our specific understandings of culture as a spatial and temporal constant. There are limitations to this approach, as Aisha Khan
cogently argues with respect to her work on the Caribbean: "Many of
these studies have been, in part, or wholly, concerned with the relationship between origins, symbolic and material continuities, and
change in the cultures of emigrant populations 'transmitted' over time
and space" (1994: 245). Her caustic condemnation of the ways in which
anthropologists have imagined the connections between India and its
emigrants questions the easy association and yardstick measurements to
a putative "home culture." The attraction of looking to India as the
source or guide for exploring British Asians can be linked to two specific
critiques leveled against anthropology: its methodologies and reluctance
to incorporate historical contemplation. Critiques of ahistorical, static
perspectives have come from both within and outside the discipline
(Marcus 1989; Marcus and Clifford 1986; Fabian 1983; Clifford 1983).
The critique is now being redressed with the use of historical sources
and the increasing interest in long-term cultural change (Davis 1994;
Fox 1985; Ghosh 1992; Toren 1994). Ethnographies of Asians in Britain,
however, continue resolutely to focus on the present-day and produce
ethnographies without time. The fact that the British were in India (and
in the Punjab for almost one hundred years) seems incidental. This may
seem an obvious omission as anthropological field research is de facto
based in Britain.[21] But even those anthropologists who worked "at
both ends of the migration chain" assumed two self-contained and
present-time societies for comparison existing "here" and "there." Such
research recognizes the economic conditions in South Asia, especially
the "push-pull" factors that produced migrants, but it tends not to set
such observations in a wider context of the creation of group identity,
culture, and community with respect to changing dynamics of power
and representation.

For example, it is commonly known that the majority of South Asian
migrants to Britain originated in Gujarat and Punjab. The reasons offered
for their preeminence among migrants from the Subcontinent include
farming stress on land, patterns of inheritance, early-nineteenth-century
droughts, unemployment or underemployment, and other economic factors (see Fox 1985). These factors, however, are invariably linked with the
policies and practices of the British Raj. Furthermore, that Punjab and
Gujarat provided the bulk of migrants is also related to their long associations as historical trade centers (especially for Gujarat) and conquest
areas (especially for Punjab). Consequently, both regions were familiar

with the British Raj's ruling arm. This inevitably produced cultural familiarity at certain levels and a changed perception, or "worldview" long
before the postwar migration. However, the influence of cultural familiarity on the "push" factor is not generally acknowledged. Instead, the
standard economically deterministic theories of migration that brought
the migrants to Britain as workers (funding the postwar industrial production) or as a result of recruitment of Indians into the Allied armies as
Indian soldiers (some of whom then migrated to or retired in Britain) are
the only ways in which Britain's migrants are connected with the history
of empire.[22]

Because British sociocultural influences in India are not considered, the
toolkit is limited to an inevitable concentration on "transplanted culture,"
or South Asian "culture," or the culture of ethno-religious group X in
which India is treated as a site of origination. One recent ethnography
innocently illustrates the ahistoric attitude pervasive in British Asian
ethnographies:

In the decades since the Second World War, the flow of migrants has been mainly
towards "the west" or "the north": the centers of former colonial power (Balibar,
1991a). Relations between global "center[s]" and margin[s]" have shifted radically
(Julien and Mercer, 1988). The resulting encounters — collisions and collusions —
between colonizers and colonized, between tradition and modernity, between
"the east" and "the west," "the south" and "the north," have precipitated enormous
social and cultural changes. In Britain, in particular, established notions of
"national culture" and "national belonging" — of what it means to be British and
who belongs — have been challenged and transformed. (Gillespie 1995: 3)

But the "encounters . . . between colonizers and colonized" are not new;
the British were in India well before the post-World War II factory
worker from the Subcontinent arrived in the Midlands or West London
(the research area for the above scholar). Social and cultural changes for
Asians began long before Asians arrived in Britain. Yet by reading the
accounts of migrants to Britain one might suppose the Raj was never in
India.

The Portuguese, trading with India since 1505, were eventually followed by the British East India Company, which was formed in 1600. In
1858 the East India Company's dissolution brought India under the
empire as a viceroyalty (1885). The cultural fascination in Britain with "The
Orient" is well represented in architectural forms and the penchant for
luxury silks and fine cottons — the Brighton Pavilion with its surreal
domes or even the "Durbar Room" in Queen Victoria's Osborne House

(built in 1890 by BhaiRam Singh of the Lahore school) all combine to reveal the earlier mercantile cultural exchanges. Moreover, the impact of the Raj on language and food in Britain is readily recognized (people live in bungalows, sit on verandas, eat kedgeree and chutney, drink punch, wear jodhpurs or cummerbunds, and read newspaper reports containing the words "juggernaut," "guru," or "pundit"); yet the long-standing cultural effects of the British Raj on creating what is now understood as "Asian" culture are ignored. Language change provides one example of Europe's influence on Asians before they arrived in Britain.[23] Ivor Lewis (1991) suggests that English and Portuguese words now currently used in Punjabi (and Gujarati) offer the possibility of considering long-lasting cultural shifts, which are the result of the colonial encounter.[24]

"Being and exuding British-ness" were challenged throughout the empire prior to anthropological first contact with migrants in Britain. The challenges to the 1925 Coloured Alien Seamen Order and the 1948 British Nationality Act reveal two early examples of institutional changes addressing "belonging" in Britain.[25] Challenges to empire by South Asians, and inclusion in the Commonwealth had taken place long before 1948. Three examples among many include: the Ghadar movement in North America (Jurgensmeyer 1979; Puri 1993), the Quit India movement activities in London, and the debates surrounding the various categories of British passport and immigration legislation from late nineteenth century onward. All three indicate that "notions of national culture" and "nationalism" had been challenged *before* post-World War II Asian arrival in Britain. Granted, these challenges may have been different, but this is to be expected with varying social, cultural, and historical contexts.

This historical amnesia eclipses prior cultural connections between Asian migrants and Britain. The migrant arrives in Britain with a post-British rule South Asian culture that needs to be researched. But the migration process starts with acquiring a passport or waiting for bureaucracy, and the familiarity with the regimes of bureaucracy have long been in place. However, the siren call of a fresh contact story between two cultures emerges from a notion of being outsiders from only one perspective. Asians are marked as minorities in Britain. They represent the trope of the successful migrant in which their cultures change because of economic changes in Britain. In this common interpretation, post-World War II migration to Britain is the "cause" of social and cultural change to Asian and British identities. Research on Asians in Britain must cut this umbilical cord and resist understanding diasporic South Asians by turning to South Asia; India, Pakistan, and Bangladesh cannot be seen as ideal cultures, fountainheads, or yardsticks for British Asians.[26] The fact that these migrants were marked as outsiders, as Vilayati, from their places of emigration, reveals a complexity for any straightforward rendering of migrant belonging and identity. For those I studied, the Indian "diaspora" is conceived in many ways across the world, and there are changing connections between ethnic minorities and their putative homelands. The movement of migrants opens up the dialogue on the ways we conceive of ethnic identity as a de facto product of migration, one in which the rhetoric of immigration continues to assume a notion of a cultural identity that has been left behind. I have brought into focus how difference is framed by the ways being an outsider is perceived: there is a double-edge in becoming Vilayati and becoming Asian, where too often difference is taken for granted to be a product of the nations in which migrants and their families live and completely unproblematic for the places that they left behind. (I return to this theme in Chapter 7.) And yet, as I have argued above, by using only one perspective of difference, that of being Asian, cultural contact and change are framed as a novelty coupled with a historical amnesia of colonialism. The very term of reference, "Asian," coalesces culture and identity with place. A similar conceptualization affects how their claim of a Punjabi identity is contingent on the power and representations of place. In particular, culture and communities are tied to the transformations of the nation-state and, in this case, to the changes that occurred during the birth of postcolonial India.

CHAPTER 3

"I Am From Nowhere"

Partition and Being *Punjabi*

Ethnic minorities share a memory of movement and a sense of collective history of displacement that helps to create their transnational identities.[1] For the Hindu Punjabis of my research, the trajectory of this historical memory can be traced to the 1947 Partition of British India. Partition was the prior event that had already disrupted the sense of ethnicity cum community cum identity based on place. Marking the *end* of the colonial period in the Subcontinent, the division of British India into India and Pakistan created specific senses of national histories and identifications based on place and religion. Muslims belonged in Pakistan and Hindus and Sikhs left their homes in that region for the newly independent India. In the Punjab, through which the resulting fault line ran, the break altered the importance of language as a common denominator. Further religious fracturing subsequently divided the post-Partition Punjab into two states, Punjab and Haryana. The ways that the HPs in London think about being Punjabi and the history of the Partition together give specific credence to my central thesis that ethnic migrants should not be marked as products of globalization. Instead of focusing on the most recent movement, I want to show how they live the multiple processes of producing a viable meaningful ethnic identity because of an earlier displacement and sense of difference. Taken in this frame, Vilayati and Asian are only the most recent manifestations of being outsiders from a homeland.

Understanding their complicated sense of homeland is critical for conceptualizing their notion of transnational identities, which does not prioritize India as a de facto homeland. For these families, the challenges of belonging to a nation occurred long before their migration to Britain. Moreover, it also shows how "Punjabi" as an identification has particular meaning for HPs; the sense of being Punjabi, an ethnic marker putatively based on location, in fact, refers not to a place on the map but to their experiences of multiple dislocation.

During my fieldwork, 60 percent of the migrant-generation life history interviews were conducted with individuals whose families directly experienced the Partition, and I met many others from Partition families whom I did not interview. The parental generation hailed from "refugee families" and were either born in West Punjab but were very young at the time of the Partition (between the ages of one and perhaps as old as seven) or had been born in India after 1947 (perhaps having older siblings born in what became Pakistan). There were a few who were young adults aged eighteen or twenty at the time of the Partition.[2] The majority did not have direct experience of the displacement, or were very young when it occurred. Many of these parents are now approaching retirement. Their children are in their early twenties to thirties and therefore have had no direct experience of the displacement. Nevertheless, Partition continues to have significance for the British children of Punjabi migrants (Raj 1997).

Other Hindu Punjabis experienced the event by simply living in Indian Punjab, where they housed refugees (especially their relatives), or may have had knowledge of refugee settlement camps that were found outside borders of large centers such as Jullunder and Amritsar. However, listening to these relatively affluent and well-educated migrants, it became clear that for both parents and children, the Partition was a framing historical moment. For example, one spring afternoon in central London, I met a thirty-year-old Hindu Punjabi man for an interview. As we walked to a café to begin the interview, he asked me about my research. I explained that my reason for studying Hindu Punjabis was the lack of research on this minority in Britain. In response to my interest in family history perhaps, he began describing Lahore and its former glory as a great and fashionable place. He also elaborated on his own family's experiences, emphasizing their prosperity before the Partition, and he told me about his great-grandfather's *foreign* car. This young man had never seen Lahore, had obviously never experienced the 1920s, and his parents were very young when they left Pakistan. Yet his description of what was once called the "Paris of the East" was vivid and spontaneous. Family memories nudged the event through the generations and into our conversation in London.

What are the memories and metaphors that inform the lives of Hindu Punjabis in London? What are the narratives that they tell themselves about themselves? People's lives shift irrevocably within larger sociohistoric processes. Social scientists have explored collective memory as a key facet of identity.[3] Memory makes identity through the body (Connerton 1995), through the collective (Halbwachs 1980), through the nation (R. Werbner 1998), and through the process of forgetting (Lambek and Antze 1996). Oral historians focus on stories people tell about the past, their reworking and revision of a known official history. For Samuel and Thompson, memory, as learned through life histories, is akin to myth and provides a "nonofficial" perspective of history. They state, "[L]ike myth, memory requires a radical simplification of its subject matter. All recollections are told from a standpoint in the present. In telling, they need to make sense of the past. That demands a selecting, ordering, and simplifying, a construction of coherent narrative whose logic works to draw the life story towards the fable" (Samuel and Thompson 1990: 7). Oral historians begin by asking people to speak about "the past," eliciting narratives and memories and thus constructing an "oral history" for their interpretation. However, I never solicited anyone's thoughts on the Partition. Moreover, no one ever offered me a formal account. Yet, during my fieldwork, repeated fragments of the past, specifically in relation to the Partition, came into the context of the present. These moments happened too often to ignore. Partition was intermingled with everyday speech and stories of ordinary events. These were not tidy narratives of reminiscences: transmission was informal, unintentional, and only momentarily elucidated. Narrative and memory are, in fact, inadequate terms for this phenomenon. These were not stories, myths, or fables of the past, but moments when the past was evoked, expressed, mentioned, forgotten, and remembered. Subtly evoked, these interpretations of the Partition can be seen not merely as individual experiences but as part of a collectively understood process. This memory is very closely tied to the processes of identification, the awareness, in Hall's formulation of "who we are and what we have become."

Any history of Punjab begins with contestations and questions: Whose Punjab? How is it defined? In which period? The term itself is a combination of *Punj,* meaning five, and *ab,* meaning rivers; "Punjab," therefore, is "the land of the five rivers."[4] In Ibbetson's 1881 Census of India pre-

Partition, preindependence Punjab extended from Delhi to beyond the Khyber pass. After the British arrived, for administrative purposes, the Punjab region also included thirty-four native states, which joined India in 1947. Depending on one's perspective, Punjab was connected / annexed / incorporated / subordinated by Great Britain in 1849. It was a late addition to the colonial landscape, and was (and still is) regarded by some migrants, and indeed those governing the former colonies, as an "administrative dream for the British."[5] If India was the jewel in the crown, Punjab provided the Koh-i-Noor[6] diamond by being a successful laboratory for the great colonial experiment.

Almost one hundred years after the British arrived, the Indian Independence Act of 1947 divided Punjab into the East Punjab Province of the Union of India and the West Punjab Province of Pakistan. Although still known as the land of the five rivers, present-day Punjab in India is actually only *Doab* (two rivers), the other three rivers run through Pakistan. The dividing line of Partition followed the course of two rivers, allotting parts of Lahore, Rawalpindi, and Multan divisions to Pakistan and the remainder of the region to India.[7] "The political decision to Partition the Subcontinent into two sovereign states resulted eventually in the largest transfer of population known to history. Nearly a million persons perished, and over 13 million crossed the borders. Over 4 million refugees from West Pakistan crossed into the Punjab" (Grewal 1990: 181). In 1948, after Indian independence, owing to the call for a Sikh homeland, Punjab was divided further to become Punjab and the Patiala and East Punjab States Union (PEPSU). In 1956 the State of Punjab was formulated and PEPSU merged into a reformed Punjab boundary. In 1966 this refigured Punjab further divided into the Punjabi-speaking Punjab State and the Hindi-speaking Haryana State. The consequences of such divisions have to this day rendered Punjab a balkanized version of its former self.

This description, however, reduces "Punjab" to questions of historical and political demands and changing borders. The Punjab most relevant to this chapter is the Punjab of experience, which makes memories and gives a specific sense of how changing borders and displacement form the base of Punjabi identification. Thus when London's Hindu Punjabis speak of Punjab they may be referring to: (a) the precolonial Punjab (everything north of Delhi into the Himalayas); (b) the colonial administrative Punjab with clean lines and marked districts; (c) East and West Punjab of the pre-Partition period; (d) the divided post-Partition Punjab; or (e) the current Punjab minus Haryana. These historical splits, especially that of the Partition, have become a collective memory of fracturing, spawning a specific set of collusions between language, land, identity, and religion, which inform what it means to be Hindu Punjabi.

Memories of the Partition come into everyday London through both explicit reference and silence. One Hindu Punjabi migrant, who has been in England since 1965 and first worked in a factory in the East End of London, has his own reflections. Since his arrival he has saved enough money to buy a small corner shop. He has three children: his eldest son was a doctor, his daughter was a pharmacist, and his youngest son was reading law at Cambridge. As we spoke, this son phoned and asked his father for some extra money. His father's response was, "Just tell me how much you need, I will transfer it tomorrow." Before the phone rang I had asked him where he came from, and he had replied, "Delhi."

Afterward, he added, "I must tell you, though, I am from nowhere," to which I responded, "Uncle, you are from nowhere?" He elaborated, "Same as you, your father comes from Bannu, then Delhi, then you're in Cambridge, then you will be somewhere else, so?" And he trailed off. I wanted him to pursue this further and asked, "So Uncle that means we are nowhere people?" He said, "Yes, our family was first in Punjab, then we went to Bihar, then we came here. . . . We were in West Pakistan, in Rawalpindhi. Then we were in East Ham, now we are in Leyton, so how many places you want to remember? For what? For just the knowing sake. Isn't it?"

To be sure, the Partition altered the sense of homeland, for some, like Uncle, so much so that he can claim to be from nowhere. But it seemed to me that it was not so easy to just dismiss oneself as being from nowhere. At the temple, at dinner parties, in many different venues, people would ask, "Where are you from?" In doing so, they were reinscribing identity and place by trying to differentiate the "Asian" ascription and break the category down into other categories of identity based on language and custom (Punjabi, Bengali, Gujarati). So I probed Uncle further and asked, "How do you answer that question — where are you from? And it is an obsession with our people to ask, 'Where are you from?' or 'What side do you come from?' How do you answer that?" His reply was enigmatic: "So I am from nowhere, because connections are just like footsteps, you move your foot and erasing the previous mark. The step is gone."

His reluctance to give a clear answer was frustrating. I wanted to probe if in fact he felt he was from nowhere, and if this was indeed something that those who had experienced the Partition believed. I asked, "What about your children then, are they from nowhere?" He was firm and swift in his reply: "They are from here; they don't know any place or any name [in India], isn't it? They do not want to remember. Sometimes we say, 'oh, your that *bua* or your that relation'; they don't want to know. It is the practice of what you do, if you meet people, then you know them. If you don't meet them for a number of years, then you don't know them [referring to relatives in India]." His sense of his children being nowhere people seemed less related to his own sense of displacement, than his sense that they did not know the kinship reference for his sister. He was clear that they were from England and that they had a sense of belonging. Perhaps that is how claiming to be from nowhere is effective — it allows one to claim to be from wherever they are. After this, some guests arrived in the shop. There was only one front entry and they passed behind the counter to a door, which I realized was the front door for his home. After welcoming them in, he paused for a while, looked at me, and then enigmatically added, *"There is nothing in story — these are realities."*

Stories, realities, narratives, myths, experiences, and imagined communities are some of the tools available to social scientists for understanding people's experiences — the "metaphors" that we are made of. Uncle ended the interview by insisting not on metaphors but on "realities." His being from nowhere made his children come from Britain. They did not have the referents for being from India. In exploring these realities of memory, and the metaphors in which they are entangled, memories are lost over the generations. Those memories that are perceived as necessary to remember become part of a collective consciousness, more of a diffuse feeling, not concrete, but repeatedly stated, assumed, or informing one's thoughts and actions, a nebulous sense of the collective based on history.

Partition is remembered and recounted or forgotten and hidden, but sometimes it emerges in specific contexts. By reviewing some of these moments, through the casual rememberings, the phrases, and the thoughts, Partition becomes a beginning point, and an anchor, for many people's life stories.[8] The past of Partition is resurrected and imported to Britain via visits by the elder grandparent generation. While on extended visits from India, grandparents inevitably tell nostalgic stories of their youth, describe the idyllic setting in which they were raised, and detail the wealth to which they had been accustomed. Their children, the migrants to Britain, grew up in India with these stories in the aftermath of the refugee experience. I explore specifically how these migrants (that is, the parental generation) referred to the Partition, how each moment of remembering imparts a certain meaning. Occasionally it was as simple as just adding the date for clarification and emphasis, "Partition, you know, 1947," and indeed many referred to the Partition only by its date. In this reference the chronological aspect of an historical event is emphasized.

Other modes of reference, however, prove more revealing. For example, communal violence was another focus of remembering. Muhammad Umar Memon, in his study of Intizar Husain's writings, reveals that the Pakistan's Progressive Writers Movement "viewed the Partition as totally negative and failed to appreciate it within a historical context. Devoid of any deeper historical understanding, this writing focused narrowly on an offshoot of the Partition, namely, the communal riots, leaving the influences that necessitated it virtually untouched. The literature produced on the theme of communal riots appears to be generally tentative and superficial" (Memon 1980: 409). The extreme violence is also emphasized in historical accounts such as the 1989 reprint of *Stern Reckoning* (Gopal Das Khosla's account of the 1948 Government of India Fact Finding Mission). This work is filled with tales of atrocities — looting, rape, killing, abduction, arson, and self-immolation — unfortunately common to many refugee experiences. But almost fifty years after these events, people in London no longer emphasize the violence. They simply assume it. Unlike literary or historical accounts where violence is the starting point, for those I worked with in London the violence was mentioned as a peripheral point of reference, something taken for granted as part of the experience: "*jadon khatra hoya*" (literally means "when the danger occurred," however, was translated by the informant as "when *the slaughtering* occurred"). Violence has become part of the collective memory of the experience. It is an additional referent for the event.

The most telling references, rather than violence, are those of loss and dislocation. Menon and Bhasin, researching the abduction of women, state, "[I]n their recall, the predominant memory is of confusion, dislocation and a severing of roots as they were forced to reckon with the twin aspects of 'azadi' — bewildering loss: of place and property, no doubt, but more significantly, of community, of a network of more or less stable relationships, and of a coherent identity" (Menon and Bhasin 1993: ws2). The bewildering sense of loss in all accounts is not restricted to the abducted woman (although no doubt experienced by her in a very specific way), but defines the refugee experience generally. For migrants to Britain the assumption of the tale of dislocation was commonly found in other terms of reference. For example, instead of using the word "partition" itself, or recalling the date, people refer to it in other revealing ways such as: "when we became *Sharnarthi* [refugees]" or "*sanu jadon bahar kad ditta*" [when we were *thrown out*], and most telling, "*jadon assi ghar chor-ke India a-gay si*" [when we *left* our *homes* and came to *India*]. Others referred to Hindustan, not to India. The geographical nomenclature is significant, as the use of Hindustan particularly emphasizes a sense of British India, which included West Punjab. In those days, the areas outside of the Punjab in British India were referred to as "Hindustan" (land of the Hindus) and most importantly they were not considered *home*.[9]

Uncle's claims "I am from nowhere" and that "connections are just like footsteps, you move your foot and erasing the previous mark," attest to the power of the decision to forget, to erase history or memory as a basis for identity. Samuel and Thompson, referring to Freud, assert that "memory is inherently revisionist, an exercise in selective amnesia. What is forgotten may be as important as what is remembered" (Samuel and Thompson 1990: 7). Perhaps the most alarming consequences of the silence surrounding the Partition are the assumptions pertaining to Punjabi identity, especially religious identities. Addressing this sensitive topic runs the risk of reifying dynamic processes and denying the many interreligious Punjabi friendships that I witnessed between Hindus and Muslims and Sikhs. These existed between young people as well as older people, but the young people's sense of the distinctions had taken on a particular religious-cultural force. Religious differences create impressions of irreconcilable differences; ignoring these divisions, however, perpetuates harmful assumptions, which occlude the complexity of Punjabi identity in the past and permit clear oppositions in the present.[10] The relationship between religion and Punjabi identity has changed since Partition; there was little sense of a Punjabi identity that subsumed religious ones.[11]

One evening my husband and I were visiting with a family for the first time. An older couple wanted to introduce us to them and we were all sitting in the front room. After the initial introductions, the man asked my husband the often repeated question: "Where is your family from in India?" My husband, whose family originates in Deri Ismail Khan (now in Pakistan), began to outline his family history. Our host told us that he had been born in Pakistan just before the Partition, but that his passport read that he had been born in Hoshairpur (Punjab, India), which was where his family first settled as refugees. To make sure that there were no further problems, when he "had his passport made" before migrating to England, he claimed India, specifically Hoshairpur, as his place of birth. An altered passport birthplace was not uncommon or even interesting in

itself (although I had mostly heard of changed birth dates). It was a common strategy of the time. However, the striking aspect of his revelation
was the look on his daughter's face. She was about fourteen years old and
had obviously just discovered her father was originally from Pakistan.
Given the complex ways race, ethnicity, and religion were being articulated
by second-generation Asians, it was not surprising to see her shock.
Perhaps it became clear to her that at that moment her parents had
become exactly that which she had sought to distance herself from in
school, and perhaps even at home: she realized she could be called "Paki."[12]

This silence and act of forgetting has serious consequences. In some
families it leads to defining Muslims as *other,* sometimes as despised and
hated *others* with whom nothing was shared. At specific moments, these
fellow Punjabis become Pakistanis or Muslims, and their shared *Punjabi-
ness* is downplayed. In these instances cultural memory is about oral narrative and actual practice. On one occasion I bought a box of Indian
sweets for a family my husband and I were visiting. They accepted the
sweets, but then later remarked on the packaging, "You know you should
not go to that shop, it is owned by Muslims; it is a dirty shop." When we
protested that the shop was in fact very clean they replied, "No, the back
of the shop is dirty, the kitchen; they even have mice." The underlying tension and constant referral to religious-based difference was revealed in
other ways as well. As one woman said on another occasion, when buying the groceries for an event she was sponsoring at the local temple, "Oh
if I would have known that it was a Muslim shop then I wouldn't have
bought the food for the temple there. I mean, I don't mind, but because
it is temple food . . . . Oh well, it is done now." The subtleties were played
out in terms of purity and pollution.

The parents' subtle and sometimes direct disdain for Muslims was
keenly felt and known by some of the British-born generation. One
young man told me about his cousin's surreptitious marriage to her
Muslim boyfriend, which had "shocked the whole family." He continued:

My dad will not let Muslims into our house. . . . You have met my girlfriend's
dad, but you have not met my dad, they are very different people in many ways
but there is one thing that they share, right, they are both anti-Muslim. It's in
every Asian. I live and let live, but I do not trust them at all. I've seen in it on both
sides, young or old. You see my friend from work, Nasir, I owe him a lot, you
know I don't consider it as a Muslim thing. It has to do with trusting each other
and being fatalistic, like the Irish and the British.

This young man's words reveal how national identity has become a
gloss for religious identity in certain situations. The current tension

between Hindu and Muslim youth is obviously a complex matter, and contemporary factors need to be considered alongside those originating with the migrants. But Muslims are glossed as Pakistanis, whether or not they originated in India. This fundamental sense of difference is constructed in the home.

Partition has become a moment of reference when the migrant generation recollects life in West Punjab. Their homes and childhood impressions would be remembered sometimes when speaking about something else entirely. For example, at a dinner party one woman said, "Yes that was what it was like in Kohat, now in Pakistan." But when I asked her when she left the frontier, she said she was two years old. These moments of remembering, when the past becomes the present for the migrants or for their parents, are an intrinsic aspect of being a British-born Hindu Punjabi. The memories passed to the British-born generation revolve around themes of past dislocation, overcoming refugee experiences, and of being permanently separated from an ancestral homeland (that is, the part of Punjab lost to Pakistan to which they can never return). These are all manifest, moreover, through an emphasis on a lost *golden age*.

Partition recarved and reshaped Punjab's boundaries as well as the boundaries of Punjabi identity. In 1947, Muslim Punjabis became Pakistanis and ruptured the Punjabi tripartite of Hindus, Muslims, and Sikhs. In the period leading up to the Partition, their Muslim-ness as Pakistanis increasingly became primary, occluding their identity as Punjabi. This tripartite was to fission further: Hindus and Sikhs would not be primarily "Punjabi," but "Hindus" and "Sikhs" (that is, their religious identity would become more salient). Punjabi identity was fractured further when, in 1966, the Haryana state was carved out from post-Partition Punjab resulting from a successful call by Sikhs to have a Punjabi-language state. These geographical changes mark the different ways of being Punjabi. Over time have they have helped to solidify a connection between the ethnic adjective "Punjabi" with the religious affiliation "Sikh."

Hindu Punjabi migrants to Britain began to arrive after Partition, and the majority arrived in the early 1960s, the period preceding the debates regarding the split of India's Punjab Province. The creation of a majority Punjabi state did not halt demands for an independent Sikh state. The Khalistan movement for an independent Punjab pursued support from Sikh emigrants around the world who executed pressures on India (see Axel 2001; Mahmood 1996). This struggle for a Sikh homeland played out in Britain in many ways. For example, "extremists" supposedly killed Tarseem Singh Purewal, liberal editor of the Southall based publication,

Des Pardes, in South London in 1995. One year, 1984, holds particular significance for Sikh and Hindu Punjabis.[13] It is referred to as the turning point, when the storming of the Golden Temple by the Indian Army and the assassination of Indira Gandhi occurred. When referred to, the date is commonly stated without explanation, as if one should already appreciate its significance. In evoking this date in connection with the tensions between Hindus and Sikhs in Britain, I necessarily refer back to South Asia as a source for understanding the experiences of migrants who had left thirty or forty years previously. However, Hindus and Sikhs in Britain did not react to the events in terms of an issue exclusive to India. Those in Britain were reacting to the perceived threat in Britain, as well as expressing concern about relatives in India who would be directly affected by the riots and curfews in Punjab and Delhi. It was in 1984 that Hindus in Britain learned of the extent of the tension and scale of Khalistan demands that were tied to global Sikh experiences and monies. Somehow, 1984 confirmed their hitherto unanticipated suspicion: Hindus did not belong in the Punjab. Sikhs have sought to separate and distinguish themselves as a community. Because of the increasing identification of Punjab, India, with Sikhs, Punjabi Hindus in Britain were left in an oppositional role.

Yet my interlocutors described how Hindus and Sikhs enjoyed and assumed a fraternal Punjabi *Indian* identity during the postwar migration to Britain (especially between the mid-1950s and early 1960s). Hindus and Sikhs shared religious sites of worship in London as during the early to mid-1960s, when few Hindu temples existed. Many of the men and women who arrived during that period spoke of frequenting a gurdwara, such as the Hammersmith gurdwara in West London. Also Sikhs and Hindus to this day in the United Kingdom continue to share overlapping albeit restricted patterns of marriage alliance (for example, the matrimonials section of local temple publications and newspapers such as *Eastern Eye* sometimes contain advertisements that state that both Sikhs or Hindus are sought as suitable potential partners).[14] Individual Sikhs and Hindus share symbols and practices of body inscription (such as wearing a *kara* and women keeping their hair long).[15] They share friendships, visiting each other socially and sometimes using fictive kin ties. Yet in spite of the sharing, there is an increasing identification of being "Punjabi" with being Sikh.

This equation of Punjabi and Sikh identity became apparent to me during fieldwork through people's reflections on the differences between the religious groups. The first generation reflects on the increasing separation of being Hindu from being Sikh and laments the loss of being Punjabi as the operative, prime identity. One of my informants, a store owner (a businessman), went into this at great length. He expressed anger that there was no recognition of a shared Punjabi culture in Britain. Even though, "the Sikhs, Hindus and Muslims all had the same culture." He opined, "In this country to be a Punjabi is to be a Sikh — not a Hindu, not Muslim."

To give me an example, he recounted the position of a university language professor who was a Punjabi scholar, but also a Hindu. He had to fight for recognition because the Sikh community would not accept him as a Punjabi scholar. Then there were the Sikh teachers at a local Sunday school who would not buy Punjabi books from a non-Sikh. "But we are all Punjabi — one identity. We all speak the same language and do the same things," he told me. He asked, "Didn't the women all keep long hair?" as if this alone constituted Punjabi culture (as a foundational aspect, or as culture inscribed on the body). Perhaps he was saying the Sikhs had no hegemony over hair. This was something he felt strongly about and he covered many different issues to illustrate his point that Sikhs, Hindus, and Muslims were all the same. Shared language was the main example — Sikhs were trying to equate Punjabi with Sikh by ignoring that Muslim Punjabis sometimes spoke Punjabi even if they wrote it in Urdu rather than Gurmukhi script.

The equation of Punjabi with Sikh identity is even more evident among children of migrants. For many British-born Hindu Punjabis, being Sikh is entirely separate from being Hindu, the negotiation of difference involves separating out. As Hindus they may wear a kara, they may have Sikh friends in their parents' generation, they may have Sikh friends themselves, but Sikhs and Hindus are distinct, and it is a distinction that is espoused without lament. The assumption of difference between Sikhs and Hindus is a perspective that the British-born generation feels it needs to explain. For example, one Sunday in the temple I began talking to a young woman whose family was sponsoring an event to mark the birth of a son to her sister. She introduced me to her cousin, a young woman who was sitting beside her, "This is my cousin Kiran; oh, she is Sikh." There was no apparent reason for this introduction to be marked by religious difference. I had neither asked her religion, nor inquired about her reasons for being at the temple. I gave no indication of disdain or difference (incidentally, this "cousin" did not have long hair and was not wearing a kara). This example provides one of many instances when acknowledgment of difference becomes necessary and conspicuous even when not explicitly sought. Why did this young woman feel that religious distinction needed to be highlighted? The response lies in the increasingly articulated difference between the second-generation Hindu and Sikhs, who see themselves as "Asians" with distinct religious traditions. Religion is not simply, in this context, a harping on a putative homeland identity; the ebb and flow of Punjabi identification has come to be equated with Sikhism, partially because of the second generation's experiences of living and growing up in Britain. As a result, the second generation call themselves "Hindu Punjabi," rather than the more familiar "Punjabi Hindu."

There are other ways in which this religious difference is constantly being referred to and evoked, and always there is an assumption of difference. The simple game of naming reveals the assumption that Punjabi equals Sikh. Repeatedly I would hear that when Punjabi Hindu students were asked, "Are you Punjabi?" they would respond, "No, I am Hindu." Conversely, when a group of active Hindu students who helped me to find young people to interview led me to a young woman who had long hair and wore a kara, I explained my research then explicitly mentioned that I was working with Punjabi Hindus and asked, "Are you Hindu?" she responded, "No, I am *Punjabi.*" How has Punjabi become a gloss for Sikh for British-born Asians?

The alignment of Sikh with Punjabi is tied to new boundaries of language use. The changing boundaries of the Punjab "left Sikhs as the prime 'owners' and promoters of Punjabi language" (Sachdev 1995: 177). This sense of language ownership was apparent when I began fieldwork. For example, I took Punjabi lessons to improve my speaking abilities. It was through the reactions of others to this seemingly inconspicuous act that it became clear that the Punjabi language had also become synonymous with being Sikh. My teacher was a part-time translator for the Borough when I met her at a bus stop in Redbridge. It was a typical gray fall morning in East London, and there was a slight chill when I approached the bus stop. Only one woman waited at the stop. She was clad in a sari tied in a manner particular to professional women — graceful, elegant with every fold in an exact place. To pass time and in a manner reminiscent of the formality of Greater London bus stops, she began to converse with me in English. I did not know if she was Hindu Punjabi, but in response to her questions, I responded by nodding and saying "*ji*" — a shortened form of the Hindi phrase "*han ji,*" which indicates a formal agreement. With this small prompt, she began to speak to me in Hindi and then switched when I responded in Punjabi. She had been a schoolteacher in

India and since migration had informally taught Hindi, Punjabi, and Urdu to children in Newham. She agreed to take me on for private tuition at her home. At the first lesson she asked why I wanted to learn Punjabi: *"Hinduan di bhasha Hindi hondi he; Punjabi Sikhan di bhasha he"* [The Hindus' language is Hindi; Punjabi is the language of the Sikhs].[16]

At our next meeting she inquired if my husband was a Sikh who did not wear a turban. When I asked her why she wanted to know, she recounted at first wondering if my husband wore a turban (that is, was a Sikh) and perhaps that was the reason I wanted to learn the language. Then, after meeting him in the temple and not seeing a turban or a kara, she wondered if he was *"mona* Sikh."[17] When I responded that he was not a Sikh, her attempts to get me to learn Hindi resumed. Repeatedly throughout our lessons she would tell me, *"Punjabi sadi bhasha ni he"* [Punjabi is not our language] or would ask, *"Hindi kyon nei sikhdi"* [Why don't you learn Hindi?]. She said that once I learned Hindi, I would find no need for Punjabi. Learning the language involved learning a script and as I was learning Punjabi she taught me to write it in Gurmukhi script.[18] A few times, of her own accord, she began to teach me Hindi, using Devanagri script. This attempt to subvert my Punjabi learning was quickly abandoned when she realized that I had begun to confuse the characters of the two scripts and in fact was not progressing in either language.

My Punjabi teacher was not the only one with strong opinions about which language I should be learning. When I recounted to friends and people I met during fieldwork my attempts to study Punjabi, I was told, "You should learn Hindi; it is our language." Despite my response that I was learning Punjabi primarily to be able to speak it and not offend anyone with informality, people continued to insist that I learn Hindi. My interlocutors explained to me that Hindi was the national language of India and the language of communication for overseas Indians. I was met with silence if I said that I was already fluent in India's other national language, English.

By asking to learn Punjabi I had unwittingly aligned myself to a longstanding language division that not only separated script from spoken language but also linked to religious identifications. My Punjabi teacher was raised in West Punjab and was twenty years old at the time of the Partition. She was born in Lyallpur (now in Pakistan) and educated as a teacher in Lahore. She had grown up knowing that language choice indicated many other subtle meanings, which I did not know but needed to learn. As inscribed practice, language was difference. She saw me as a Hindu who, as such, should be learning Hindi. If I learned Punjabi, especially the Gurmukhi script, it might be assumed that I was a Sikh. Oblivious to the nuances between written and oral language skills, I approached my fieldwork with the idea that I needed to learn a more formal Punjabi for research purposes. I soon become aware that my choice of language instruction unknowingly had evoked a political-historical divide. I thought about discussing with her the deSaussureanian arbitrary nature of signs but knew that it would be meaningless — to learn Gurmukhi was a fixed sign.[19] Not surprisingly the only people who did not comment on my learning Punjabi were Sikhs, who took me to be Sikh because I was learning the language. By learning it, I was fixing myself and making a statement about religion, language, loyalties, body practice, and home and belonging.

Central to understanding this language separation is the difference between the written and spoken languages. Historically, the high language of the Punjab, Urdu, was written in Persian script. English, the language of the colonial overlords, was also both a written and spoken high language. Thus, of the grandparents' generation the men would be literate in Urdu and English, yet speak Punjabi, Urdu, and English, as well as a home dialect (such as Multani). Men were often proud that they could not read and write in Hindi. It was not until I started to gather my data and hear people reminiscing about language that I began to appreciate my Punjabi teacher's gentle admonitions about my choice of Punjabi. One Uncle recounted that in Pakistan the Sikhs would go to the gurdwara after school and learn Punjabi and the Muslims would go to the mosque and learn Urdu and Persian by learning the Koran. He used to tag along with the Muslims to the mosque. Although all spoke the Punjabi language, the languages in which one was literate depended on religion and social standing. Urdu and Hindi were languages taught at school, but Punjabi written in Gurmukhi is associated with the gurdwara. Exceptionally, some women of that generation, such as my teacher in London, would have the same written skills as the men. More often women had limited abilities in Urdu (Persian script) but were proficient in written Hindi. Most women of this generation were comfortable with conversational Urdu, fluent in oral Hindi and Punjabi, and a few had had some basic schooling in English. Of the parental generation (that is, the migrant generation) men spoke Punjabi, Hindi, English, and Urdu. Yet, depending on their age, whether they were born before or after Partition, and location of birth — West Punjab, East Punjab, or Delhi — they had differing oral and written skills in Urdu, Hindi, and English. Often the men spoke but did not write Punjabi.

The separation in terms of language was seen as an active choice or lamented as a strategy of survival. When the refugees moved from West Punjab into Hindustan (often Delhi), they were embarrassed about their seemingly parochial, rural accents, which distinguished them as West Punjabi refugees. Some parents remember the conscious effort made to sanitize their Punjabi language and how it became a *home* language after Partition because the Delhi-ites would jest at their language abilities. The language choice of Hindi by those who remained in India relates very much to being a Hindu, supporting the Indian nation and its official languages. Thus the migrants, before leaving India, had already assumed language choices (of Hindi) and definitions of self in terms of the strategies of nation building because of their refugee experience. The British-born generation presupposes the preference for Hindi and the differentiation in spoken and written language along religious lines.

An example of the diversity in languages in one home illustrates the changes in language over time. During the Diwali celebration at one family's house, the "Sanskrit" Hindu prayers read by Uncle were written in Persian script, the same prayers were read by Aunty in Hindi script, and their daughter (British born) read part of the prayers, the Hanuman Chalisa, from a booklet that contained Hindi and Sanskrit and transliterated English. Thus even within one family, language abilities and proficiency in written script vary tremendously.

The question of which language to speak was eloquently observed in one man's reflections, in moving out of India: "The relationship of language for the Sikhs is actually [the change of] one language, Punjabi to English so there's no medium in between. For the Hindu Punjabis," he continued, "it was exacerbated after Independence [because] there was a certain degree even before — 'do they belong in Punjabi or do they belong in Hindi?' and that has had the effect accordingly." The shifts rationalizing language choice were clear for the migrant generation. They moved from Punjabi to Hindi to English and had usually grown up with oral and written abilities in all three languages. The move toward identification with Hindi (which began pre-Partition and was solidified after 1947) was revealed when people reflected that their relatives in India (again, usually in Delhi) did not speak Punjabi at all with their children, and the children of migrants (that is, the British-born and -raised generation) remarked that their language skills in Punjabi are indeed better than that of their Indian cousins. But for Hindu Punjabi migrants to Britain, language is not so easily compartmentalized, and the move away from Punjabi into Hindi not easy to trace. Language choice is a constant struggle in Britain, but now it is defined by specific boundaries of identity where language use is synonymous with religious affiliation.

Language, both oral and literate, provides a further indication of absolute separation and difference. I knew some young Hindu Punjabis who were friends with Sikhs or Muslims and did not know that they all heard the same language in their parental home. For example, when I met Ravi, who had attended a local college and worked for his father's company, I asked what language his parents spoke at home. He responded "Hindi," adding that to him they spoke English or a mixture of the two languages. Later that evening when I met with his parents, I asked them what language they spoke at home and they replied, "Punjabi." When I sought clarification, they said that they rarely spoke Hindi as most of their friends were Punjabi. This instance is not simply one of a young man who did not know the differences between Hindi and Punjabi. At issue is not what language people speak, but which language they claim to be speaking, and the symbolic political meanings of the language. The young man was not alone. Many Hindu Punjabi young people increasingly claim that Hindi is spoken at home, or that Hindi is their parents' mother tongue. At first I thought that this was something exclusive to the children of migrants, reflecting the fact that they are not speaking their parents' mother tongue (replete with concerns of language attrition in a community). But some of the migrant generation claims Hindi, although certainly not in the same manner as the British-born generation. However, because of their parents' assumptions, they have been given Hindi as the language that should be studied and Punjabi as the home language for which formal tuition is not encouraged. To be prophetic, Punjabi is a dying language for young Hindu Punjabis.[20]

Hindi is the claimed language of London's diasporic Hindu Punjabi community. An example of the assumption of Hindi is found in the fact that children are sent to study Hindi during evenings or weekends, or are taught it by the parents themselves.[21] People also claimed that informal learning of Hindi occurred during regular doses of Bombay Hindi films that young people watched as children with their parents. They understand these films but usually cannot translate them.[22] In London, the Punjabi language is taught in Sikh gurdwaras and increasingly it is offered as a second language in some schools (GCSE examinations may be taken in Punjabi).[23] By contrast, for Hindu Punjabi children there is no formal training in Punjabi. It is often picked up from hearing the parents speaking or from hearing it at social gatherings. Often the most intensive periods of language learning occur during periods of immersion, for example, when children visit India and have to communicate with their grandparents. But even then, many of their grandfathers speak and read English and may only deliberately speak Hindi or Punjabi for the benefit of their British-born and -raised grandchildren. These moments of immersion are not regular and not sustained (five- to eight-year gaps in between visits to India were not uncommon).

For the British Hindu Punjabis, there is a *home* Punjabi, a language that they understand and speak with their parents and their parents' friends. Home Punjabi involves parents speaking to children about domestic matters, usually helping with the housework. While the children's understandings may be proficient, oral home Punjabi is very basic, most often consisting of phrases of greetings, or responses to usual questions (such as "How are you?" "How is school?"). Moreover, code-switching is normal and conversations, even within a single sentence, change between English and Punjabi. Some young people who are more comfortable with the language speak basic Punjabi to each other. For example, friends phoned by Punjabi friends would follow "Hello" when answering their mobile phones with "*Oh yar kidhan*" [Oh friend, how are you?]. Such code-switching was common, occasionally providing a comic base and lightheartedness to their exchanges.

During my first meeting with Karnal Bhandari, he reflected on the use of Hindi and Punjabi in England and in India, and the changes in England in the use of Punjabi since his emigration to London as a teenager in the early 1970s.

I grew up with Urdu and Punjabi — they were not a problem. Hindi was more of a problem. When I first went to Delhi I found I had to get myself around Hindi. The conversations there are invariably in Hindi and only this [last visit] partly because we were relaxed and talking about language, I found us slipping into the Punjabi language. . . . We were in a party and clearly there were a lot of Punjabi speakers. They were all speaking in Hindi but when they actually want to tell "a real thing" which could be a joke, or which could be a particular reference, they always switched into Punjabi.

It was almost like a secret language, which only this particular group of people shared. But in a way that's a bit like us, the immigrants here. What is noticeable in schools is that amongst particular groups, the Punjabi speakers, the Gujarati speakers, the Bengali speakers and now perhaps also the Tamil speakers whose kids are absolutely proficient in English — they speak English with the same accent, they have a local accent but the secret language in school when they get together just like any kids who have a second language, that is Punjabi or Gujarati or whatever, they will slip into, that is their secret code.

That is when they really are themselves and, in a way, . . . [it's] partly also an echo or a reflection of what happens with West Indian speakers, in the end their language is Creole but what they really want to talk is patois, that is cool. . . . The Indian kids are doing the same things. Which I find . . . a very curious way of the language remaining alive. That's been certainly something that I was surprised by, but also very glad that, in fact, the language is surviving.

I responded to his thoughts: "Yes I have seen that and I have seen the reaffirmation. I have seen it with some of the young people so that when they pick up the phone they will answer with 'Hello' and then switch to a Punjabi loud and long '*Oh kidhan*,' that is the way they start their conversation." He quickly cut in:

But also the peculiarity, in this particular community there is another strand which is sort of an echo of what you are talking about which is a complete and utter denial of wanting to speak the language — "I don't know a language" — I find it amongst Hindu Punjabis that there are these kind of two poles. There is one which is, as you say, now that is a part of a particular youth culture which is a part of the Bhangra rap scene which is done, even a sense of the language as a positive language. It's been rid of the association of it being a traditionalist language, my parents' language — there's no way we want to speak that parents' language. It's rid itself of that association because it is now coming via these types like Apache Indian and others — it's cool to speak Punjabi.[24] But I actually don't think that amongst the Hindu Punjabis there is the similar feeling for the language as there is say amongst the Muslims for Mirpuri or for Urdu, or as there is amongst the Gujarati kids for Gujarati. I don't think that is quite happening in our community.

I would agree. The association of language for the British-born generation is not happening, perhaps because they do not know which language is theirs — Hindi or Punjabi. At home, their parents converse amongst themselves and with others of the migrant generation in Punjabi, but they speak English at home with their children, interspersed with Punjabi and Hindi.

The language attrition is not only due to the migration, as the counterexample of the Sikh and Muslim youth reveal. The shift out of Punjabi use for the Hindu Punjabis is, in effect, not separable from their shift of territory, and in the case of Partition, the creation of the territory is not separable from highly demarcated religious boundaries. The younger generation did not experience the Partition directly, yet in their language choices, they embody the ruptures of the Partition. As my friend, quoted above, later stated:

[The Punjab and Haryana split] has had the effect of more affective speech for the HPs — what is their territory? Compared to any other Indian you know, you talk to a Kannada speaker then you know it is Kannada, for a Malayalam it is from

Kerala, for Punjabi you think Sikh, Gujarati, Gujarat. So what's a Hindu Punjabi's territory? Now there's been an attempt, like Haryana state. These are all fictions; there is no actual language base. Really they belong in Punjab in the sense they are Punjabis so there's been this kind of mental thing of being between two worlds.

Between two worlds? What two worlds are being constructed here? He questions a division between two worlds based on two languages and attempts to move beyond the issue. However, the connection to language still lingers.

Understanding the saliency of memory in making identity can only be explored through the assumptions and thoughts of this British-born generation. The young man in Leicester Square who sparked my quest for understanding is among many for whom memories of the Partition are an aspect of "becoming" Punjabi. Identity is as contingent on that historical juncture as on their future in Britain. This is not a deterministic manner of connecting diaspora with the homeland and of reducing experiences of being in Britain to an aberration of a pure ethnicity. Nevertheless, the building blocks of identity through memories include Partition, language, and religion.

What makes the British-born generation Punjabi? The memory of the Partition, and remember this is not a coherent myth, forms part of their Punjabi identity. This is even true for young Punjabis who were born in East Africa. For example, Karnal, ever reflective and always eloquent, migrated during the Amin exodus from Uganda. His parents had migrated to East Africa and were from refugee families:

I think that, for example, the whole Partition thing is in a way much more exacerbated. The Partition experience is much more exacerbated in the Hindu Punjabis wherever they are irrespective of whether they have actually had direct experience of Partition. Because in a way what it really touches upon is on the very deepest sense of, "Well who are you now?" You know before Partition one still had this ambivalence of, What is our state? Who are we? Kind of flipping in several ways in a way that was fine, that was comfortable because there was no question then of a nationality. Part of the modern disease is that unfortunately nationality is primary and [in this] Hindu Punjabis find themselves in a very peculiar problem.

For this British Hindu Punjabi generation, being Punjabi (and their Punjabi identity) is constructed through the accumulation of memories, partially informed by the Partition, which they experience indirectly through unintentional tale telling. Karnal's words reveal that Partition is also being connected to issues of homeland, belonging, longing, and being a part of the larger diaspora.

The importance of theorizing diaspora for Punjabi Hindus underpins this discussion of the formation of the Punjab and the many entanglements of the shifting Punjabi identity via the Partition. The diaspora phenomenon is not a new one. As my friend from East Africa later claimed, Hindu Punjabis were always nomads:

I think this is most interesting that we really are a [true] migrant community and have been for generations. Way before we ever arrived here we have been migrating from ourselves. I have just started to read John Irving's *Son of the Circus* which has a similar sort of sense because, I am a foreigner overseas, of course, and I am a stranger at home. John Irving has got this character who feels a foreigner in Toronto and a foreigner in Bombay where he was born and that the essential nature of the Indian in the book is to be the foreigner wherever. But I think that this is the essential nature of the Hindu Punjabis.

This quotation stresses the dislocation of the Hindu Punjabi experience. The dislocation is related directly to the formation of the Punjab and the many complexities that have fractured the Punjabi identity to the point of its assumption in the British-born generation as meaning Sikh identity. Most importantly, however, it is the displacement from West Punjab that "took place . . . years ago but still reverberates in the general consciousness" (Menon and Bhasin 1993: ws2). These experiences cast Hindu Punjabis as a diasporic population and as nomads, with a specific sense of being Punjabi.[25]

Identification, then, for British Hindu Punjabis is not a stagnant static retention of tradition and values that renders them Punjabi. Memories of language and Partition are crucial aspects of the negotiation of Punjabi identification. In terms of language, religion, and geographical reference, Punjab and its adjective "Punjabi" are being identified in the British-born generation as Sikh attributes. Moreover, these are attributes from which Punjabi Hindus seek to separate themselves and yet to distinguish themselves from other Hindus, usually Gujuratis, by calling themselves "Punjabi." Through these changes and shifts of identification away from Punjab, the British-born generation does not refer to themselves as "Punjabi," or "Punjabi Hindu," but as "HP." When I first heard the phrase during fieldwork I thought it was a brown sauce, but I was told that it was an acronym for "Hindu Punjabi" and that this was the term that was used for (and by) British-born Hindu Punjabis. This identification is all the more striking because of its specific articulation, which can be seen to have been initiated when the British left India, through the demarcation of religion and language groups. It has only found its full form when HPs were born in Britain, because of the specificities of being a minority among other Asian minorities in postcolonial Britain.

Punjabi identification for Hindus has changed due to their changing experiences of Punjab's shifting landscape, which disaggregated the tidy associations of ethnicity, culture, difference, and land. As a group, their self-identification has changed from being Hindus in the pre-Partition period (whose practices overlapped with the Sikhs and even Muslims) to Punjabi Hindus in India, and then to Hindu Punjabis in London and finally to HPs in the British-born generation. These conspicuous changes in name indicate the sense of a changed but shared identity. Partition is manifest as a memory of loss (of property, of homeland, of family, of friends, and of identity), which has become a means of collective identification: everyone suffered a loss. Most interesting is the manner through which this collective memory is then rearticulated and understood by the British-born generation as a lack of homeland and a former status of glory. The articulation of loss of homeland makes the specific transnational experiences for Hindu Punjabis all the more powerful. Their families' histories as refugees and then the migration to Britain gives a complex sense how of difference is articulated because of movement. It is a sense of a connection that is informed by a shifting past while entering present-day London through the recollections, silences, and strategic ignorance (see Gershon and Raj 2000) of the grandparent and parent generations that create a notion of Punjabi identity.

An unnuanced sense of the adjective "Punjabi" renders a construction of ethnic identity connected to a faraway and exotic land, an essentially timeless land, important only insofar as it becomes an ethnic adjective for British Punjabis. My task has been to de-exoticize this use of "Punjab" by rendering problematic a putatively simple geographical referent of identity. In revealing how my interlocutors can respond to the question "Where are you from?" I have shown the complex historical implications of thinking through the identity politics preceding immigration. Introducing their complex history with the specific articulations of Hindu Punjabi identification, I have begun to explore the spaces of difference created by the connections of name and place. In doing so I have begun by interweaving the complications of their Punjab identity namesake without stifling them in a taken-for-granted "cricket match test" approach to ethnicity.[26] By uncovering the various ways that they can claim and create being Punjabi, ethnicity becomes part of how difference of culture and community are articulated. In examining how they are not able to claim Punjabi, I have shown how ethnicity needs to be understood through a specific lens of power and representation. Central to their sense of Punjabi subjectivity are both the prior sense of displacement and the movement that preceded immigration. Bringing forth the complex connections to place, Hindu Punjabis in London exemplify the narration of the dialectic between ethnicity and identity within transnationalism. Amazingly, as the case of Hindu Punjabi shows, people can simultaneously acknowledge the disjunctures of movement and then fix identity to a certain place irrevocably full of meaning.

CHAPTER 4

Becoming a Hindu Community

Compared to India, we are more Hindus. We are more Hindus because we feel that we have to stick to something. I will tell you the number of times that you have visited the *mandir* here you would have never visited in the whole of your life over there, is it true? And here we go 100%. I have got a friend of mine, they are from West Indies; they moved from India in the 1890s. They are more Hindus than us, because they moved a hundred years back. We are twentieth century, they are nineteenth century. They are more practicing and they stick to it. They may not be able to speak Hindi but they can recite mantras in English [laughing]. We are in active practice; we go to functions, we celebrate festivals, and that is active, and active participation. When you think of losing something then you try to grab it hard.

This eloquent quotation from Uncle Ram, who migrated in 1968 and currently owns a small business, ruminates on the changing nature of belonging to a Hindu community. By comparing himself with his friend from the West Indies, he reveals his views of the different ways to be Hindu in the diaspora. His words acknowledge the fundamental importance of space and time in the construction of a diasporic Hindu community. He attributes some of the differences between himself and his friend from Trinidad to the time of migration and the location. Like others of the parental generation, he associates being a Hindu in England with going to the temple. His perspective is that migration has given them a sense of "losing something" and as a result trying "to grab it hard." The British-born young people of my research have a different sense of being Hindu and have their own interpretations of what this entails. For them, certain ontological and epistemological questions of identity come to the fore.

The historical memories of the Partition indicate how changing social practices and locations inform the subjectivity of ethnic identification. The notion of "being Punjabi" is not fixed in a straightforward equation of identity and ethnicity, but rather is the product of constantly changing larger shifts in geography, politics, and language. Below, I examine ethnographically the ways identification is also about the production of a "community." The words of Hindu Punjabis in London are used to examine what it means to be a "Hindu" in Britain. What is a Hindu? By chronicling shifting religious identity for London's Punjabi Hindus and changes in how people are aware of shifts in what it means to be a Hindu, I reveal how community "identity" changes and is created in specific moments, while remaining nominally constant. The Hindu Punjabi community occurs in moments within specific places, temple as well as home-based worship. This again disrupts the equation of community, culture, and ethnicity based on religious identity. Hindu rituals are prescribed yet the practices are not rigid (see Humphery and Laidlaw 1994); therefore the notion of being a part of this "community" dynamically changes. The different arenas where these changes are evident — in temples, in home ritual practices, and in the second-generation's sense of being Hindu — collectively indicate the various sites in which being a Hindu has meaning for people. At the same time, I wish to reveal how they have become British Hindus with a particular sense of how creating a minority religion has been informed by their experiences of difference in Britain.[1]

What Is a Hindu? Becoming a Political Community

In 2001 the government of the United Kingdom asked a religious question on its national census. The debates on this were furious: faith-based groups argued that it would help to allocate resources; and "free thinkers" and "atheists" were upset that their identities were being counted as "none." The Office for National Statistics conferred with the Religious Affiliation Sub-Group, composed of representatives of various faith-based religious organizations, academics, and others. The debates held in the House of Lords and the House of Commons are instructive about the many pros and cons considered before the question was finally approved.[2] The ultimate inclusion of the question is interesting for the ways that the numbers and identity game of multicultural states influences how minorities define themselves in terms of difference.[3] The census not only is an arm of bureaucracy but also helps shape the very identities it seeks to count. There is no natural reason to think of religious identity as fixed.[4] Uncle Ram, for instance, sensed changes between eighteenth- and nineteenth-century Hindus, which were dependent on their location. The historical notions of "Hindu community" in pre-Partition Punjab carries insight into how twentieth-century understandings of "Hindu community" have developed. Historians and anthropologists of the Punjab have argued strongly against the idiom of a fixed religious identity that explains the belief system and practices of the Punjab region. "In the West we are used to thinking of these three elements — tradition, church, and ethnic — as fitting together in a coherent scheme, but in the Punjab they do not coalesce so predictably" (Juergensmeyer 1982: 2). Historically, the most important identity marker was not discretely religious (either Hindu, Muslim, or Sikh) but a combination of geographical, linguistic, and cultural factors. Punjabi identity was paramount. For example, Sikhs (both *keshdhari* and *sahajdhari*) participated, contributed to, and helped the early-nineteenth-century beginnings of the "Hindu" Arya Samaj movement.[5] The Amritsar Golden Temple defended by Sikh militants and stormed by Indira Gandhi's military in 1984 held Hindu deities until 1905. The Brahminical wedding ceremony is now associated with Hindus exclusively, but in the nineteenth century Sikhs and Hindus married and intermarried according to these rites. Sikhs once visited Muslim shrines (devoted to a Muslim saint) and Hindu shrines (devoted to specific deities). Similarly, at one time Hindus regularly visited Sikh and Muslim places of pilgrimage (see Fox 1985; K. Jones 1976).[6] This sense of religious fluidity was a mainstay of Punjabi religious identity, and indeed of many other religious traditions. By definition, fluidity cannot be a part of the rules of the numbers and identity game.

There has been a shift away from thinking about erstwhile fluid religious boundaries. One significant influence on Hindu Punjabis may be traced to nineteenth-century British policies that sought clarification through classification.[7] Similar to the changes in Punjabi identity, the formation of a religious identity for Hindus can be linked to the historical implications of the British Raj in creating "community consciousness." The precise connection between colonial reforms and the establishment of discrete religious categories in India, especially in the Punjab, and their role in reifying and fixing erstwhile fluid boundaries is hotly debated (C. Bayly 1985; Pandey 1990; Thapar 1989). However, it is generally agreed that this reification of religion is most closely connected to the classification procedures of the British census, to the impact of Government of India job and educational allocations that between 1890–1920 linked employment access to social identities, and to subsequent reforms that took on these discrete categories as natural forms (such as the Land Alienation Act of 1900–1901).[8] Combined, these three events cemented distinct religious communities that, once constituted, competed for limited resources.[9] The argument regarding colonialism's long-term social effects is not my focal point; instead, I want to stress that the colonial regime needed the notion of "community" to govern and that it is arguably their sense of English, Scottish, Welsh, and Irish that informed their ideas about what constituted a community. In the Punjab the institution of identity was based on relative religious difference, that is, people were made aware of the importance of difference and of labels in new ways (Baumann 1996: 28–29).[10]

The effects in the Punjab of the census and the resulting competition for placements, recognition by the government, and preferential treatment because of minority status are well reviewed (see, for example, Barrier 1989; Dusenberry 1995; K. Jones 1976; Fox 1985). Early-nineteenth-century Sikh and Arya Samaj reformers responded to the colonial state and competed with each other for limited resources. Fox, for example, argues for the creation of a distinct Sikh identity (that is, the "Singh" identity) as a product of the colonial encounter. He notes that early census takers such as Denzil Ibbetson (Census Commissioner in India) expressed concerns about the difficulty in marking Sikh and Hindu as distinct religions. "In the censuses after 1901 the British acknowledged their inability to determine and apply a strict definition of the category Sikh; whoever claimed to be Sikh was so recorded" (Fox 1985: 112).[11] These difficulties in boundary definition were due to the fact that some individuals were sahajdhari and evidenced no outward indices of being Sikh, while the keshdhari were visibly so. In time, a Singh identity (that is, keshdhari) became coterminous with the Sikh identity in reaction to (a) the activities of the wider reform movements, such as the Arya Samaj, and (b) British colonial rule.[12] Similarly Kenneth Jones, a historian reviewing the development of the Arya Samaj Hindu reformist movement, suggests a syncretic religious identity for Hindus — untangled and fixed through the growing "orthodoxy" espoused by Arya reformers.[13] For example, the

Arya Samaj reformers became vegetarian only after internal divisions over whether being a vegetarian and a Hindu reformer were coterminous requirements — did one need to be vegetarian to be a Hindu?[14] The Arya Samaj eventually answered "yes" and their return to tradition (specifically the Vedic orientation) therefore was a restructuring, rebuilding, reappropriation, and creation of symbols both from the past and present in response to the colonial state.

The long-term reverberations of these reformist movements in the Punjab cannot be overemphasized. At work since the late nineteenth century, their changes have echoed throughout India. Hindu reformers strengthened their position after independence from the colonial state because of reservations (setting aside places in education, government, and so forth for minority-status individuals) based on religious communities (note the separate rules and laws in India for minorities such as the Muslims and "Untouchables").[15] Thus, the creation of boundaries and distinction based on religious categories has become more entrenched over the last century through the process of reforms, powerful associations of territory and religious identity in Partition (Pakistan was created because of the adherence to ideas of fixed religious difference), and growth of the Indian state (the subsequent fragmentation of Punjab into Haryana and Punjab).[16] The end effect has been that syncretic traditions have been disentangled, and now specific behaviors define discrete religious communities.

Nevertheless, syncretic practice among Punjabi Hindus continues, albeit modified, challenged, and changed. Indeed, some of London's Hindu Punjabis, especially young children but also young adults and adults, wear the kara (the steel bangle — one of the five Ks of Sikhism). Meat eating is another example, as well as the general tolerance toward those who are nonvegetarians (among my informants, I observed no proscriptions regarding vegetarians eating with nonvegetarians or eating food cooked by nonvegetarians; some women who are vegetarians, in fact, cook meat for their families, even though they themselves do not eat it).[17] Moreover, during fieldwork I observed Sikhs celebrating the goddess, praying in Hindu temples, donating to Hindu temples. Likewise I saw Hindus attending and donating to the local gurdwara. Some London temples and those altars in the home displayed a framed picture of Guru Nanak (the founder of the Sikh religion) or the Cross of Christ.[18] In fact, I met one "Hindu" family who sent their children (boys aged five and seven) to the Sikh private school in Chigwell. These examples reveal that syncretic practices of a specifically "Punjabi" kind continue. However, what is most important is that people claim the existence of discrete religious "communities" despite obvious overlap in practice.

The experiences of the Subcontinent, the historical factors of British census taking, the colonial encounter, reformist activities, as well as recent Indian religious politics contextualize the wider processes for Hindu Punjabis in Britain. All of these factors influence how Hindus experience themselves as a community, which is perhaps unsurprisingly linked to questions raised during colonial rule in India, namely "What is a Hindu?" It is important to understand the need to substantiate Hinduism in Britain as a complex process of many varied influences. This question is still asked, albeit in a different manner (on the need to substantiate religious Sikh and Hindu identity, see Appadurai 1998; Das 1995). One response has been an overt boundary marker connected explicitly to ethnic community formation, a factor in creating discrete religious communities for Hindu migrant groups (see Vertovec 1990; van der Veer 1995).[19] A good example of how community is experienced in late-twentieth-century Britain is the site of the Hindu temple.[20]

The Temples: Becoming a Community in Moments

Temples in Britain, like elsewhere in the diaspora, depend on local government authority zoning approval.[21] Beyond the establishment of the temple, zoning issues govern the use of the temple space, as evidenced in the mid-1990s by the legal scuffle between the Department of the Environment (DOE) and Bhaktivedanta Manor, which brought to light the delicate balance between the right to public worship and zoning issues. The politics and negotiations involved within the temples also illustrate one side of how temples are both active sites for Hindu practice and the negotiations of being able to be a Hindu in Britain. The temples are also changing the ways people pray and congregate as Hindus in the diaspora. The temples concurrently establish the community and mark the changes of belonging to a Hindu community. Their formation also reveals how the sense of belonging to a Hindu Punjabi community is changing. The temples are part of the British landscape; there is a massive Hindu temple in Neasden, West London, which is an amazing ornate vision of ancient India carved of white marble and set against the backdrop of gray rows of terraced housing. This large Swaminaryan temple opened its doors in the late 1990s and has become a touristic alternative London landmark because it is the largest Hindu temple outside of India.

Other temples, such as the Sri Hindu mission that was once an old warehouse in East London, have long been established in Britain. I was first invited to the Sri Hindu Mission, an East London temple, when Nishma's parents suggested I join them for Shivratri celebrations. Nishma made it clear that she was not going. Prior to their invitation, I knew the temple existed; I found it was entered in the local phone directory under "Hindu temple." Paul Weller's *Religions in the UK: Multi-Faith Directory* (1993) also listed its details. But I had little idea of who used it. There were, at the time of my fieldwork, more than 203 Hindu temples and cultural organizations in London alone, but their naming systems — either based on principle deities, for example, "Sri Ram Mandir" (Southall), or general names, such as "Hindu Society" — hid any obvious markers of "ethnic"-based affiliations (except, of course, the Gujarati caste-based Samajs, such as the Patel Samaj [a caste or religious society]). At first I tried to find Hindu Punjabis by locating a temple where they might congregate, and I tried to make tactful enquiries by phone by contacting temples listed in Weller's directory. I realized that I needed to find Hindu Punjabi people to take me to their temples and then find more people, rather than use temples to find people. I was glad that Nishma's parents invited me to the Sri Hindu Mission early in my research, and I anticipated meeting more people there. I had arranged to meet her parents at the temple in the evening, but they rang from the house of their friend Mrs. Kapur with a change of plans. We were going to a different temple, and I was asked to meet with them at Mrs. Kapur's house in Waltham. Their changed plans introduced me to two centers of Hindu Punjabi worship in London's urban sprawl.

I had heard about the Sri Hindu Mission and was curious to attend. I was surprised that they choose another temple at the last minute for this important festivity. The change in venue forced me to reconsider how I conceptualized "community" for these people who are dispersed. Working within an ethnically clustered population, one strategy would have been to locate a "local" temple and then locate people. Like many researchers my focus would have been on finding "ethnic individuals" via a temple, mosque, or gurdwara. This approach assumes community ipso facto. In retrospect, the change in venue also made me realize the role of the temple for these dispersed people. Researchers look for community and find it in the religious space. Therefore it is assumed the religious space makes the community.[22] Yet it became clear to me during my fieldwork that the temple was only one of many places these dispersed Hindu Punjabis visited. It was by no means the focal point for them. The role of the temple was to mark collective social space in Britain (Uncle and Aunty changed their place of worship because Aunty Kapur wanted to go to a different temple). In this it had a function and role.

Subsequently I did visit the Sri Hindu Mission temple. Uncle Aggarwal gave me the address and suggested that I go on my own because he was not sure when they might have a chance to go to the temple again. I also went to the local library to gather historical information. The history unit, like many archives, was filled with old pictures related to specific places. The Sri Hindu Mission was one of the first temples established in East London. The site had been consecrated in 1883 as a mission church. During the Second World War it had been bombed and was used as a commercial premise until 1962. It then remained empty until 1970 when it was reconsecrated as a Hindu temple. It was neither in an area inhabited by many Hindus, nor in the past had there been any great number of Hindus who had lived nearby. It had been chosen simply for its availability and affordability at the time. In the late 1960s, when migrants were settling into life in Britain, the ad hoc temple committee, taking into account their limited funds, selected the old warehouse as the most suitable location. Plans were underway by the temple committee to change location to closer to the A406 North Circular for easier access by car. In the meantime, lack of parking space was a persistent problem, because the warehouse is actually in a residential area of row houses where there is very limited parking, especially on Sunday evenings.

When I first entered the temple in the autumn of 1994, the structure struck me as odd. Only later did I attribute the peculiarity of entering into the temple to the lack of a formal entrance. There was only a side entrance, which seemed a makeshift shed tacked on as an afterthought. There was no welcoming space, no foyer, no antechamber signifying a change from the secular to the sacred. In place of an antechamber was a shoe room with shelves for shoes. Only one interior wall seemed to have been added to the original structure to demarcate space to perform the first act that shifts one out of the secular — the removal of one's shoes before entering the temple. At the back of this twenty-year-old, seemingly makeshift entrance was a sink to help complete the second act of separation — the washing of one's hands as an act of purification after touching one's shoes and feet.

After washing my hands I proceeded into the temple proper where the deities are on a low dais. Usually after entry into this hall people approach the dais and each deity in turn for *darshan*. Each deity (or set of deities) is contained in a minitemple of its own, on a white stage built of four pillars with a peaked dome canopy. Everywhere assorted gaudy and sparkling decorations are hung: tinsel garlands, shiny metallic balloons, lights on each of the deity's domes. The devotee greets the pantheon of statues in the following order: to the left side are Hanuman (the monkey-faced god), Shiva (the destroyer), and Ganesh (the elephant-headed god whose blessings are sought for new beginnings). On the main stage facing outward are the temple's main deities: Sita and Ram (Ram, the hero of the *Ramayan* epic, is an incarnation of Vishnu and is celebrated during Diwali; Sita is Ram's virtuous wife); Radha and Krishna (Krishna is a later incarnation of Vishnu, who is the popular god of the *Bhagavad Gita;* Radha is his consort), who are the temple's principal deities; Mata (the eight-armed goddess, bestower of boons); and the Ram Darbar (consisting of Sita and Ram, Laxman, and Hanuman). To the right side is Baba Balaknath.[23] Approaching this particular statue requires some conviction, because it is blocked by a pundit who sits to the side during festivals and special Sundays for people to approach to have a *mauli* tied around their hand. On most Sundays, people pass quickly in front of all of the deities with their hands joined in *namaskar,* the sign of respect and prayer, while some pause longer in front of their *ish-devta.* Each deity has a small donation box and *jot* (or *jyot*) in front of it; often people will offer coins and then pass their hand over the flame of the jot. Unlike the temples in India, there is no possibility for circumambulation. In fact none of the temples that I have attended, except the new Swaminarayan temple in Neasden, allows one to circulate around the deity.[24] Normally the deity may only be approached from the front, because all deities face outward to the devotees. On the walls just beside the statue of Baba Balaknath are pictures of Satya Sai Baba and Shiva.[25] In other temples in Greater London that I have visited, photographs of Guru Nanak, the first Sikh guru, are also found (usually to the side of the main dais). On the other walls are various announcements — notes from the temple committee, advertisements for other Hindu events (for example, the poster for a protest march in support of Bhatkivedanta Manor), a list of contact numbers, *preeti bhojan* dates, and a list of founding members.[26]

The above description, at first glance, seems a fairly accurate picture. However, to let it stand would be to commit the same social science crime that I seek to prosecute — to see "community" as made up of religious action and then to describe this action as making community. I return to the permanently makeshift shoe room looking into the temple. After the first visit I realized that proceeding to the stage is not the first thing that people do when they enter the temple. It is the first *ritual* action, but preceding that most people, upon entering the temple, quickly glance around the room looking for friends and family to join after they approach the deities. Thus, after coming off the dais to where people are seated on carpets covered with sheets (some of the elderly are sitting on chairs against the back wall), people already know where and with whom they are going to sit. In fact, a repeated action of those already seated in the hall is a constant turning of heads to see who has just entered the room, to wave to their friends, and to indicate that they have kept a space for them. It is an action so often repeated in this sacred space that the distinction between ritual action and social action blurs for the anthropological instant. The first time I entered the temple I was also greeted with this rhythmic movement of heads, but the waves and indication of a kept place did not come until much later in my fieldwork.

There is no gender separation in seating in this particular temple (unlike some other London Hindu temples, Sikh gurdwaras, and Muslim mosques). In other temples, especially in India, even if no formal division is prescribed, men and women separate, with men sitting on the right and women on the left (from the deity's perspective). Nevertheless even in the Sri Hindu Mission temple groups of women tend to form and pockets of men are found sitting together. This is perhaps because often people attend temple when their friends are sponsoring the communal eating, the preeti bhojan, held after the religious prayers: wives move toward wives and husbands to husbands. In this case, those attending would more than likely know many of the people who were also present that Sunday evening. On my first visit, however, there had been no sponsor for the preeti bhojan and consequently there were not many people present, perhaps thirty. One week after my first visit, during Navratri, the room was packed with at least five hundred people. This was an unusually large crowd, but of course festival days always attract the greatest numbers.

Festivals are usually celebrated on the night of the actual event (as deemed by the lunar calendar). For some festivals, such as Diwali, the Sunday just preceding or following the auspicious date is also a time of celebration, and if a festival falls on a Sunday, that day is particularly well attended (such as during Navratri). Sunday evening from 7 to 9 P.M. is the usual time of gathering in most of the temples I have visited. Because there are no prescriptions of a holy day to meet, why was Sunday evening preferred?[27] Later I was given two explanations: Sunday allowed those who were in business to come, and Sunday evenings marked the end of the week. Saturday daytime was for running errands, and Saturday evening was social. Sunday evening was preferred because daytime was reserved for *ana-jana* and people were busy doing other things (such as recovering from Saturday evenings out) so they would not come.[28]

Each temple has a slightly different regular Sunday event and starting time. At Sri Hindu Mission temple the evening begins with a reading and lecture given by the resident pundit. However, it is poorly attended and temple committee members are constantly seeking people to come slightly earlier and using every opportunity to advertise the lecture that precedes the collective singing and *kirtan*. Despite the pleas, most people arrive for the kirtan between 7 and 7:30 P.M. They join in the singing (mostly in Punjabi, but also in Hindi), clap along, listen, or just talk to their friends. The kirtan lasts until 8 or so, when temple announcements and requests are made for donations.

Afterward *bhog* is performed (when the preeti bhojan is blessed by the resident deities and then added to the rest of the food to be eaten by all). After bhog, *arti* (*Om Jai Jagdish Hare*) is sung followed by a litany of various prayers ("*Sat Sai Baba ki jai; sabday apne apne guruwa di jai; poore Sanatan Dharm di jai*" [Victory to Sai Baba; victory to everyone's personal gurus; victory to the whole eternal Dharm]). Following these prayers, someone takes the jot around the room on a steel tray. People approach this jot to pass their hand above the flame and give money (usually small change). At the same time others circulate distributing *parshad*, which people have brought to the temple to share with others (most often fresh fruit, dried fruits and nuts, or a sweet mixture of brown flour, butter, and sugar). Following this, everyone proceeds to the queue already forming for the food. The food is served in an adjoining hall and kitchen (which are located in an adjoining terraced house that was purchased by the temple committee and then joined into the main hall). After queuing for the blessed food, one returns to the main hall through a separate doorway to find a place on the sheet-covered carpeted floor to eat. The meal is in the grand tradition of communal eating. The noise level and sense of fun increase as groups of friends gather to dine together.

This is the average Sunday evening experience for those who come to the temple to pray, meet friends, and form "community." The ways that this space and these rituals have come to pass are fraught with tensions about its establishment.

HISTORY OF THE TEMPLE: TWO NARRATIVES

The aspect of the temple I have outlined above concerns its role as a focus for dispersed and overlapping networks of friends, relatives, and fellow

Hindus. Yet the temple's contested history makes evident that it is much more than a focus for worship and social gatherings. The establishment of a temple is not simply a reflection of an existing "community," but rather the very formation of a temple generates ongoing politicking, struggle, schisms, and debates.[29] As I learned more about the temple it became clear that the establishment of the Sri Hindu Mission as a Hindu center with an almost exclusive Hindu Punjabi membership resulted from continuing factionalism. This was not unusual: other temples with which I was in contact were just as rife with political struggle. At one temple the conflict had escalated to the point of involving the English judicial court. The two narratives presented below reveal how definitions of "community" and "identity" are contested internally and externally. The first, offered by a temple founding trustee and life member, outlines the conflicts and changes since the temple's establishment; the second narrative was elicited somewhat unexpectedly one evening and reveals further details about the temple's establishment and recent factionalism.

After spending the evening with Uncle and Aunty Aggarwal in their comfortable, large, north London house, Uncle was driving me to the underground station. Uncle was a founding member of the temple, but I had never initiated any discussions with him about it. I only responded to his queries. He seemed comfortable with me and since we had a long journey ahead, I took the opportunity to talk about the temple.

The temple was established by myself in the late 1960s. I had been in the Hammersmith gurdwara — we all used to go there as there was nothing else around in those days. Just once a week, sometimes less. I went to get my son who was in a room, you know children they just go wherever. There were a group of Sikhs in there who were talking and saying really bad things about Hindus. I don't want to repeat them, but they were really bad. Right then and there I decided that I would make a mandir so that our people could go somewhere and not have to listen to this kind of talk.

First it was for everyone, all Hindus. Everyone used to come and sit there, then slowly the Gujaratis started coming. They were coming before, but they started coming into the executive and then tried to take over the temple. It was bad and we had to work to get them out. In the 1970s some Bengalis approached us; they wanted to put in their Durga Murti and use the temple. It was put to the committee and we all agreed to allow the Bengalis to use the space. It was agreed as they used the temple at a different time than us so that their schedule did not interfere with ours. They did different things. One time, though, there was an overlap. They [the Bengali Hindus] had just finished [their worship] and had got up and were eating their parshad. They were really noisy and we kept asking them to stay quiet as our *puja* was still happening. Now as we were coming to do arti, I asked them to stand. They did not stand up and they just continued eating their food and talking. I lost my temper. Here we allowed them to come and use our temple and they cannot even stand for one minute for the arti? They had no respect for our gods; they had no respect for Hinduism, so there and then I told them to get out. We had them removed and had their Durga Murti removed as well. It took some time, but they were gone. Since then it has been only us.

It was clear that by "only us" Uncle meant Hindu Punjabis. Indeed for the last ten years the majority visiting the temple has been Hindu Punjabis, although a few Gujaratis worship there as well (one of the women who helps with the temple is Gujarati and there is also a Gujarati among the trustees, so it is not an exclusively Hindu Punjabi space).

The second account was the result of fieldwork serendipity. I had met Ravi at a bhangra comedy gig and after our interview he introduced me to his parents, with whom I began to chat. Ravi was getting restless because he had plans to go out dancing that evening, and his parents invited me to stay on. After I told them more about what I was doing, I asked them for an interview and then began to ask them more about their lives in Britain. It turned out they were also regular visitors to the Sri Hindu Mission temple. Uncle Chawla began to talk about his involvement with the temple.

A friend of mine and myself, we just got talking that we should do something in East London [because] there was nothing there. So we had a first meeting at a friend's house, five of us were there, Mr. A, myself, Mr. B — it was in his house — Mr. C, and Mr. D. [The meeting was held in 1966]. So the five of us, we contributed, on that particular day, five pounds each, which in those days was quite a lot of money, and we started the fund. After that, for a little while, we used to hire a hall and do some functions over there. All the expenditure we put from our own pocket. I think it was six months later we registered ourselves as a charity. There was a Hindu Centre in Chalk Farm — it is still there actually — and we just took their constitution word for word as it was; nine of us became trustees. Then after that we used to hire a hall every Sunday. The income was coming in [from donations on Sundays] and the expenditures we were still meeting ourselves — postage; parshad; and the rent, which used to be five pounds. It was Durning Hall, which was a sort of social center.

Accounts of establishing a temple often involve the practicalities: the primary concern initially was financial. The organizations needed to be able to sustain themselves and to be able to grow. In a few years this temple gained a large following while still in a temporary location.

It was a church in Forest Gate and they gave us a place over there on a permanent basis and we stayed there until 1972, then we bought our own place in Stratford.

It was a derelict place, completely derelict. . . . The rainwater used to come in and puddles were on the inside, very bad. So that church hall and the house next to it we bought that for six thousand pounds and after that we started work over there, which cost us a lot of money to put it right and then we opened up for the public. We moved the *murtis* and everything from Durning Hall . . . and we have been here ever since.

The temple's establishment in a permanent location was not without politics, however all were seen to be working toward a common cause. Thus, places of "community" interest tend to develop a complex politics around them, for people were well aware of the need for overt representation.

In today's day there is a lot of politics. You see when you're starting nobody wants to know you at that time. You know all the hard work and once you're successful other people like to come in and take over the place. But we have had a lot of problem on that side. Since we began there have been nearly four to five attempts by different groups to come over and take over the place, but we have got a very strong constitution. Although the temple is run by the executive committee . . . the executive committee consists of the eight elected members [elected by the general membership annually] plus the nine trustees, so there are seventeen people. Of the nine people, four of us are still there, Mr. A, myself, Mr. B, and Mr. C, then there are other people as well. Yes over the years there have been quite a few changes.

It was an opportunity to explore the problems to which he was alluding: at the beginning of my fieldwork this particular temple was embroiled in acrimonious disputes, which threatened to end in court. I said, "I have heard of some of the recent problems and politics of the mandir." He replied:

There were two trustees who were taking sides with some of the other members who were on the executive committee and what they really wanted to do was, they wanted to take over the temple and the only way they could do it was if the trustees could be removed, which is impossible. It cannot be done. So they convened a special AGM last year; the trustee took an injunction against them, against the General Secretary who was the main ring leader and the whole thing failed. They did hold the AGM but the court put an order on them that they couldn't hold it. The case was due to be heard, I believe it was in March, but then myself and another person we mediated between the two parties and it was mainly Mr. A who was the chairman of the board of trustees and Dr. X on the other side, the ex-General Secretary. At the last minute we avoided the case going to court.

I asked, "What was the injunction specifically about?" This was a question that I had posed to others, but few were able to respond with any details. Being directly involved, he responded:

For them to hold the AGM to change the constitution. First of all the AGM had been called illegally in the sense the executive committee had not authorized it and Dr. X had done it on his own. The other thing was even if the special AGM had been called legally, unless the proposals are approved by the trustees the Constitution cannot be changed. There was a real danger that the temple could have actually been closed. If that had happened, according to the Constitution, all the properties would have been disposed, but none of the money could have remained in this country. That is in the Constitution, that is to deter anybody from trying to make an attempt for a takeover. The money would have gone to charities in India; that is what the Constitution says. We did not write this constitution; we took it word for word from the Hindu Centre in Chalk Farm. Apparently they have had a lot of problems over there as well. Because the [Chalk Farm] temple has been going for a long time — a lot longer than us — and whomever drafted the Constitution, he really thought of everything. It's very simple, tomorrow you can go out make two hundred members and bring your own party and make it a political thing and they do it, this does happen [referring to temples where there are not strong constitutions and at election time people try to stack the vote by signing memberships just to vote in a certain candidate].

But it is the trustees who hold the real power in that sense. The day-to-day running of the temple is in the hands of the executive committee, and the history shows over there that the trustees have never interfered. Never ever. But the purse is held by the trustees, so whatever money that the executive committee wants to spend, they have got to go to the trustees. The trustees would say, "Yes you want £20,000 for this project, we approve that." You see the thing is that we have got loans from the bank as well. The trustees have given their personal guarantors for that. If something goes wrong, I don't know how much loan we have got at the moment — it's not much actually, but at one stage it was a lot of money. Now if anything goes wrong, the bank can close in on any of the trustees and say, "Right you've got the money, you sell your house and you pay us." And we would have to; we have no choice, as we have given our personal guarantees. Whereas the executive committee members they do not have this thing, the treasurer of the elected members is always a trustee and is elected by the trustees, the President [is elected by the trustees] and the General Secretary [is elected by the member public]. . . . Now nearly four times we have had a General Secretary who was not a trustee and every time the same thing has happened. You see today people would literally give their right arm and right leg to become a trustee. I can't understand why, but it has become a real prestigious thing for anybody to become a trustee. I don't know, they've made it into a big thing, these people who wanted to take over, they wanted to become trustees, that's all they wanted.

I had heard murmurs in the temple that the politics were actually about money and embezzlement and asked him about it. He replied strongly:

No there is no truth in that *whatsoever.* This is one thing right from 1966 onwards; there has never been one instance that anyone has said that someone has done something with the money. Never. Never. Never. Ever. That is one thing which has never happened in this center. I don't think we would ever let anything like that happen in any case. No, everything and everybody has always been aboveboard.

When I tentatively suggested, "It is more to do with power," he agreed. "One hundred percent. There have never been any allegations against anybody, even whatever they raised against Mr. A that was on tactical rather than financial grounds. In the end the whole thing was dropped. They wanted him out really." I thought I would try to approach the topic of money again; perhaps it was something being used by those in opposition to take hold of the political power of the temple. I again asked, "Did they try to use money or embezzlement of funds?" He again replied, "NO, no embezzlement no. In any case Mr. A is a multimillionaire, if anything he has given more money to the temple than anybody else."

This candid account was exceptional. During fieldwork most people were reluctant to speak about the injunction and political factions, and as my research progressed the temple regained its strength and popularity. It was a place where people came to meet with their friends and where people could carry out their religious duties. It is in such a space that "community" is constituted: the temple is a focus for aspects of shifting identity, especially the contested arenas of establishing and maintaining a space more or less exclusively Hindu Punjabi. This building of community has concomitantly involved the building of boundaries.

Temple As Community Space

As Uncle Ram's quotation, which is this chapter's epigraph, suggests there is a consciousness of the changing role and significance of the temple in Britain. This is not to state that there is an increase or decrease in "Hinduism" (as if such a measurement could be ascertained), but rather a change in practice. Temples have changed because of their centrality as community centers. The temple in London is a social and political space used to meet other people, to meet friends, to educate children, and in some cases to meet prospective marriage partners.[30] As such, it has encouraged the development of a clearer sense of "Hindu" identity in a non-Hindu world.

For those accustomed to Hindu temples named after principle deities, the nomenclature of the temple I discussed above, "Sri Hindu Mission," is striking. The names of temples in Britain have begun to incorporate identity labels such as "Hindu center," "Hindu society," and "Hindu mission" (see Bowen 1981b). This shift reveals how the temples are recognized as central aspects of "making community" and indeed of "calling attention not to the deity in the temple but to the community that worships the deity" (Burghart 1987: 232). According to one London temple's letterhead, temples are "religious, cultural and social institute[s]." Burghart connects this nomenclature to the "idea that Hinduism is an ethnic religion" (1987: 232). An ethnic religion is one that is conscious of itself as marking "a community" and of the name by which it is known. The consciousness of using the temple to act as a focus for the representation of a group is obvious from many official annual temple publications that reprint letters from VIP non-Hindus, including the Prime Minister, Prince Charles, MPs, local mayors, and councilors. These letters are solicited through invitations to major events and the printed responses of these officials reveal how integral representation is to creating a Hindu community in the temple space.

The Sri Hindu Mission, one of many "Hindu temples" in Britain with an almost exclusive Hindu Punjabi membership, is a fixed place where members of a "religious minority" gather (members of the "Hindu community," or as we might argue in some cases, members of the "Hindu Punjabi community"). As such it is a community bound in space and specific times. Hindu Punjabi identity is tied to this temple in complex ways. Historically it was formed by Hindu Punjabis and others, but over time Hindu Punjabis have clustered there. This could be because of the language spoken in and around the temple (Hindi and Punjabi); it could be because the food served is generally cooked in the Punjabi style; it could be because the kirtans are sung in Hindi and Punjabi. People know each other in and through the temple, but aside from the executive and active members (including previous or aspiring executives) they do not all attend the same temple regularly. The fact that Uncle and Aunty Aggarwal spontaneously changed plans and attended a different temple confirms this. There were other instances as well, when people would go to a different temple for a friend's function, or perhaps they moved among two or three temples. Others attended the same temple regularly; still others participated only in the temple's large events and celebrations. Each temple maintains a membership list, but their membership was by no means exclusive. Nor was the temple the only way to practice being a Hindu in Britain. The temple was a place to congregate, even though the actual site of congregation could change. For those I studied, their temple outings were usually around large-scale events, rather than regular Sunday meetings. This undoes a notion of Hindu community for these people, because there is no regular contact. Instead they come into and out of different physical places of worship, yet there is a persistent sense that they belong to a Hindu community in Britain.

Evoking "community" for the Hindu Punjabi temple involves an understanding of a spatially bounded place temporally coherent with a specific organization and structure and with sharp boundaries. As such, the temple is a community that is spatially defined and comes together at certain moments. While the physical structure of the temple always exists, the people are not always present in the structure. Can the term "community" be extended to refer to people when they are not in the physical space of the temple? Probably not. It is useful to employ the term "Hindu community" when people are in the temple. It is a complete misnomer to speak of a middle-class Hindu Punjabi "community" outside of the places such as the temple where they come together. In London, apart from the Southall Hounslow area, there are no significant Hindu Punjabi clusters of settlement, nor do Hindu Punjabis attend the same temple (regularly or otherwise). Individual members, as Hindus, may not hold the same beliefs or conduct the same rituals or practices. Many do, but this is not a requirement. Some are vegetarian, some are nonvegetarians; some hold one deity as most important, others emphasize a guru; and so on. Within the temple I observed smaller social groups, cliques, or "circles of friends" whose existence challenges a view of the temple community as a "unified" group. Their unification was a nominal part of their common experience of being a minority, and they have an ethnic religion very different in its many forms of practice to the dominant majority. Individuals may see themselves as nominally part of a Hindu "community" when they are not physically "in" the temple. There is no Hindu Punjabi "community," therefore, but only moments when community occurs, when people gather as a whole, because of a certain criterion of religious identification. Conceptualizing community in moments moves away from understanding "ethnics" either as static and unchanging or (more dangerously) as part of a group defined as those who practice the Hindu religion.

The "imagined community" (Anderson 1983) of Hindus is constituted via temple worship and wider practices. The temple is a focus for a dispersed group of people who lead much of their lives in separate social fields; this is an imagined community. There are certainly "communal" tensions revealed in the ways informants spoke about this temple, especially in separation from Sikhs. Also, as the account above reveals, there are tensions within the "Hindu" community between Punjabis, Gujaratis, and Bengalis because of differences in religious practices and languages. These discussions lead me to understand the temple, not as a site where "community" meets (unlike the Muslim ideal of the *umma,* the global community of all Muslims, or a Christian congregation), but as a place where "friends" socialize. This is not to say that people do not use the term "community" to refer to their experience. Indeed, the notion of a Hindu community is being increasingly evoked to "promote Hindu solidarity" (see Raj 2000).[31]

The analytical utility of "community" has, of course, been questioned and debated extensively (Bell and Newby 1972; Cohen 1985; Macfarlane 1977; Calhoun 1978; Carrithers and Humphery 1991); yet it remains integral to many accounts of ethnicity (see Gillespie 1995: 164, who explicitly connects "community" to locality). Recently some scholars have sought to use the example of South Asians in Britain to engage in debates on the connections between community and ethnicity. For example, Gerd Baumann in his work on Southall has sought to separate the "demotic" from the "dominant" discourses on community and examines how the term is used and understood by those of his Southall study. Baumann, like Gillespie, begins with a locality and argues that the place itself imposes shared boundaries on its inhabitants. He concedes "that the relationship of culture to community and indeed the meanings of these words themselves, are matters of continual contestation in the culture that Southallians share" (1996: 32). His emphasis on the different ways people use the term "community" is insightful, but he does not examine the ways in which he, as an analyst, might use this term (in fact, he dismisses the analytical utility of "community"). Marcus Banks is less reluctant to dismiss the analytical purchase of community in his study of Jains in Leicester. He argues, "A notion of community is perceived by the actors themselves" (1991: 258) and that "'Community' is not an a priori quality of a group of Jains, or of all Jains, it is something that they, from the conceptual category of 'Jainism' create for themselves" (1991: 258–59). This clarification is very helpful because it implies inscription and ascription of practices as integral to "making community."

Living in transnationalism, the changing nature of belonging to a community has meant a specific sense of being a minority. "In the diaspora, and especially the diaspora of the first world, the Hindu constitutes a minority, surrounded by societies which are not Hindu. He can develop the mentality of the ghetto and a minority consciousness, and see his identity in those terms" (Thapar 2000: 607). This is borne out by the experiences of Uncle Ram, whose words reflect on the strength of the temple. During our interview he indicated that one of the experiences of being a part of the Hindu diaspora included a feeling of being a minority. I had asked Uncle if the act of going to the temple constituted "active practice" as a Hindu, because his initial words seemed to imply this. He responded, "No, no, there [the temple is a place where] socially you get together. Then, suppose you are gone somewhere, and you are standing in a field and one in only a hundred people looks known to you. So you start moving that way and out of one hundred where will you go first? To the one that is known to you." Uncle Ram's abstract reflection contains the sense of being a minority, that one goes to those who "look known." The temple is one of the main places that people cluster toward those who look familiar. But, as I have argued above, although this clustering is a key location in the transnational terrain, it is only a community in moments. It remains to be seen if this sense of minority identity, leading to a need to occasionally congregate in the temple, will be sustained in the second generation. For now, it seems that, as the second generation gets older, marries, and has their own children, the site of worship is changing to the migrant's home (especially for events such as Diwali, where a home-based celebration are customary).

Home Rituals — Being a Hindu in Everyday Life

Domestic practice informs transnational Hindu worship as a personal and social activity. When my husband and I were invited to Aunty and Uncle Aggarwal's Diwali celebration at home, the functions were all held in their kitchen, the site of the home temple. In many of the houses I visited, people kept their mandir in a kitchen cupboard. The home temple contains statues or pictures of deities and gurus, incense sticks along with the accoutrements of daily ritual, including matches, cotton balls, and ghee. The door to this cupboard stays slightly ajar, or may be made of glass. More recently, as their children leave their parental homes, some families are dedicating entire rooms to a home temple. Aunty Kapur had done this in her box room — the smallest bedroom in their home.

The same deities may be worshipped at home as in the public temple; however, home mandirs are generally more heavily decorated with various pictorial or statue representations of deities than public temples. All deities are present (such as Krishna, often without Radha if he is represented in a statue, Ram and Sita, Hanuman, Ganesh, and so forth) and some duplicated in form (that is, Krishna may be found as both statue and picture, depicted as a baby and as a warrior). Pictures of gurus that the family currently follows or has followed in the past are represented as well. As one woman whom I met only for an interview explained to me, "My father-in-law [now deceased] used to believe in that [Sai Baba's picture still kept in the temple] so we have got that as well. There is another one there, which is my mother-in-law's guru; she's taken vows from him. He's in Kilburn." Often home temples have a string of colored Christmas lights that are lit during daily worship, and which often stay lit during festival days. Others have silver or gold garlands or other tinsel decorations. In public temples purification rituals form a significant part of the daily activity. This is not the case for home temples, which are differentiated from the secular space when the jot is lit daily.[32] The jot is kept in a small steel or brass container that perhaps was purchased in India and brought to England at the time of migration. In the cupboard temple, or nearby, in addition to the deities are religious books and a container of parshad filled with dried fruit or nuts.

The location of the home mandir in the kitchen implicitly connects the idea of a symbolic hearth and the well-being of the family. This connection is often understood in terms of the behaviors and roles of women.[33] The gender divide in home worship is not uniform across families, but in the majority of cases, the female head of the household took responsibility for daily prayers and lighting the temple area.[34] Only in one family did I meet a woman who claimed that she did not conduct rituals on a daily basis, but she pointed out that her husband and mother-in-law pray and read every morning: "My husband does the jot and he just prays, I don't pray [laughing]; I don't do nothing. I just do *matha tek* in the morning. That's it." She says hello to the gods. Her home temple was kept under a purpose-built imported canopy in the front sitting room.

Day-to-day activities at home vary. Some women told me that they performed a variety of rituals. The form and duration of these depended on whether the woman was working and the age of her children. The range of activities usually at minimum included lighting a jot. Aunties told me about doing daily reading from either the *Gita,* the Hanuman Chalisa, Ram Chalisa, or the Sikh book *Sukhmani.* Time permitting, these might be combined, or she might read certain texts on certain days (for instance, on Tuesday she might read the Hanuman Chalisa, the day associated with that particular god). Other Aunties and a few Uncles mentioned that they might recite a mantra, or small prayer. In the evenings,

Uncle and Aunty Aggarwal would together do the evening arti. Nishma and I would sometimes hear the ringing of a small hand-held brass bell. Other aunties would light an incense stick and just the smell of incense meant that the evening prayers had been done. The children usually did not participate in the prayers, but they might go into the temple and ask for blessing (especially on the eve of an important interview or exam). In other families, uncles and aunties at the morning prayer might seek each deity's blessings by touching the feet of the deity and applying a *bindi* of red powder or sandalwood to the statues. In the handful of cases where the grandparents lived with the family, when the elder woman did any of these activities the young preschool-aged children might join her in her daily prayers. But there are other forms of domestic devotion. For instance, certain regular household activities can be seen as part of the globalization of Hinduism through technical commodification.[35] Watching religious videos, such as the *Mahabharat* or *Ramayan* or Bollywood films with a religious theme, falls into this category, as does listening to religious tapes of bhajans, kirtan, or lectures either at home or in the car.[36] Such tapes are also used at times of social home worship. When my husband and I attended Diwali celebration at the Aggarwals' home, they read the Ramlila Chalisa (the story-dramatized portion of the *Ramayan* based on the two Sunder Kand and Lanka Kand chapters) as well as from the *Gita*. The arti was delayed as family members tried to find it on different audiocassette tapes. Finally after Nishma and Aunty rewound and fast forwarded a series of cassettes, punctuated with short bursts of kirtan, Aunty found the appropriate arti and we all stood singing or clapping along, accompanied by the singing and music of the personal stereo.

Increasingly, religious symbolism is incorporated into more general patterns of personal consumption. Religious iconography was once restricted to a single cupboard in the mandir. More recently, however, in some family homes pictures or statues of deities are also found as decorative pieces, hanging on the wall or sitting on the mantelpiece above the fireplace (Ganesh seems particularly popular for this spot, but as it is fashionable and decorative to display the Ganesh murti, this may not have any religious connotations). Hindu styles are not yet as obvious as those of some Sikh and Muslim families in Ilford, where an *"Ek Omkar"* symbol or a Koranic phrase in beautiful stained glass is placed above the front door (other houses on the street have the usual assortment of stained-glass flowers and birds). Nevertheless, interiors are changing, and in one or two homes I saw a wall clock with the *Gayatri Mantra* inscribed in circles.[37] As part of a display of material wealth, cars are also subject to this public declaration: Sikhs might have "Ek Omkar" stickers, and Hindus might have Satya Sai Baba or ॐ. Small photos of a deity are sometimes placed on the car's dashboard. A further example of this public display of Hinduism is the jewelry worn by both men and women. It was fashionable for women to wear elaborate jewelry of Hindu iconography (Krishna pendants or mounted goddess coins). Men as well wore religious pieces, such as ॐ pendants on 22-carat gold chains. Thus, both in the home and on the body sacred images are becoming "decorative" and definitely much more public.

These practices make Hinduism visible and act as an affirmation of "community" identity. All of these practices indicate a more overt and self-conscious Hinduism, which has emerged from behind the doors of the temples and homes into the public. Such a public display is not uncommon in India, or indeed in any other country in which Hindus are found, but while the material forms of collective religious expression may be similar to India, the social composition of the identities signaled are distinctive to the United Kingdom. For the parental generation, these overt and conscious patterns of practice contain the essence of what it is to be Hindu. For the younger generation, however, "Hinduness" is something that needs to be learned and has some specific manifestations.

Young Hindus: Learning to Be a Part of a Community in Moments

Young Hindus learn about being "Hindu" from a variety of sources, including the home and the temple. Their sense of Hinduism is privatized, because of the requirements of being a minority religion. One young woman told me:

Our religious experience is just basically just sitting around and with my mum cooking. It's really nice. Religion has to mean what it means to you at a personal level. I do have the books and look at them if I have to, I have watched the whole of the *Mahabharat* in the New Year with my parents. You pick up little bits and bobs from that and apply them to real life. I don't think more than that. I am not kinda overly into religion. . . . We just did our thing at home. . . . Religion is kinda a home thing.

Some parents, concerned about the "Hinduness" of their children, teach them mantras, read to them religious comics imported from India, or show them religious programs. Young people recall participating in religious functions, such as *havans* and pujas, at home. and taking part in the preparations. They also recall the celebrations, such as Diwali, that take place in the home with friends or relatives.

Children also learn about religion in the Hindu temple. Many young people I studied had attended one or more temples regularly as children, but the frequency decreased as they grew older. Most of the young people I met during research went to temple only on special occasions such as Janmashtami, Diwali, or Navratri. Another common time that young people attended the temple was when their family had an event (a special puja) or their parents, friends, or extended family sponsor a preeti bhojan. This does not imply that the parents attend the temple regularly on Sundays and that the children only go during festival events. Youths will not usually attend without their parents, and often parents do not attend regularly. Most youths said they did not attend the temple except on festival days (three or four times a year) because it was just a social thing, a place where parents can meet their friends. Some young people recalled, "Nothing religious in it really," or "Religion is the excuse [for our parents] to meet with friends." Only parents who were directly involved with the functioning of the temple, their families, and certain individuals trying to maintain a high profile because of their jobs or positions, attended every Sunday. In fact, the Uncle who initially invited me to the Sri Hindu Mission had not been there himself for at least one and a half years.

My Punjabi teacher (as well as many others) commented to me that the children's behavior at the temple was "uncontrolled." Their dismay was not hard to understand; at temple one would regularly find youngsters running up onto the dais, taking fruit offered to the deities, or playing with the jot. When families did not retrieve the child immediately (often older sisters or cousins or a friend's older daughter would bring the child back to where the parent or group of friends sat), the pundit or a temple member gestured with both hands, pointing at the child then to the crowd, as if to gently push the child off the dais. Not all children would behave like this, but there was usually at least one acting in such a manner every Sunday. The older children were different. The boys were often near the back playing tag or play-fighting, or just running around their parents (or the group of family friends). At the entrance to the temple there was a group of teenage boys who remained outside until arti. Or the teenaged boys congregated in the room where the food was served. The girls seemed more sedentary, often staying close to their mothers or aunts or, if younger, with their fathers. They helped relatives and friends look after straying younger children, or they sat with other girls their age.

Despite regular complaints from the adults about lack of knowledge about the religion, only one of the temples had an established program for children. In a way it was assumed that simply bringing children to the temple without any instruction would be sufficient to make them Hindu.[38]

Many young Hindu Punjabis I knew did not see themselves as Hindus exclusively but were concerned with what they termed "spirituality." During the ritual practices they participated in with their parents, they can be seen as Hindus, but their identification as Hindus is not framed in exclusive terms.[39] They not only grew up with Hindu practices but also with the Lord's Prayer, which does not challenge the ways that they experience community in moments, or how they frame their identification as Hindus. They may have taken various sojourns to the temple and participated in family religious prayers, which are the ways they learned to be Hindu. But they may also have participated in other religious practices, which do not challenge their "Hinduness." To borrow an analogy, which one uncle shared with me, the youths see the world's rituals and religions as "many paths up the same mountain." In this way they resemble the anthropologist who sees the diversity in cultural and religious practice as meeting the universal human need for a belief system. They are relativistic while underscoring universal underpinnings to religious belief and practice. They undergo *sanskar* rituals, alter them, reform them, rewrite them, or just dismiss them as unnecessary ritual without thought to their meaning beyond pleasing one's parents.

However, these young people are generally aware of holding religious identities that are different from other minorities. For example, I asked the young woman quoted above (who spoke of religious experiences in terms of her mother's cooking) what she thought it meant to be a Hindu in Britain. She remarked, "I think it means, it has to mean what it means to you. There's not a big organized community set up in the sense that there are of other religions. I mean they are getting there, there's mandirs that are starting and happening. As with the Sikh community where everything gels and works together, I don't see that with mandirs — bits and bobs coming together and that is about it."

In interviews with young people I would ask, "Are your parents Hindu?" The response would be a definitive yes. When asked, "Are you a Hindu," they would respond, "Well, no," or with a qualified yes. Some would add that they believed in God, and that they had been bought up in a Hindu manner, but that they did not think of themselves only as Hindus because all religions were the same. Baumann (1996) notes a similar emphasis — on what he calls "encompassment" — among Hindus in

Southall. When I asked them what it meant to be a Hindu they would speak of everyday practices such as vegetarianism, or the exclusion of red meat, or ritual such as a regular prayer in front of the murtis. At the same time these young people were often perfectly prepared to use religious images in a kind of generalized spirituality. Take, for example, the Kapurs' home. Despite the picture of Sai Baba on Aunty Kapur's bedroom door, she did not exclusively follow Sai Baba as a guru. Aunty did attend his kirtans regularly and had even taken a pilgrimage to his ashram in southern India, but she also attended the Vishwa Hindu Parishad (VHP) temple and the Durga temple with equal regularity. And she has completed many different pilgrimages around India. At home, there were many different murtis and photos in her mandir, where Sai Baba blended into the many representations of god, in front of which she lit her daily jot. On her daughter Arti's bedroom door was an image of Sai Baba, an eye-level sticker of Sai Baba's feet. Inside the room, among the usual clutter of a young working woman's bedroom, including eau de toilette bottles, Body Shop creams, and hair accessories, at the head of the bed was a photo of Guru Nanak with a rosary hung around it. She hardly ever went to the temple, and on one occasion when I was with Aunty at a kirtan, Arti was at a pop music concert by the artist formerly known as Prince at Wembley Stadium.

I do not mean to suggest her ideas were insincere. She would often talk about spirituality, about being at peace with oneself, about wanting to meditate, and about keeping up her yoga classes (given through the local authority). She was a vegetarian of the sort who did not eat eggs but would eat egg tagliatelle. Food, in fact, proved to be a very apt medium for exploring the flexibility in young people's understanding of Hinduism. One evening, for example, I was interviewing a young woman who said that she was not really a Hindu, but that her parents were; nevertheless, she did not eat beef. Later when we went to a restaurant we both decided to order the "all you can eat" pasta and pizza. When she took the spaghetti with meat sauce, which obviously contained beef, she clarified her position: "I don't eat beef if I know that it is beef. As I don't know that this is beef, I'm not really doing something wrong." While such beliefs and practices are flexible in a way that parental beliefs are not, among young Hindus there is a growing awareness of how one's religious difference matters (see Raj 2000).

Perhaps the most interesting development is how Hinduism is being promulgated using Internet technology, both via e-mail and the world wide web. The following e-mail circulated in January 2001:

"OM"

Just send this prayer to seven people or more and let me know what happens on the fourth day. That's all you have to do. This is a powerful prayer of Ganesh. Prayer is one of the best free gifts we receive. There is no cost but a lot of reward. Let's continue praying for one another. Make a wish before you read this prayer. Did you make a wish?(if you don't make a wish, it won't come true) (Last Chance to Make a Wish). Let us start,

SHREE GANESH VANDANA

SHASHI VARNAM CHATURBHUJAM;|

PRASANNA VADANAM DHYAYET;

SARVA VIGHNOPA SHANTAYE;|

AGAJANANA PADMASANA;

GAJANANA MAHARNISHAM;|

ANEKA DANTAM BHAKTANAM;

EKA DANTAM UPASMAHE;|

Send This to 7 People within the next 5 mins and your wish will come true Somewhere, somehow.

This chain e-mail wish, fortified by religious Sanskrit prayer, certainly has a lot of appeal in the world of instant communication/gratification whereby "community" is taken to be an omnipresent force. Prayer e-mails, religious screen savers, and websites that allow one's scanned photo to be immersed in the Ganges (www.webdunia.com) exemplify the ways technology is being used as a vehicle for Hindus to be constantly aware of their Hinduism, to literally become a virtual community, one that extends beyond temple gatherings and home worship to moments of receiving e-mails, listening to bhajans online, and sending Diwali e-greetings.[40]

The experience of Hinduism as a community in moments has aided the transformation of Hinduism into an ethnic religion. The transformation has also involved negotiations between Hindus, between Hindus and non-Hindus, and within a changing sense of Hinduism for the children of migrants. One of the first acts migrants undertook as they "made community" in Britain was building a Hindu temple. By questioning how we understand "community" in relation to the temple, I have challenged how Hindu temples are ipso facto sites of community. Rather, these exist as physical spaces in which a community occurs in moments. The temple is one site of contested identity and also provides an apt example of the processual nature of identification. Such a processual view of lived religious experience and the various negotiations involved return us to the ways in which transnationalism is created by people's everyday lives. The experience of a community in moments creates globalization; establishing a temple, practicing home rituals, and being aware of one's minority religion are all the microstrategies that create collective agency and cultural knowledge.

The experience and diversity of beliefs, which I observed in London, are various aspects on the continuum of Hinduism. At one end of the continuum are those who claim not to be Hindus, but they ritually perform Hinduism; at the other are those who are active Hindus in the temple and at home. The Hinduism of London's Hindu Punjabis is not only a product of living in Britain but also of a religious transnationalism. The experiences of the youth and the parents, the temple politics, and domestic worship all indicate the contextual nature of understanding what a Hindu is and what it means to be a Hindu and have a community in moments. In sketching the historical details of syncretism alongside details of temple politics (recall Uncle Ram's narrative above), space and time factor into the notions of a changed religious community. Migration is only one factor in which this production of diasporic Hinduism occurs that requires a certain accountability of one's identity. The inflection of this has separated out the easy conflation of community, identity, and community.

The processes of being and becoming Hindu allow my interlocutors to discover and establish a religious identification that assumes a community located to a specific place. Religious boundaries have often functioned in prosaic ways as markers of difference, indicating those who are counted as insiders and outsiders through ritual, belief, and practice. In focusing on the maintenance of Hinduism in Britain, academics have promulgated certain notions of difference across time and space, in which Hindu identity is perpetuated as omnipresent entity outside of locality. By infusing "community" with time, I have also questioned the easy equation of ethnicity and culture. Does identification as a Hindu necessarily mean that one is part of a Hindu community? The people I studied, like other minority groups around the world, have various ways of refusing and entering into the production of difference. Like other religions, Hinduism has become a touchstone of irreconcilable and unquestionable difference connected to the ethnic minority group. The production of this difference and their own sense of making an ethnic religion reveal how people in their daily lives are creating alternative transnational realities. There is a sense of the ubiquity of Hinduism in which being part of a community in moments can occur at the click of a mouse. There are also active processes by which ethnicity, community, and religious identity become exchangeable. For Hindu Punjabi migrant families, the intergenerational experiences especially reveal the processual nature of identification as Hindus. In fact, the survival of religion depends on these very quotidian changes, creating the possibilities of claiming Hindu as a changeless social form, while it is inflected by space and time. What it means to be Hindu is a part of their lives that is constantly changing.

CHAPTER 5

The Search for a Suitable Boy

My parents took me to meet this guy. He was all the things they wanted: he was fair; he was tall; he was a banker, or investment guy, earning £200,000 a year. All the things I hate. We went in; it was me, my parents, my brother, and my *bhabi* [brother's wife]. There were five of us; there were thirty of them, just sitting there in the room — all over the place. He was on one side; I was on the other. It was silent and then someone would ask a question and everyone would be focused on me or him. So then his Aunt asks him (in front of everyone), "Do you like her?" And before he answers, then she says why don't you go into the other room and talk. So we went into the other room. Basically there was nothing wrong with this guy, nothing at all that I could tell them. On the way out I asked my brother, "Please I have never asked you to do anything in your whole life so tell them you didn't like him." And so my brother later said that he thought the guy was too arrogant and stuck up and that is why he didn't like him. So I just said, "Yeah I found that too when we went into the room to talk." And that was that. I have seen a couple of others. Last week I told my mum about Ashok [her current boyfriend], he is South Indian but at least he is a Hindu. I just told her, "What do you think of him as a possibility?" And that was it, she hasn't said anything else to me since then. (Anu Sharma)

Thus far we have examined how culture, ethnicity, and community are disrupted when looking at the terms "Punjabi" and "Hindu" through the lens of power and representation. In the following discussion on Hindu Punjabi marriage, the ethnography illustrates the subtle ways ethnic identity is produced and challenged though practice, specifically youth practice. Intergenerational narratives are the strongest challenge to the nostalgia for culture, because they create a disruption between community, identity, and culture. I want to think through marriage as a way for talking about being transnational. The focus is on "arranged" marriage and the complexities involved in matching parental and young people's expectations. At one level, the whole chapter revolves around reflecting on the differences between what people say and what people do, their sense of cultural knowledge and agency. At the same time I use their negotiations to understand how community building occurs with a simultaneous engagement with marking identity and difference (of choosing an acceptable partner). Alliance in this way provides an additional framework for thinking about how these people live transnationalism in the sense of place and the complexity of meaning making produced by their engagement in a specific sociohistoric location.

In what follows, I focus on a gender perspective of arranged marriage. For Anu, and many other young Hindu Punjabi women, the system is flexible enough to allow for the possibility of rejection, but the rejection must be expressed in culturally specific terms. In a way the focus on young woman is a result of my fieldwork, because most of the young men I met were not looking for wives or were already married. Ethnographically, the examples are from both the young women and their parents, as bride givers. The families are extremely self-conscious of their role and responsibilities in the process. Examining arranged marriage for this relatively prosperous and educated "noncommunity" highlights the centrality of marriage for ethnicity. By detailing the Hindu Punjabi parental concern with one modality of ethnic boundary maintenance and their children's reaction to it, I explore identity negotiation at a personal level in which there is verbal affirmation of maintaining a notion of community, ethnicity, and identity as exchangeable under the umbrella of culture. What this actually involves for the parents and the young women is completely variable.

Research on South Asians in Britain has linked arranged marriage practices to an assumed culture clash between parents and children (see, for example, Anwar 1976) and the clash between British and Asian cultural patterns.[1] Perhaps in response to this "problem"-orientated approach, anthropologists during the 1980s and 1990s tended to stress the integrative role of marriage and to treat marriage choice as relatively unproblematic, instead focusing on the wedding rituals or the event itself (Bhachu 1985, 1993, 1995; P. Werbner 1990b). Others have argued against the limitations of such a focus on symbolic interactionism. At the base these scholars challenge the ways in which the research on Asians in Britain treat weddings as metonymic windows into Asian culture, as symbolic ceremonial wholes that encompass the putative central threads of the whole culture (in a vein similar to Geertz's treatment of the Balinese cock fight). Some younger scholars have even argued that marriage is among the most "exotic racist categories" that characterize accounts of Asians in Britain (Sharma, Hutnyk, and Sharma 1996). A focus on marriage is not inherently racist, although, the ways in which South Asians have been typified through marriage may be. By highlighting its salience, I do not wish to perpetuate a sense of fixed otherness. The difficulty with arranged marriage is not with marriage per se but with its treatment in the literature. Rather than viewing the wedding as the finale of a lengthy period with its own rules of cultural performance and social interaction, some scholars often concentrate on interpreting a single day or the events immediately preceding the day. Ignoring the mechanisms and activities of finding a suitable partner neglects that aspect of marriage concerned with the transformation or reinterpretation of identity in favor of collective ritual. Bhachu highlights why the prewedding details are often absent:

In general, information about the very early stages of matchmaking is difficult to obtain because of the *delicate* nature of the discussions. The whole procedure is handled secretively, in case the proposition falls through. Often even the close relatives are not aware of such activities until it is almost certain that the match will be fixed, at which time there are intense consultations among relatives to check the background of the family members with the help of the wider kinship network before making the final decision. It is only after the *rokna* that people first find out about the match. (1985: 183, emphasis mine)

The "delicate" processes of arranging a marriage are precisely the most interesting ways to think through issues of agency and cultural knowledge. Like Bhachu, I found that this information is difficult to solicit, or even to obtain systematically in the field. Nevertheless, the arrangement of a marriage alliance is replete with meanings giving insight into the changing nature of Asian identification in Britain.

Matchmaking allows people to reflect on changing cultural attitudes and social structures. The period of intense prewedding activity and the grand finale of the wedding are the culmination of a range of activities that may have spanned one, two, or even five years.[2] The search for a suitable boy or girl balances the social need to "save face" and to protect one's status and that of one's daughter or son with the need to use kin and friend networks necessary to perform the search. During my fieldwork

Aunties, Uncles, and HP friends stressed the delicacy and secrecy of the process. I was often directed, "Don't tell anyone," or "We have not told anyone," or "This is something we want to keep amongst us." Children, while keen to solicit my opinion or experiences, would explicitly ask me not to relay any information to their parents. The focus on Nishma's story below is an outcome of her family's unusual openness with my husband and me. Of all the families we came to know, Nishma's seemed the most candid regarding all aspects of their search and their concerns. This confidence partially stemmed from my close relationship with Nishma and partially because my husband and I did not know many others in their immediate kin or friendship networks. Only one other family I knew discussed their activities and concerns in detail. But they never told me about their arranged meetings until at least two weeks after they occurred, even though we were requested to "keep our eyes open" for suitable boys. Other women would talk about the potential partners they rejected and elaborated on their own concerns about the arranged-marriage process.

"Arranged marriage" seemed to be the norm in the parental generation, albeit variations among households were common. Some migrant parents told me they had "love marriages" and that they would allow their children to choose their own partners. However these same parents would nevertheless articulate preferences or prescriptions, especially regarding religion; "The boy must be a Hindu" was important for many. A few parents said to me, "She [their daughter] will choose their own person to marry and then we will see." In these cases, daughters had to find their own partners, and parents would not organize introductions unless explicitly requested. Most parents, however, were more interested in playing an active role in finding a partner for their children. From the children's point of view, some were keen to find their own partners while others reluctantly agreed to meetings arranged through families. Negotiation is thus a necessary part of the process. How does one negotiate in cultural terms? Due to parental expectations, marriage becomes a time in the second generation's life when negotiation of ethnic identity is the most calculated and explicit. In turn, marriage can be used to demonstrate how parents negotiate ethnicity. They are not the "traditional" (read: unchanged) migrant, but have altered and been transformed in response to living in Britain.

During the first meetings with many of my London informants one of the initial questions I was asked by both parents and children was, "Did you have an arranged marriage?" My deliberately teasing reply, "No, I met my husband before our wedding day," allowed me to explore individual understandings of the phrase "arranged marriage" and elicited many different qualifications about what the original question had meant.

For the anthropologist, arranged marriage is defined as "the degree to which persons other than those marrying participate in the process of selection" (Freeman 1968: 457). In the South Asian case, intertwined with this are a variety of prescriptions and proscriptions such as caste endogamy, subcaste exogamy, and incest taboos.[3] Beyond these "rules" lie other more loosely defined ideas of what characteristics might be detailed to "make a good match," that is, to effect a proper and acceptable alliance between families. Unlike for British Muslim Pakistanis and Bangladeshis, for Hindu Punjabis there is no preference for reinforcing kin alliance through marriage between close kin, such as the preference for mother's sister's son. Also, unlike the British Sikhs of Gell's Bedford study (Gell 1994), regional exogamy is not required, although families do prefer that the couple are not known to each other.[4]

The term "arranged marriage" subsumes various understandings and social practices. For my informants it is the introduction of a "boy" or "girl" whom parents have found "suitable" because of their own requirements and restrictions such as ethnic background, caste, and profession. When my friends and informants would talk about having an "arranged marriage" they meant a marriage that developed from an arranged *meeting,* an introduction service performed by parents. Arranged marriage should not be confused with *forced* marriage. Moreover, it is not the only way to find a life partner, and as Nishma's story reveals, young women who are agreeable to an arranged marriage and respectful of their parents' wishes are often simultaneously negotiating their own requirements and desires into its framework. Often, parents state that a partner had been found in more traditional ways even when those closer to the family know that the couple had been dating for some time, or, as I learned in one instance, cohabitating.[5] Arranged marriage for young people is one method among many for introduction to their life partners. As Nishma's narrative below shows, they are open to the possibility of meeting someone in this manner while viewing the potential of its success skeptically.

Nishma was in her late twenties and worked in the media. She had gone to a very posh private girl's school in North London, and her schoolmates had gone to Oxford and Cambridge. She opted for college and read accounting. This was for her parents; she never had too much interest in business studies. My first encounter with Nishma was unexpected: I had a meeting with someone else for an interview and she was waiting for a friend in the reception area. We began to talk and slowly became friends over the course of the fieldwork. During the first months, Nishma would hint at "marriage" concerns, mostly by joking about it. But it was clear that her parents were putting pressure on her to get married. We would often meet on the weekends, and once when I rang to confirm our meeting on a Sunday she told me that a family would be coming to "see" her on the day. As she explained, "These people phoned from Nottingham and they want to meet me for *Riśtā* so I have to be here. I really wanted to go out with my friends." Explaining that I had neither seen one of these meetings nor had any friends or relatives who had gone through the process, I asked her for details of how the meeting would take place. Did they come for dinner? Did the families meet beforehand? Did the children meet independently? Her responses were blunt and seemed to reveal a slight irritation with the process.

They come over and sit for tea, they ask my father some questions, in this case it will be Mum, as Dad is in India. They ask questions like *"Eh baby ki kardi he?"* [What does the young girl do?]. What bugs me is they don't ask you any questions [directly], but always asking about you through your parents; it's as if you are not even in the room.

After this, then what happens?

Then we go somewhere, usually into the kitchen, and talk.

Are you nervous?

No, I just don't even want to be there.

Are the boys nervous?

Yeah, sometimes, they just sit and talk about things, like there was this one guy, he was a banker or something in the City and I asked what his idea of a good night on the town would be like. He said, "I have a book of all the best restaurants in London and I just put my finger on a page and go there." He was a real loser; they're like that. Or there was one guy who was a schoolteacher. Really nice, and I could talk to him, but he just had no oomph, you know. He just needed some spark. I felt like putting a firecracker in his ass.

Did you tell your dad that this was the reason you didn't want to see the guy again?

[Laughing]. No, no. There was one guy, a dentist. He was totally into being a dentist. Like that's it. That was his life. All he talked about was how much money he made, about £50,000 a year. I still remember, he was a total coconut.[6] I even told him that to his face. . . . He was from a small town in England, total coconut. They are not around any other Asians — it is really hard for them to deal with London and the many cultures that are here.

How do you find people?

Well, through mandir or agencies [referring to the marriage bureaus that offer a matchmaking service]. There is a list that goes out every month from the mandir so then people just call you up or you just call them. Not me, but Dad, and then we get together.

What do they say when they telephone?

They're really rude. They say things like "Is your daughter fair?"

For older Hindu Punjabis, skin color is one of the many criteria of a suitable match. "Fair" skin is preferred. For Nishma, who could be classified as "fair," and other women, this question is seen as blatantly racist in favor of light skin color. The fact that many young women do not view skin color as an important aspect of "suitability" indicates changed perspective and priorities of the second generation; they are not interested in the subtle social markers of graded skin chromatism by which the parental generation still seems to be obsessed. This was part of what irked Nishma about the process. She was trying to reconcile her needs, while finding out the needs of those who were looking for girls, meeting the expectations of her parents.

She continued:

Or, like these people who are coming on Sunday, they first phoned and asked if we could go to their sister-in-law's or someone's house in Heston just to see if it was worth their while. I just said to my mum, "No, forget it. Why should she be involved?" and then you go through the whole thing again when the family comes. . . . I was not going to go there at all.

They just treat you like shit — you feel like shit.

These statements were harsh, but familiar. My previous conversations with Nishma made me wonder why she bothered with the meetings, because she seemed so negative about the whole process. On the phone, she was always more scathing. When she paused, I asked her, "Do you think you're going to find someone like this?" She responded:

No, well, two of my friends did. But I don't think so.

Why do you do it? For your parents?

Yes. I don't like it at all; it just makes you feel like shit, the whole process. I am going to find someone on my own, I'm not too worried though, I'm in no hurry.

What happens when they come over? Do you have to serve tea?

No, I refuse to do that. I did it a couple of times when my mum wasn't here [she was in India], but no, I'm not serving tea. They just ask stupid questions. It's all really stupid, really.

In our other conversations about marriage, Nishma was not always this bitter about the subject. At times, she even conceded that her two close friends had been married this way and were happy. Her questioning, reluctance, and openness echoed in my conversations with other young women. It reflected their ambivalence to the process of finding a partner through their parents.

The topic of arranged marriage, in the sense of arranged meetings, arose many times with different women, mostly because parents were "looking" for a partner or had "put the pressure on." Pressure began usually in the final stages of a university or college degree or just after finishing postsecondary education. Pressure was not direct, and marriage was rarely addressed openly. The articulation was much more subtle, like a well-landscaped English garden, contrived but seemingly natural. Hence, the topic would be slipped into conversations carefully but casually. For example, once I asked Nishma's father when he next planned to visit India, because he had been every year at Christmas. He replied, "Well, we are waiting for Nishma to get married; when she does, then we will go and do the wedding there." On another occasion when speaking about his forthcoming retirement he said, "Our future plans first depend on Nishma's wedding. First we do that then we will see what we can do next." Parents would make these kinds of statements publicly in a variety of social situations. Family matters are usually guarded or secretive. These remarks, by contrast, were conspicuously made with their children deliberately within earshot. It was masterful indirect communication. Friends and family would also broach the subject. Often others would raise the issue at a wedding ceremony or reception. "Next is your turn!" or "When are you getting married?" were the asides made to young unmarried women. The young and unmarried mocked these comments and "girls" would taunt each other in imitation with these same words. As one friend exclaimed, "It's as if they think, OK one down, who's the next to go?" The pressure for marriage is subtle, often veiled in fun and given in jest, but is nevertheless felt by the girls, and perhaps even more so by their parents.[7]

Parents experience pressure regarding their children's marriage in different ways. Primarily pressure stems from their sense of duty and obligation as parents. Seeing their children married is something to be completed before retiring from active responsibilities. As one Uncle stated, in the course of a conversation about "looking," "In 1997 we are retiring and I want this work [the wedding] to be finished by then; I want to enjoy my retirement." This sense of profound duty and obligation applied especially to daughters: most parents felt strongly that they must ensure that their daughters would be married into "good families" and taken care of long after their own deaths.[8] This is related to a broader sense of marriage as the moment when responsibility for the daughter's welfare is transferred to her new household. As one father explained to me, "I told my daughter when she got married, we are your birth parents, and they [in-laws] are your real parents; girls are *kanyadaan,* the greatest gift that one man can give to another family."

This is not incompatible, however, with pride in their own daughters' achievements and ability to look after themselves. Daughters were raised to be able to stand on their own. For mothers, this was often linked to what was seen as the potentially difficult nature of traditional Hindu Punjabi marriage arrangements. As one woman confessed, "I raised my daughter to know that she must be independent, I did not want her to be like me, dependent on my husband for everything. Don't get me wrong, we have many things, but I wanted her to be strong, to be able to fight, so this is how I raised her. She has to go into another family, and make her own home. You are always dealing with his relatives no matter where you are and you have to be strong about it — this is what I have given her." Thus the sense of parental obligation and of being *bride givers* implies giving skills to the daughter that will enable her to negotiate in the family sphere. Some women explicitly hoped their daughter's life would be different from their own. Others' comments made it clear that patrilocal residence in an extended family was an experience they were happy to leave behind when they migrated to Britain, and which their daughters would be lucky to avoid. As one Aunty said to me about my own circumstances: "You have it easy, mate. I did too after I came here, but still you have to be careful about them [referring to in-laws]."

The biggest fear that parents have is that their children are not ready for marriage, or not open to the idea of marriage when the parents think it is necessary to begin looking. Parents make subtle comments to their children and to others to "test the ground" and plant ideas. For example, one Aunty from London telephoned while I was writing this chapter. I recount the conversation here to show how parents assess their children's intentions and seek to apply pressure through social networks. Aunty began our conversation with the usual, "How are you, how is your husband?" Then the predictable, "How is school?" and "When are you going to be finished?" to which she added, "First you must celebrate Anita's [her daughter] wedding and then leave us." To which I responded, "Aunty, you have to find a boy first." She quickly cut in: "Well, when Anita is ready, then I can find one. But I am looking; I will keep looking but it is up to her in the end. Why don't you ask her [if she is ready]."

I was surprised because although I had previously heard mother and daughter talking about marriage, and Aunty was always steering my conversations with Anita toward the topic, this was the first time she had spoken to me directly. Aunty was attempting to co-opt me into her fact-finding mission: I was being asked to find out if her daughter was ready to get married or open to the idea of being introduced to men. I replied, "Aunty, please don't stick me in the middle of this. She is my friend. Give that duty to her sister. Don't worry, you will know when the right time comes; she will tell you." But this, of course, was not the response she wanted. I was rejecting her attempts to draw me in and with these words, Aunty quickly ended the conversation. I suspected that she only rang to co-opt me into her fact-finding marriage mission. Aside from quickly ending the call after my response, she had called during the long-distance, prime-time rate from London to Cambridge. It was before noon and her daughter was away at work. In the end, it had some effect. By speaking with me, Anita's mother hoped to exert indirect pressure on Anita, because, as she rightly presumed, I related the conversation to Anita.

Enlisting the help of others is not straightforward and also increases pressure on the parents. They must depend on their network connections to promote themselves and their marriageable child. Yet, as they engage kin and friends in finding a suitable partner, they implicate family honor (*izzat*) and name (*nam*). The network inevitably "keeps tabs" on the number of "suitable potentials" met by young women and men. A stream of rejections leads to questions and speculations: often the "boy" or "girl" is said to be "too fussy," or rumors of a hidden girl- or boyfriend circulate. If family friends offer details of a "potential" from their network, then inevitably they query the results. They want to know the reasons for a rejection for their future reference. Additionally, if friends and family members know that a family is "looking," even if they do not provide contacts, they remain interested in knowing if a suitable boy or girl has been found. One Sunday afternoon when a family and a "potential" were coming to "see" Nishma, one Aunty [Nishma's fictive kin] had come around for tea unexpectedly. She was told that Riśtā were coming but only left after the boy's family arrived. Afterward she quizzed me on that meeting and asked me many times: "So what did Nishma think of that boy?" and "Did she like him?" I never answered her persistent queries directly. Instead, I only hinted that Nishma did not seem to like him and suggested that Aunty speak to her longtime friends (that is, Nishma's parents) and ask them. Finally, the reasons for her immense curiosity were revealed. Her own daughter had met the same boy and family a few weeks before Nishma's meeting. Her daughter had rejected him as a suitable boy as well.

The fact that two friends had seen the same boy independently points to another type of pressure experienced by families with daughters — their sense of a distinct paucity of boys. This concern was related to me in many forms: "There are not enough boys" or "Boys' families have so much choice; there are so many girls but there are not enough boys." Despite the fact that this is a common complaint, it is not possible to explore the demographic basis of this assertion since British Hindu Punjabi population statistics do not exist. The lack of men can be explained by a number of reasons: too few young men with appropriate educational qualifications, too few men of adequate financial status, the impact of arranged marriages of men to women outside Britain (in America and India), as well as the preference for caste hypergamy for women.

Related to the claimed "lack of men" is a second parental concern about their daughter's age. Parents correlate age with availability and maintain that as their daughters get older choice diminishes because the numbers of potential males decreases. For parents, the ideal age for marriage seems to be after completion of higher education once their daughters have settled into a job. Thus, young women (who are twenty-two to twenty-four) in their first years in the workforce experience increased pressure, and for those who had been working for a number of years (and who were twenty-five to thirty years old) the pressure was intense. The young married women I knew during research had married shortly after completing their higher education, and they all confirmed that their parents had increased pressure to marry after graduation. Nishma, for example, was twenty-eight and her family was getting anxious. As her father said, "I want to get it done within this year; it is too late already." He then spoke of two of his nieces, one of whom was in her late thirties and the other in her early forties and who were not married.

Look at them. She [one of his nieces] wanted to concentrate on her career. Then when she was thirty-five she said she would look at consultants, not even a doctor, but he had to be a consultant. So I found one, but she did not like him. You do not have so much choice at that age. Look at how many problems my cousin is facing trying to find someone for his daughter.

Thus parents' sense of their obligations, the sense that their daughters' agreement was crucial, the use of social networks (which involves its own related set of pressures), the putative lack of men, and the sense that age mattered more for women than for men are all factors involved in the active search for a suitable boy.

There are many different ways in which a search is activated and most families use many methods, including temple matrimonial lists and kin and friendship networks.[9] A search may be initiated by informing those whom the parents know and trust that a search has begun. Some of those who have been dropping hints and applying pressure to the parents and daughters are brought into the search and involved in a variety of ways. They may be in England or elsewhere in the diaspora, and they may or may not have been in contact recently. Friends and family are approached with enquiries about boys, or about others they know who are also "looking." Parents place faith in the judgment of character, trusting that their own family name and honor will be considered and respected within the network search. The extended family, namely the parents' siblings, will not necessarily be involved in the matchmaking process. Some of them, often those in India, are excluded. However, occasionally Indian relations are approached so that contacts they might have *outside* India can be exploited.

Soliciting help from social networks outside the nuclear family is delicate. To seek help of this kind, from the start, is to risk involving them in the whole arranged marriage process including the initial ceremonies. Some parents were happy to do this: for example, as Nishma related above, one of the families she was to meet initially requested that she visit the boy's maternal aunt's house. There were practical considerations. The boy's family lived up north and they would have to make a special trip to London to see her; therefore, it was easier for the prospective grooms' maternal aunt to be involved in a preliminary meeting. Whereas Nishma only wished to meet the boy and his parents, others I knew were more flexible. The extent of involvement of family both nuclear and extended depends on each individual meeting and the families involved.

Middle-class Hindu Punjabis live throughout Greater London, and their personal networks inevitably span the globe. Immediate family may not live in Britain, or the girl may have a particular preference for marrying abroad. While some young women explicitly state that they do not want to leave Britain and do not even want to leave London, others are actively seeking an alliance in America or Canada. In these cases families draw on networks of relatives who may have migrated to North America from India as professionals or as students. Others may have moved to North America after first migrating to Britain, especially during the early 1970s when the trend for South Asian migration from Britain to Canada or the United States began. Many of these people who left were manual laborers who left when economic decline was foreshadowed in Britain. However also included were the "professional classes," often those who took secondary degrees in Britain and then moved to America or Canada. Another potential source of "American connections" were the children of family and friends who married North Americans of South Asian descent during the early 1980s.[10] The diasporic search involves an active schedule of telephone calls and traveling, both dependent on the accoutrements of middle-class lifestyles.

One Uncle, for example, casually told me how his cousin from America had expressed an interest in coming to England for a visit and had called on his cellular phone.[11] Later Uncle added that his cousin and perhaps his wife would be coming to "see some boys." The proposed plan was for Uncle to meet with prospective grooms and their families before his cousin booked the trip. The cousin wanted to ensure that it was worth their time and expense to come to Britain (this was not unusual and was in fact similar to the request made to Nishma's family by the family from North England). Uncle, however, mailed to his relatives a "mandir list" and suggested, both by letter and by telephone, that "you can make your own arrangements." The cousin telephoned again: he had chosen three boys from the mandir list but wanted Uncle to make the initial contacts with the boys' families; after which he would decide on the necessity of a trip. Uncle repeated to his cousin that it would be better if his cousin initiated contact with the families himself. At the cousin's insistence, Uncle reluctantly agreed to meet the boys and their families. Uncle stipulated, however, that the first approach to the families must come from his cousin in America.

In this case, Uncle was aware of being used by the network and chose to act cautiously, negotiating the level of responsibility he was prepared to take. If he had initiated contact, Uncle would have been partially responsible for the outcome. This was a difficult situation because in this case he did not know the boys' families personally. They lived outside London and thus he could not vouch for them. In the same way, Uncle would have been partially responsible if the marriage had not been successful. Negotiation is necessarily delicate and not clearly defined; the extent to which individuals continue to be involved in matchmaking activities for others involves balancing one's own sense of duty against self-interest and cautiously playing the matchmaker and go-between. Activating diaspora ties differs from the use of local networks because personal contact between individuals may often have not occurred for a number of years. Those from North America often visit relatives in England, for example, only while on a stopover to or from India. Otherwise, individuals have contact only via post or via telephone, the latter increasingly popular because of both the migrants' growing prosperity and affordable international telephone rates. In this instance, Uncle felt it was more appropriate to leave negotiations entirely to the father. In the end, Uncle's cousin never came to Britain, and he and his wife are still looking for a suitable boy for their daughter.

Diasporic relations follow a certain pattern. Many Hindu Punjabis living in Britain have family friends who migrated to the United States and Canada after living in the United Kingdom. Previously, the trend was for movement westward across the Atlantic and a number of British-born Asian women married boys from Canada and America during the 1980s.[12] In Canada, for example, the population of marriageable South Asians in the 1980s was the children of the "early-third-wave" migrants — the South Asian economic professional migrants to Canada who had arrived in the mid- to late 1960s and early 1970s. These children preferred someone like themselves, that is, born in the diaspora, to an Indian bride. Indian brides were seen as "too traditional," while Canadian girls particularly were "too modern." England was perceived as a perfect pool of potential brides. However, in England, while men were prepared to take a bride from India, it was less likely that British women would seek Indian partners, unless the boy had kinship ties in the United Kingdom. As one Uncle told me, a boy would not choose to move to Britain where he would be dependent on the girl's family and have no house. For men, migration to Britain for marriage complicates the status of being a wife receiver as well as challenging one's own sense of worth as defined by material status. During fieldwork, I met one woman married to a man from India. They had been students at the same university and he was introduced to her parents after they had decided to marry. I also met one mother whose daughter was married to an Indian man, now living in Delhi with his very well-to-do family. However, the trend for differences in male and female preferences for Indian spouses is changing. Today, many men do not want a bride from India. "Suitable" matches for these boys would come from affluent Indian families. British Asian boys, along with their mothers, are wary of the fact that an Indian bride, accustomed to servants and a comfortable lifestyle, will not know how to do any housework or cope with demands of daily living and work in "the West." Indeed, the only London family I met who were waiting for the arrival of their daughter-in-law from Bombay were sufficiently wealthy to not have to worry about adjustment; they even had a servant themselves.

Global connections are an option for many, and it is clear that marriages made in this way reinforce the sense that the Hindu Punjabi "community" is in fact a transnational one and will continue to be so. But often girls do not want to leave Britain, or even London. Anita, for example, has two sisters who married in America and one who lives more than two hours outside London with her husband. However, as she put it, "I want to stay in London. I am not leaving my job for some guy and I want to be close to my Mum. . . . If I leave, Mum will not have anybody." For some young people, local ties (which are not necessarily ethnically exclusive) may seem more important than global ones.

How do parents initiate the search when the larger diaspora is not the preferred option and when local kin networks are limited?[13] The mandir is one place where the search for a suitable boy begins. Regular attendance at the temple provides introductions to potential marriage partners as well as offering an informal arena to explore their suitability. The mandir lists are another, more formal and also more structured option. Usually known as "matrimonials," the lists are found in the back pages of the regular publication of certain temples. Many temples have begun to publish separate matrimonial lists for which they charge an additional fee. The seriousness of this issue may be seen in the fact that some temples have an elected officer appointed to oversee the duties of organizing these "matrimonials." These lists give basic details of potential marriage partners. For example:

> A suitable match is required for a young Brahmin lady. She is British, single, born May 1967, height 5'3" and is vegetarian. She has passed M.Sc. Biology from Glasgow University and has a full time job as a medical representative in the top British Pharmaceutical Firm. Caste immaterial but a Brahmin professional young gentleman is preferable.

This is a typical advertisement. British temple matrimonials, which permit the assumption of shared religion while commonly listing the caste of the prospective bride or groom, do not list any of the other criteria, which ethnography on South Asian marriage describes as significant in marriage choice.[14] Equally characteristic is the statement "caste no bar," indicating that caste is not important. This standard phrase, taken in isolation, might seem to indicate a loosening of marriage alliance prescriptions. However, as in the example above, often a specific caste preference paradoxically follows the phrase, or may be qualified by a series of exclusions: "caste no bar, but no low-caste" or "caste no bar [may be] . . . preferably a Khattrī young lady & vegetarian is being considered." After caste, the most conspicuous preference expressed is for professional status (see Bhachu 1985). Matrimonial advertising may specify, "The gentleman must be professional" or "Only professional graduates need apply," or even specific professions, "A Punjabi Khattrī gentleman is preferred especially a doctor, dentist or chartered accountant." It is significant that professional status is demanded for both males and females. This reflects the sense that shared professional status is critical for the maintenance of a certain lifestyle and standard of living.

To be clear, these lists circulate widely and are not only used by those who attend a specific mandir. In the marriage search, many lists are subscribed to and consulted; each list contains perhaps only one or two people that could potentially be met. Here again, there is an explicitly "global" dimension. This global dimension takes two forms. Firstly, the information offered makes clear citizenship and current residence and sometimes, more subtly, hints at the individual's sense of identity based on the nostalgia for culture. For example, "British-born woman" and "Indian-Born British woman" carry two different meanings: the latter indicates that, like the first, the young girl is a British citizen, but she is Indian "in outlook." Hence, the necessity of specifying her Indian birth. Secondly, matrimonial advertisements might also indicate a willingness to travel outside of Britain or mention that the prospective bride or groom is studying in the United States or has gained U.S. qualifications. For example, "She is B.D.S. (London Hospital) and has passed National Dental Board Examination (U.S.A.) and is a dentist."

A further specification relates to religious divisions. I have reviewed the increasing separation of Punjabi Sikhs from Hindus, but here I want to bring attention to the fact that this separation is not absolute. There are also advertisements that indicate the willingness to enter into Hindu/Sikh alliance such as:

> A suitable match is required for a Punjabi Sikh (Ramgarhia) young lady doctor. She is British, single, born September 1961, height 5'6" and nonvegetarian. She is M.B.B.S (Kings College) and is a general medical practitioner. She enjoys travelling, music, theatre and socializing. A professional clean shaven Sikh/Hindu gentleman is required.[15]

Or:

> She would prefer a clean shaven Sikh, professional gentleman but would accept a Hindu male aged between 29–36 years, single, good looking, loving, reliable, with a good sense of humor.

These advertisements, although few, trace the remaining bridges across religious divisions in Punjabi identity that are encouraged and actively sought in some families (particularly Khattrī ones in which Hindus and Sikhs have historically intermarried).

Matrimonial advertisements also contain indications of the "children's" concerns; because of this, British matrimonials read very differently from those originating in the Subcontinent, or East Africa.[16] In Britain, preferences for looks, aside from "being fair," and personality are given in addition to caste or professional status. For example, "He must be tall, handsome, good natured from an educated family with a modern outlook." Or "caste no bar, preferable a lady doctor, dentist or highly professional young lady with lively personality" or "caste no bar, but the young lady must be beautiful and [a] computer accountant," or "caste no bar but the young lady should be slim, beautiful & qualified." Compare these to the following:

> A suitable match is required for a Punjabi Brahmin young lady. She is Kenyan, single, born 1960, height 5'4"/ She is Doctor of Medicine (M.D.) and is cardiology consultant and is teaching medical students in India. (matrimonial in London's *Eastern Eye*)

Or, for example:

> Wanted a suitable match for a young Punjabi gentleman from Kenya. He is British, single, born May 1959, height 5'7" and is vegetarian. He is BSc (Hons.) & A.C.C.A. (London) and is an accounting supervisor in a U.S.A. firm. . . . caste immaterial. (matrimonial in London's *Eastern Eye*)

The popular Asian youth-oriented newspaper, *Eastern Eye,* carries a section, which at the beginning of my fieldwork was called "MATRI-MONIAL" and was promoted "as a service for parents/guardians seeking a suitable marriage match for their sons and daughters. Individuals seeking genuine marriage partners can also write in for themselves." In December 1994, *Eastern Eye* changed this section to "Connections" describing it as "[t]he sensational way to make new friends and even meet that someone special." While the section began to include requests for "discreet encounters" or same-sex partners, the majority of advertisements in *Eastern Eye*'s "Connections" contained an explicit statement such as "with view to marriage" indicating "matrimonial intentions." Some closely follow the phrasing of mandir advertisements (and perhaps are written by the parents themselves) such as:

> Hindu Punjabi female slim, very fair, attractive, graduate and qualified chartered accountant, 26, 5'2" and seeks Hindu male, 5'7" plus, 26–31, should

be a professional, i.e. doctor, dentist, smart, independent, sincere, caring, sociable and have a good blend of east/west culture. Genuine replies only.

However, most of these advertisements for long-term commitments and matrimonials read much more like the singles columns in the main-stream press than those of the temple lists. A particularly striking exam-ple, of the children's changed tone in advertisements for partners would be:

Raja Raver [King of RAVE] seeks Rani Raver [Queen of RAVE]. He's 5'10", hippy, funked up, designer space baby who's raved from here to Islamabad. Seeks inter-continental babe to share my space pram. She's got to be funky, intelligent and babe worthy! As I am? Sorry no bhangra babes? Crazy pho-tos appreciated.

Or the one found just below it in the same issue that reads:

Attractive Asian prince, 21, VGSOH, [Very Good Sense of Humor] medium build, sporty and sexy, fair complexion, and clean shaven, caring, honest, loving, down to Earth, enjoys most good things in day to day life, into bhangra and jungle music, and respects Eastern/Western values. Seeks beautiful attractive Asian princess between 17–21 for friendship/relationship (religion unimportant) ALA [all letters answered] . . . London-based. You won't be disappointed! (*Eastern Eye,* November 15, 1994, 19)

These advertisements, although not Hindu Punjabi, reveal the language of London, specifically of a young "Asian London," which includes bhan-gra gigs, raves, and jungle music. Those reading these advertisements have some understandings of specific identities of high-fashion and middle-class lifestyles, not to mention reference to the transnational. They reveal a very different agenda from the parents; although, as the latter notes a concern with "fair complexion," they may also echo parental concerns.

The World Wide Web is also increasingly used as a potential source of suitable mates. These generally take the same forms of the temple or news-paper matrimonials. The sites containing these advertisements are nu-merous and include: Matrimonial Online, Indian Matrimonial Link, Hindustan.net (with a specific section), Cyberproposal.com, marriage .com, hindumatrimonials.com, matrimoniallink.com, Indian alliances, shaadi .com, and many, many more. Usually the sites are free and allow the potential bride or groom or family member to search by certain categories. Their databases are large and international. As Matrimonial Online claims: "Currently we have 17,558+ Profiles of Indian Men and Women from Aus-tralia, Canada, India, Korea, Malaysia, Singapore, South Africa, Switzerland, Thailand, United Kingdom, USA, New Zealand and many other countries." Often, the main page has pull-down menus for religion, caste, preferences, marital status (never married, separated, divorced, widowed), citizenship and current residence, and sometimes horoscope details such as birth time and place. Also, some sites allow one to specify in pull-down menus the suitable categories of a potential mate such as age range, height, religion, and so forth. Other categories include "cuts hair, drinks alcohol, spiritual values" (see, for example, http://www.hindumatrimonials.com). Amazingly, family status can also be specified, and on one site a pull-down menu allows one to fill in high class, middle class, or other (http://www. matrimonialonline.com/addbride.html)!

The ads provide examples of how these categories come across on the Web, differently from the newspaper advertisements:

Male, 28, 6ft-0in, 183 cm, Never Married
Religion: Hindu
Culture: Indian
Occupation: Other (graphic design)
Location: United Kingdom

I am Hindu born in Kenya with origins in Punjab, working in London in Product and Graphic Design. I come from a cultured modern family all of whom are well educated and settled. I have travelled extensively and know a great deal about my own and other cultures. I have an interesting outlook on life and would love to meet the right person who can share this with me. What else? I am 6' tall, fair complexion, age 28 and very funny to those who know me. http://www.matrimonial.com/IML/Ads/ao8fu6/

Female, 32, 5ft-4in, 163 cm, Never Married
Religion: Hindu
Culture: Indian
Occupation: Unspecified
Location: United Kingdom

Dynamic and fun-loving Hindu punjabi female, slim and considered very attractive.

Lawyer (corporate finance) with a US law firm based in City/London, UK (relocatable).

Fluent in French and German, travelled world-wide, lived/worked in New York City, USA and France.

Photograph available upon request.

Prefers to meet a professional male over the age of 32, over 5 ft 9 in. tall, of slim build, non-smoker. No divorcees please.

http://www.matrimonials.com/IML/Ads/ob4dg4/

These matrimonials combine technology with the genre of personal advertisements. The categories of identity that were traditionally part of the matrimonial are now in a separate cluster, which is followed by a more personal note. Also, each advert seems to have been written by the person seeking a spouse, in the first person, rather than by the family (usually written in the third person). There seems to be a lot more individual personality in these messages and an overt reference to both their sense of being transnational and their seriousness about finding someone in this way.

Other advertisements reveal how the personalities of the potential spouse come through. For example:

> Male, 28, 5ft-7in, 170 cm, Never Married
> Religion: Hindu (love/ishq)
> Culture: Multiculture (punjabi/western)
> Occupation: Other (telecoms consultant)
> Location: United Kingdom

> HI name is XXXX i am 28 yrs old i am searching for my soulmate whom was my partner in heaven. we promised to love and to cherish in sickness and in health in the presence of god. i deeply miss your sweet voice and your sweet smile. i can remember that we used to meet under a large tree and your name was pooja or priya, in the last janam 100,000 yrs ago if you are reading this ad please reply soon. http://www.matrimonials.com/IML/Ads/nw4dt9/

This person seems to want to show that he is "multicultural" by code-switching and gives further evidence of this by mixing the metaphors of "in sickness and in health" with reincarnation (reference to a love known in a previous life). Not all are about love, as this next advert clearly shows:

> Female, 32, 5ft-0in, 152 cm, Never Married
> Religion: Hindu
> Culture: Punjabi
> Occupation: Educator (teacher)
> Location: United Kingdom

> Here are some bullet points about me!

> My name is XXXX. I am 32 years old, have a very fair complexion, 5ft tall and have a medium build.

> I am a primary school teacher. I did my degree at XXXX University in England.

> I am a hindu khattri but happy to meet a hindu or sikh partner.

> I enjoy swimming, watching Indian movies and travelling.

I have one brother who is younger than me. My father is a doctor and my mum is a housewife.

I would like to meet someone who is caring, fun-loving and has a good balance of eastern/western values.

If this sounds like someone you want to meet, drop me a mail.

http://www.matrimonials.com/IML/Ads/zn3yj9/

This message is probably the most personal that I have read, it is one of the first that actually gives the person's name, her hobbies, and details about the family that do not indicate the usual categories of caste, region, but does highlight her father's status (he is a doctor). The presentation of self is mixed with that of her potential spouse. There is a sense that she is looking who is East/West balanced, and, as mentioned earlier as a Khattrī is open to marrying a Hindu or Sikh.

The global references in these advertisements show the sense of transnational identity that they seek in a marriageable partner. The following advertisement calls attention to this by clearly stating that a U.K.- or U.S.-based person would be welcome.

Female, 27, 5ft-4in, 163 cm, Never Married
Religion: Hindu
Culture: Indian (punjabi)
Occupation: Management (sales and marketing)
Location: United Kingdom (England, UK)

thanks for visiting my site. A little bit about myself . . . I am a caring, attractive, loving girl born and brought up in England with strong Indian cultural values. I have graduated in Applied Biological Sciences and currently work for Glaxo Wellcome in England in the field of Sales and Marketing. I enjoy keeping fit, music, travelling, cooking and dining out. I have a very fair complexion, hazel eyes and overall a smart person. I am looking for someone who is professional, honest, sincere, caring , smart and fun to be with, preferably of a similar background to myself. I would prefer you to be of UK or USA origin. I would be happy to send further details and a photograph once we have become better acquainted. Contact details: http://www.matrimonials.com/IML/Ads/nd9x04/

The transnational nature of these advertisements is also apparent in their reference to origins (from Africa), to workplace (working for a U.S. company in the United Kingdom), and to choice of potential spouse (United Kingdom or United States). It is also relevant that this might implicate how they wish their culture to be perceived, and indeed how they perceive themselves as variously Indian, multicultural (Punjabi/West), Indian (Punjabi), and Punjabi. Their own various choices about what to call themselves with respect to cultural background foreground a sense of being Punjabi while making it very clear that they are a "blend of East and West." These advertisements are changing the ways people look for spouses and also reveal that their cultural identity is a product of many different negotiations. To say that one's culture is Indian on a website aimed at those who are Indians, looking for potential mates is curious choice of categorization. Unwittingly these advertisements indicate how the transnational sense of being Punjabi in Britain gets inscribed in certain ways, how the nostalgia for culture plays out in typifying oneself as "traditional" or "modern." The subtlety between these seemingly two opposite ends of cultural outlook, and all the variations in between, is part of how people look for potential partners across the globe.

Leaving aside the advertisements, the search for the suitable boy also occurs within London at social functions, such as dances, religious events, parties, and especially weddings. One young woman recounted how, while she was dancing with friends at a wedding, her mother was approached. This was not uncommon: mothers or Aunties will enquire about the prospective boy or girl through mutual friends who will then approach the parents to ask if they are looking for someone. In an exceptional instance, a boy's mother casually spoke to a young woman I know, independently of any networks. Sometimes the boy himself approached the girl and asked her if she was working or if she had a degree. Thus, others who are "looking" in the marriage process approach both the parents as well as the young woman directly. As indicated earlier, the search for a suitable boy via parental introductions is just one of the many different avenues through which children seek a partner.

A lot of my friends are in that space where this is happening to them. Their parents say, OK you can choose a partner but it has to be Hindu and Punjabi so really they have no choice at all. I mean I don't know who I am going to fall in love with — that's all it is. But they, my friends, are trying, they really are. I have this one friend who does the Asian dinner dating scene — they all get together for a dinner and dance. She's invited me to go next Saturday; a whole bunch of us might go along. (Anu Sharma)

Anu was open to having an arranged marriage, that is, being introduced to potential partners via her parents. Her friends were also in the same process, but they explored a number of alternative avenues, such as the Asian dinner dating. In London a few such networks exist for young Asians to meet. Participants can be of any religious background, and the dinners are not intended as a matrimonial introduction, in the ways that all necessary background caste and family checks are done before people enter a room. Asian dinner dating may have included special Thames River events, or gatherings at restaurants with an Asian dinner night advertised in the ethnic press as a place "to look for that someone special." There are occasionally public events when parents and children are both present, which may act as arenas for cross-sex contact, such as wedding ceremonies, temples, and *melas*.[17] At one *Dusshera mela* in Victoria Park, I noticed how well the teenagers were dressed, more for a night on the town than a grubby North London park taken over by the autumn evening chill. I was told, "This was one big pickup joint for young people — you just watch and see — a meat market." It was true. The young people seemed to be "checking each other out." Young people can meet independently, sometimes via formal organizations, like the dinner dance scene, and sometimes through their own circle of friends. This circle often becomes "more Asian" as the young get older and is established through friends from university, college, and work. It is entirely separate from their parents' social circle. These friendships are another obvious place where relationships leading to marriage form. After eighteen, most children I researched did not socialize regularly with their parents except when: (a) there was a religious function sponsored by their family; (b) they were directly invited by their family or friends; or (c) if their parents absolutely insisted that they come along. This is not to say young men and women did not have occasions to meet independently of functions where their parents would be present, but unless involved in an Asian youth group, or some sort of Asian activity, the opportunities for meeting other Hindu Punjabis were rare.

Through these different avenues for meeting a prospective partner, some Hindu Punjabi women I knew had boyfriends or steady partners already. However, if a girl's parents were looking for a suitable boy, their daughter would not introduce her boyfriend to them until she was absolutely sure that she wanted to marry him and that he was ready for this commitment. This was because the parents, especially if they had been encouraging marriage, would take the introduction of their daughter's boyfriend as their child's indication of a lifelong partner. It was a delicate situation and only rarely was the boy just brought home and introduced as a "boyfriend." This was the case for one family I knew; the daughter had introduced her partner as a friend in the first instance, leaving her mother to ask if the relationship was serious. Anu and Nishma, by contrast, went along with the mechanisms and procedures of arranged meetings, only introducing their boyfriends into the marriage process at a late stage. Nevertheless, the parent's role remains to ensure that the partner chosen by their daughter meets their suitability criteria and requirements and to vet his family. It is only after complete consideration that the parents accept or reject their daughter's choice of partner.

This final parental decision was a crucial factor in all of the marriages that took place during my fieldwork. Hence, "arranged marriage" is not easily separated from "love marriage" in the British context. Of the four weddings I have attended in Britain, none were the result of arranged meetings and, in fact, only one was between a Hindu Punjabi couple (two were marriages between Hindu Punjabi women and "English" [that is, white British] males, another was between a Gujarati woman and an Hindu Punjabi male). All cases, however, involved introduction of partners to parents only after the young couple first seriously considered marriage. In addition to these weddings, I heard details of other alliances, such as one between a Hindu Punjabi female and a Gujarati male. In fact, only one of the marriages that I heard about was a product of parental introductions, or so it was claimed.[18] Other alliances were in various stages of prewedding negotiations, including one between a Hindu Punjabi male doctor and an English woman. In this case, the parents consulted with the extended family and only after the family accepted the marriage did they officially announce the engagement. In the example mentioned above, where the girl had introduced her boyfriend as "a friend" and then let her mother inquire about the seriousness of the relationship, their engagement was not announced until six months after I had learned of the alliance and the preparations for the wedding were in place.

In Nishma's case, she was uncomfortable with the whole arranged marriage process. Nishma met "boys" partly to keep her parents happy and to let them know that she had an open mind about arranged marriage. In my analysis, like others in her situation, she used it as an opportunity to communicate that she was not opposed *in principle* to her parents finding a boy for her. The procedure, as her father indicated, allowed her to become skilled in assessing her own needs in a potential partner, and indeed skilled in negotiating the process itself. However, during many introductions, she continued with her one-year-old serious relationship with Manoj, a Hindu Punjabi man whom she had met through friends at work. Moreover, her boyfriend knew that she was being introduced to men through her parents. He too was involved in his family's search and had been introduced to women. The pressure from her parents and the introductions that had been made allowed Nishma to broach the subject of marriage with her boyfriend. By meeting these "potentials" she was also convincing her boyfriend to consider marriage. In fact, after Nishma told her parents about Manoj, her father accusingly asked her if her boyfriend had planted the idea of marriage into her head, to which she retorted, "If anything it is me who has put this idea into his head." With these words, Nishma admitted her decisions and manipulations to her father as well as making known her own desires. Introducing Manoj as a "potential" began new negotiations between Nishma and her parents; it became a marriage that needed to be "arranged."

The arranged-marriage process must be flexible enough to balance parental concerns with that of their children's, including the possibility that they might introduce their partners into the arrangement process. Children involved in the active search for a life partner have methods of subversion and resistance to these parental introductions; the meeting itself is the first site in which their subversion may occur. We began this discussion with Anu's negotiation of rejection through subversion. She needed to reject all of the "prospectives" in order to introduce her boyfriend. Subversion is used by those who are unsure of the success of their parents' efforts as well as by those who want to introduce their boy- or girlfriends to their parents (these are not, of course, mutually exclusive). Subversion of arranged marriage often occurs at the time of the meeting. Women recounted stories of meetings to me after they had occurred, and during fieldwork, I was fortunate to have the opportunity to observe one of these meetings. As indicated, the whole process is secretive and delicate. I was surprised that I was permitted to remain during one such meeting.

One Sunday I had visited Nishma and her parents and was unaware that people may be coming to see her. While at Nishma's, Aunty (Nishma's mum) sent Uncle to buy some fresh samosas and sweets from the Indian stores. I went along too and asked why he was buying these "special foods." He replied that a family was coming to see Nishma and invited me to remain. When we returned home, I asked Nishma for permission to stay as well. I was in Nishma's room when they arrived. She was still in bed, resting: she had flu and was tired from a late night. The visitors were already seated in the sitting room when she got out of bed. From a large under-the-bed drawer, she pulled out a *salvar* (bottom of a Punjabi "suit," a matched trouser and tunic outfit) and then looked through the disheveled pile for the matching *kameez* (a long tunic top). Not finding it, she looked for another matching suit in the tangled mess of silks and cottons, all stuffed into the drawer to await ironing before being worn on special occasions. She asked me which suit she should wear and rejected my suggestion of a silk suit with gold border, instead opting for a plain, light-pink, cotton suit in need of a good pressing. I took this choice of outfit and its messy condition as her first act of rebellion; she never ironed the suit. Her second act was not applying any makeup, except lipstick. She was sending a message about herself, via her appearance, which expressed her lack of enthusiasm for the impending encounter.

Ten minutes after their arrival, her mother called us to the sitting room. Just outside the door, Aunty held me back with a hand signal so that she and Nishma could enter the room first. After a second, I followed and took a seat beside Nishma. Nishma was very quiet and shy, looking down at the carpet. She was obviously nervous. The visiting family watched her carefully as she entered while trying to continue their conversation with her father. The boy's mother sometimes stole a glance at Nishma and, at other moments, kept her gaze for long periods and did not partake in the social pleasantries exchanged between Uncle and her husband. The boy said nothing. He was not looking down at the ground, as was Nishma; his eyes avoided the side of the room where we were sitting. He was smartly dressed in a suit and tie. I helped Aunty bring in some tea for all, because Nishma was not going to serve the tea or show her skills at being a hostess.[19] This refusal to serve/entertain was another act of resistance, but one with which her mother agreed. Then the boy's mother said to no one in particular, "Why don't they go talk." There was some hesitation, and then Aunty agreed and suggested that the young people go into the kitchen. It was a deliberate statement suggesting that this was the first time Nishma was meeting a prospective partner and she was unsure of the protocol. With these words, Nishma and "the boy" uncomfortably left the room. During the time that the children went away, the parents tried to get to know each other by speaking about their last visit to India, sharing details about how long they had been in England and where they had lived. They also engaged in general social conversation about the changes in economic climate. Uncle was a good talker and kept the conversation alive with skill. I passed around more of the food that we had bought earlier. It was just before dinner and the rejection of food at this house could have indicated an earlier tea and perhaps an earlier meeting with another girl and her family. This was pure speculation on my part, but since it was not appropriate to ask, I was left with only a clue. In fact, as the father declined but the mother took another samosa, I could not determine if they were "doing the rounds" that Sunday.

When Nishma and "the boy" returned to the room, Nishma seemed to have changed. Within a few minutes, the reason for the change was obvious: she had rejected him in her mind. She was ready to subvert the process a bit more. They had entered the sitting room while their parents were speaking about religion and beliefs. Uncle had taken the opportunity to demonstrate his daughter's excellent qualities. He was extolling her belief in a particular guru and her strict adherence to Hinduism and vegetarianism. It seemed that the boy's family had also visited the same guru's ashram in India because of some troubles they'd had and mentioned that after the visit all had been resolved. Nishma, quiet before the kitchen meeting with "the potential," was now ready to speak. The boy's father's comments provided her with a point of entry into the conversation. She spoke about the appalling lack of spirituality of the people who went to ashrams and how many sought gurus because of material downfall or sickness but not because they were in tune with God. Not being specific but implicating the family, she criticized people for being too attached to this world and its accoutrements and not concerned about beliefs. She spoke abstractly but her intentions were clear. She added, "I know that this is my last life; I feel it. But I know that my dad is coming back; he is too attached to this world." She had addressed their interest in religion unexpectedly by claiming to be more in tune with the goals of Hinduism than they were. It was her final act of resistance. They left shortly after this; the whole meeting lasted no longer than one hour.

"He just had no spark, you know, just nothing," Nishma replied to Uncle's question about suitability. Uncle said, "They seemed nice, but he was quiet though and a little fat." It was a negotiation of rejection. Both Nishma and Uncle had to let each other know that this was not "the boy" but to also be sensitive to the other's feelings; neither could make the dismissal too early or too eagerly. Nishma was especially cautious about not criticizing the process as she often did in our conversations. Uncle added, "The family was nice, but not very religious, and they eat meat; that would be hard for you." This allowed Nishma to return to her religion diatribe, "No, they are just people going to gurus all the time to change things, or because of money. That is not why you go to a guru." The negotiation was increasingly negative until Uncle stated to no one in particular: "I won't call them. If they call, then we'll see. But I won't call them."

As Uncle's words indicated, who calls whom first and initiates further meetings is a critical part of the postmeeting negotiation. In Parminder Bhachu's work (1985) on Ramgarhia Sikhs (migrated from East Africa) the *bride givers* are seen as the primary negotiators and those who are always initiating contact and then following it up. Pnina Werbner, writing about the Muslim experience, emphasizes the active role of the *bride receivers* as those asking for the bride's hand in marriage (1990b: 266). For these Hindu Punjabi families in London either party may make initial contact; however, the bride givers have stated that they are expected to instigate all contact and indeed claim to take all initiative. The time between the meeting and the telephone call is replete with negotiated meaning: too early and one may seem too eager, but too late and the "potential" may be engaged or married because it is possible for a wedding to be celebrated within six months of the initial meeting. Another factor is that often families, especially those just beginning the matchmaking process, want to meet more people and families before making a commitment. But the time delays can be very long. One of the temple matrimonial lists, concerned with the potential misunderstanding of such time lags, states: "May we request members who are in the process of matrimonial negotiations to please note they must inform the other party of their intentions and not just stop all contact."

The postmeeting telephone call takes the negotiation of rejection or acceptance outside of the family. In some instances after a lengthy two months, and meetings with other families, the girl's family may be contacted to request a second meeting. However most families express interest within a week and a half. The bride takers may initiate the second telephone call. If the family they contact is not interested in the alliance, they have to state reasons for rejection that must not offend. One young man told me that if his uncles and "everyone" did not want a match, then they consult the pundits or merely say that the pundits were consulted to "confirm the horoscope match": a "bad horoscope match" is then used to negotiate rejection.[20] He said, "We did it once; we said that the charts did not work out and just said no." Another form of rejection, which saves face, is to use their children as an excuse. In this case, both "she is not really ready yet" and "we were thinking about marriage in two years' time" do not reject the other person or family and ensure that the rejection is not made public. Negotiations thus involve parents, children, extended family, friends, and the family of the prospective bride or groom.

It is clear that after several unsuccessful meetings, parents, together with individuals in the network who may be involved, as well as the young girl, begin to get anxious. The parents begin to reassess, apply indirect pressure, and wonder if their daughter is, in fact, ready for marriage. The pressure becomes especially acute as the girl gets older. I knew of girls who were twenty-three and twenty-seven who were being told that their chances were diminishing. At this moment, the girl, like Anu, might introduce her own choice into the arranged marriage process. "Less suitable," perhaps, but a choice that could potentially resolve the mounting tensions. This, indeed, was Nishma's case.

One evening Nishma and her boyfriend had come to our flat for a visit. They had wanted to talk to my husband and me about our wedding and find out how I had introduced my partner to my parents. That evening we discussed their situation and were asked advice on how Nishma should introduce Manoj as her choice and a "suitable boy." Her parents already knew of Manoj's existence and that he was a part of Nishma's regular group of friends; her mother suspected a relationship between Manoj and Nishma but never broached the issue with her daughter. The couple had already consulted a pundit. They had wanted to make sure that their charts worked together and that there would be no major problems of compatibility before they introduced the idea to their parents: "The reason we wanted to do that was we wanted to make sure it would be 'OK.' We both knew it would be 'OK' but in the deep recesses of the mind we have to have approval of the stars." As we discussed the situation Manoj said:

I gave Nishma a good lecture and told her not to blow up at them like she usually does. If you go in there with your guns ready and shoot off, they are going to laugh and say "oh you missed" and then they are going to take out an uzi and blow you away. You have to keep an even head; you have to be ready for what they deal out. See, I know her parents; I know how they think. I can handle parents; you just have to know how to be cool. But she lets the slightest thing that they say get to her head and just screams at them. I have seen it with my own eyes; it is wrong. This is too sensitive to take that attitude. You have to expect what they will say and then have a response.

Then Nishma and Manoj methodically anticipated her parents' objections. His parents already were comfortable with the match. They knew what to expect. Nishma's family is Brahmin so Manoj's caste (Ksatriya, Khattrī) was going to be seen as a barrier, even though her family was introducing her to both Khattrī and Brahmin boys. Nishma had already said, "I'm going to have a difficult time with my parents; he's Khattrī. For me, I don't believe in this shit, my cousin is married to a Khattrī. . . . With my family it will be hard; they will come around at the end of the day; they're OK. The thing that's going to bug them most is that I found him and not them." She had also second-guessed their main concern: "They want to know if he'll look after me financially; they're really into that shit." Then she also hinted at another potential objection, "They have images of who they want you to marry — he must be fair and tall. Manoj is my height and dark. This will come up."

Nishma had guessed her father's disagreements perfectly. After a meeting with another "prospective," Nishma introduced Manoj as a potential partner to her father. This was at first an unpleasant surprise for her father, who sought to dismiss the suggestion: He stated, "I knew I should not have let you spend so much time together. You said you were friends; he was always coming here and you were always together. It is not love; you have just grown used to him." She responded to her father by pointing out that this was precisely the argument her parents and many others had used in favor of arranged marriage: that one grows accustomed to the person over time. Before she approached her parents, she had told me on the phone, "As far as Manoj goes everyday we get stronger, it reinforces more and more, the pundit reinforced it." Over the next few weeks they talked about Manoj and Uncle gave an indication of his willingness to consider the proposition with the words: "Well, there is no point in us looking for other men."

The discussions continued, and Manoj's caste, dark skin color, and earning potential were all discussed at length. In the interim, Nishma had told Manoj not to visit or to call, until things had "cooled off." When Uncle found out she had done this, he was annoyed and reprimanded her: "No, he should not be told that he cannot come here. You shouldn't have told him that." Nishma was confused by this response. How could they tell her to take some distance and time to reflect away from him and then also say that he could visit. This baffled me, too, but over time Uncle's objection to Nishma's handling of the situation has come to make more sense. Manoj was his prospective son-in-law, and Uncle did not want an initial rejection entering their relationship. His negotiation skills came into play for saving face and making a relationship between himself and Manoj, while he still insisted that Nishma see less of Manoj. When Nishma had first talked about Manoj to her parents she said, "I'm telling you what I'm thinking — it's all the things you're looking for in a family; they are good, religious, decent, and treat other sister-in-laws good [*sic*]." For support, Nishma looked to her mother, who then reiterated what her father had already said. Nishma knew that her mother suspected the relationship: "Manoj bought me ten roses for my birthday. Mum knows; she twigged to it, but she just never said anything at that point, you know, nothing against my dad." In the end she told her parents with tears in her eyes, "I have no other family, only the two of you. I want to get married. I am sick of your pressure. This is what I'm thinking [referring to Manoj] but I am not doing it [getting married] without you. I need your support." At this, her mother cried and her father gave her a hug. She was making some progress.

Much has transpired since that conversation. Both sets of parents met each other and agreed to the marriage alliance. Uncle did not give his immediate approval because he wanted to consult an Indian *jyotshi* during his next trip to India. They have tentatively planned the official engagement and both wedding dates — one for a Hindu ceremony and one for the "registry wedding."[21] They have not told anyone of the forthcoming marriage and have requested that Manoj's parents also delay the announcement. Only time will determine if the marriage will be presented as an arranged marriage to their friends and family. For the moment, whenever anyone inquires about Nishma, her parents are quick to respond, "We are still looking."

Nishma and her parent's negotiations are part of the subtle processes through which assumptions about identity and cultural continuity are made explicit. It is precisely at times like marriage when people are actively thinking about who they are and, in fact, who they "will become." Discussions of whom to marry and how to marry at one level fixes Hindu Punjabi identity. It invokes the sense of being Hindu (especially the discussions of an acceptable wedding ceremony and family traditions during that ceremony), the sense of being Punjabi (in terms of who is an acceptable prospective partner), as well as a more specific sense of who one is, by who one is not (proscriptions and prescriptions about the alliance). In this way marriage can be seen as a moment when culture, community, identity, and ethnicity all coalesce, and yet as I have shown through Nishma's story of marrying her boyfriend, this claim for cultural fixity is itself quite fluid.

In the process of finding a partner, as Nishma's marriage to Manoj shows, there are microstrategies that construct community, identity, and ethnicity as distinct. The actual negotiations reveal how "community," "identity," or "ethnicity" comes to be thought of as "culture" outside of those negotiations. Through the negotiations of Nishma and her parents, their family, and family friends, we can see these ideas do not immediately coalesce, but rather are given meaning through practice. This is part of the inscription and ascription of experience, which makes people who they are and conscious of the boundaries of cultural difference. It is clear that for many young people, as for their parents, the ideal of a "suitable boy or girl" is linked to claiming fixed cultural identities — being Hindu, being Punjabi — rather than the multiple and complex processes of identification. And yet, for the people I studied, these very categories of being seem to be contested and fluid — in arranged-marriage alliances between Hindu Punjabis, as well as in marriages between Hindu Punjabi, Gujarati, and "English" partners.

Moreover, in these moments of active negotiation participants also reveal their sense of the transnational connections that make up their identities. Explicit markers of transnational connections need to be read alongside markers and negotiations of difference in which certain meanings of culture are refused and others are taken up, in this instance as potential alliances. In this way, marriage, although seemingly a prosaic anthropological concern to some scholars, provides an example of how minorities can be "endogamous" and yet rupture categories of difference and complicate notions of fixed cultural boundaries. In the end, Nishma had to show that Manoj was "suitable" to her parents, and she did so by separating out community, identity, and ethnicity in her discussions. In doing so, she revealed the complex negotiations involved in the processes of identification surrounding alliance. As such, marriage is one instance of the dynamism of cultural agency and structural constraint through which people can claim and uphold the necessary nostalgia for culture, and yet can live their lives in much more complex ways.

CHAPTER 6

Becoming British Asian

Intergenerational Negotiations of Racism

Negotiations and markers of difference help to separate culture from "ethnicity" (Punjabi) and "community" (Hindu). Thus far, I have drawn on familiar terms for understanding "ethnic minorities," such as language, religion, kinship, and alliance. Continuing my focus on the negotiation of culture cum ethnicity cum identity cum community, I want to now discuss racism as experienced in everyday lives. Race is a seemingly primordial factor of identity, culture, community, and ethnicity. Having looked at the complexities invoked in producing identification as Punjabi and Hindu, I compare middle-class Hindu Punjabi parents and children's perspectives of two additional categories of identity: "Asian" and "Black." Each of these emerges as a choice of identity resulting from the movement of people from India to Britain. Each is also experienced as anything but a choice of identification.

Race relations have often been overlooked in anthropological works on "Asians in Britain": indeed some writers (Modood 1988) have challenged the utility of using *Black* identity as a marker, denying that it can fruitfully contribute to discussions of *Asian* identity (see also Baumann 1996: 161–72; Brah 1996). Discussions of race in modern social science parlance have turned "from the biological ground of 'phenotypical differences' to the social ground where differences are drawn, defined and made to matter" (Greenhouse and Greenwood 1998: 3). Discussions of racism are fraught with concerns about the accountability of exclusion because of limited access to education, housing, and health care resources. Such an understanding makes "race" somewhat a misnomer for the middle class, who, in this official interpretation can be seen to experience no racism because they have secure housing, education, and health care resources. Implicit in the academic literature are notions that Asians do not experience race in the same ways as Afro-Caribbean populations (Modood 1988), they deny racism (Gillespie 1995), or they do not self-ascribe as Blacks (Baumann 1996). In exploring the dynamics of HP identification in London, one challenge is to understand the ways new racism creates a specific experience of difference in everyday life that allows culture, ethnicity, and identity to coalesce.[1]

Taking up this challenge, I propose to explore issues of racism as they affect the Hindu Punjabis of this study by asking how the experiences of racism have affected their identification as Hindu Punjabi. Importantly, examinations of race and racism have often focused on political racism, antiracist organizations, activists, and institutional exclusions. But I do not wish to present a straightforward catalogue of incidents regarding housing, economics, or physical violence. Instead, I examine how "Asian" and "Black" are lived as nominal identities by my interlocutors, by comparing and contrasting the reactions and interpretations of the migrant parental generation with their British-born and -raised children. Such an "everyday" approach to racism involves thinking about how experiencing racism has changed parental strategies for living in Britain and, one could argue, their understandings of ethnicity.[2] The juxtaposition with their British-born children's experiences reveals how the politics of new racism encourages them to self-identify as Black or Asian. I conclude with a discussion of the significance of "nominal identities" and its implications for a discussion of culture and community. The terms "Black" and "Asian" subsume heterogeneity and are rejected in favor of a religious, specifically Hindu, identity that fixes identity to correlate with culture, ethnicity, and location.

An exhaustive account of racism and European racial thought is neither possible nor appropriate here.[3] Earlier explorations of race and racism in contemporary Britain focus on a few main themes: "number-crunching" exercises (usually exploring the connections between "race" and economics in the areas of jobs and housing); histories of racism (concentrating on the pathology of race and reproduction involved in the colonial context); as well as various explorations of the official, structural

racist nature of British society. There is also a large body of autobio-
graphical and anecdotal work, some by Asian activists and journalists
such as Sivanandan (1990) or Hiro (1991), who document racial prejudice and offer accounts of racial attacks. The "number crunchers" and
those giving journalistic or polemical accounts enhance our understanding of racism in various ways. However, they miss a crucial aspect
of racism in Britain: the everyday experience of racism and difference by
ordinary "visible" ethnic minorities.[4] It may be countered that examination of the "grand themes" of racism (housing, employment, education)
tacitly incorporate the experiential: statisticians offer "proof" of racist
experience; historians demonstrate how racist ideas developed and how
they have been pressed into service in the lived relations between Britain
and its empire; while accounts of the race relations industry, of government responses and community struggles (see, inter alia, Werbner and
Anwar 1991) detail understandings of racism by the "ethnic community
leaders" who act as "ethnic brokers," "antiracist professionals." Much of
the work concentrates on those who fight against "the racist state" and
ignores those "ethnics" not actively and explicitly involved in an antiracist
struggle.

Moreover, much of the work does not address "new racism" where
ideas of nonnegotiable cultural difference have replaced "old" ideas of bio-
logically immutable racial hierarchy (Barker 1981). From previous biological understandings of "race" and "racism," "new racism," or xenophobia has developed as a subtle exegesis of racism, not simply a matter
of phenotype as a diacritical marker but instead as the conceptualization
of exclusion based on claims of irreconcilable cultural difference. The
attraction of new racism to a broad section of the white population of the
United Kingdom and Europe is connected to responses to immigration
and postwar, post-Industrial Revolution economic crises (see especially
Stolcke 1995; but also Fryer 1984; Solomos 1991; Yuval-Davis and Anthias
1992), as well as to the ways in which such ideas fit with contemporary
ideas of the natural, the biological, and the social. Color is inextricable
from cultural difference, indeed in everyday conversation the two are
equated, thus allowing skin color to be one marker for asking the question, "Where are you from?"

Ethnographic research on South Asians in Britain has often neglected
to include race as an important dynamic in the experience of ethnicity
(two exceptions to this tendency are reviewed below). This predisposition
in anthropology more generally was noted by Harrison, who commented, "Critiques of the biological concept of race have led many

anthropologists to adopt a 'no-race' posture and an approach to inter-group difference highlighting ethnicity-based principles of classification and organization. Often, however, the singular focus on ethnicity has left unaddressed the persistence of racism and its invidious impact on local communities, nation-states, and the global system" (Harrison 1995: 47). Although recent trends in cultural anthropology have moved toward examinations of racial inequalities, in Britain race remains separate from ethnicity. Critiques by "race relations specialists" of the so-called ethnic-ity school have accordingly centered on their neglect of the power dynam-ics of racism. In "ethnicity accounts" (primarily anthropological research), race-based divisions and racism often are subsumed as cultural differences between the "host" majority society in Britain and the ethnic minority, and therefore as an inevitable (but not insurmountable) outcome of the meeting of two cultures. The strongest critique is the absence of *power* and the assumptions of an "inward-looking culture," which reduce the utility of the *ethnicity only* view (Centre for Contemporary Cultural Studies 1982 provides a trenchant critique). While the ethnicity school has its limita-tions, the race relations school is not beyond reproach. Moreover, a con-cern with "race" or "race relations" implies the materialistic (in a Marxist or neo-Marxist framework) such as the difficulties in housing, job dis-crimination, racial tension, educational achievement (or lack thereof), and physical violence. As a consequence race becomes a "working-class phe-nomenon." Moreover, these works tend to concentrate on Afro-Caribbean populations (Benson 1996). While not articulated as such, the underlying assumption is that race/racism does not occur, or is not important to the middle class, especially the middle-class Asian.[5]

Social scientists are beginning to recognize and question this impor-tant silence on the question of race and racism for South Asians in Britain (Benson 1996; Sharma, Hutnyk, and Sharma 1996). Yet, cultur-ally understood experiences tacitly depend on people's perceptions. Is racism insignificant if one's informants are silent about it? How should anthropologists think about the silences around racism? How can we examine what people understand by racism, if they do not wish to speak about it? I explore these questions through two recent publications about Asians in Southall, West London, that open up an anthropologi-cal discussion of racism for South Asians in Britain.

The first is Marie Gillespie's (1995) ethnography of Punjabis in Southall. In Gillespie's account of the racially motivated murder of an Asian minicab driver, her informants' reactions to racism were difficult to elicit. It was clear from police and newspaper reporting that the basis of this attack was racial hostility. But Gillespie asserts that the young people she spoke to were ambivalent about this interpretation: instead, they "would mostly prefer to believe that it was the act of deeply disturbed character rather than the cruelest manifestation of racist violence" (1995: 128). There are a number of possible explanations. It may be that "racism" for young Southallians is narrowly defined; it may reflect an active forgetting, a silence, a failure to remember the painful experiences of racism (aside from the dates and names of "the riots"); or perhaps it reflects the differences between those who were activist and those who were not, indicating variations in strategic approaches to a "shared" experience (the activists complained about the lack of institutional support, as well as the frustration and anger of mobilizing support). How, in this case, did the young people's understandings of racism relate to their sense of being British? What does racism mean to these young people? If they understand racism to mean getting beaten up on the street and the fear of walking alone at night, then perhaps these young Southallians know no racism, regarding it as part of a "historical" Southall that culminated in the 1979 "Police Riot." Contemporary racism, if understood in its violent guise, is reserved for the East End and serves to distinguish East from West London, thus the attack on Quudas Ali may not be seen as their experience of racism because young people of Southall are not getting attacked on their own streets.[6] This raises the question of how neighborhood and social class relate to experiences of racism. But despite claims that Gillespie's subjects are not experiencing this physical (fear of being beaten on the street) racism, they do encounter difference through the convoluted concoction of race and ethnicity called "new racism."

Gillespie's exploration of racism reacts against the earlier anthropological silence and emphasizes the lack of tools we have to address racism. Anthropological accounts of South Asians in Britain are contingent on people sharing their experiences. If informants are not willing to "share" certain aspects of their lives, these aspects are invisible and therefore remain unexplored. My sense in the field was that racism is not a topic that people discuss openly. The weakness of an anthropological account may be precisely the willingness of the anthropologist to take informants' accounts at "face value": yet what is not said may be as significant as what is articulated. The ambivalences people express in acknowledging racism are bound up in questions of how they are prepared to enter into and bridge the identifications others place on them.

Gerd Baumann's work, also based in Southall, explores racism through language. A local gazette published an article, which sought to separate

the term "Asian" from the term "Black," and Baumann reacts to this article by examining racism as nominal difference and stressing the importance of naming (1996: 162–72). His exhaustive account of the flurry of
letter writing that followed the original article outlines the many ways
Asians in the 1990s understand "Black" identity. The process, which
gave rise to the political use of the term "Black," is detailed and the rejection of the term by most of the newspaper respondents is documented;
however, the ways in which racism is experienced and understood by the
Asians he researched is not. Thus, despite these recent attempts to incorporate racism into ethnography, many questions remain unanswered.
How have experiences of racism changed? How has this affected ethnic
identity in Britain? This ethnography of racism examines these issues from
the perspective of Hindu Punjabis in London.

Racism in Britain has dramatically changed since its nineteenth-century
anthropometric beginnings. From a biological construct, race theory and
resulting racism transformed easily into "natural" ideas of social hierarchy
and evolutionism. Postwar migrants, at the end of empire, arrived when
there was only "a rare Asian face." Initially, the earliest migrants recall
being faced with a relatively benign reaction. However, a number of factors precipitated increasingly hostile and violent racist attitudes. Overt
"Paki bashing" in the 1970s followed the era ushered in by Enoch Powell's
"Rivers of Blood" speech that stirred up racial hatred in 1969. Changed
attitudes, and perhaps even a realization of the severity of the situation,
prompted the implementation of antidiscrimination policies such as
Equal Opportunities in the 1980s. More recently the 1990s have seen
explicit attempts at the local and national level to create a "multicultural
Britain."

The dynamics of racism, the manner in which it is perceived, and the
ways in which it manifests itself in the lives of the migrant generation have
changed since their arrival in Britain. The main change in racism
recounted by the Hindu Punjabi migrants of my study was that "things
were better in the past." Aunty Krishna, who migrated in 1965, explained:

When we first came, life was quite smooth; there wasn't much racism as you see
today. Then you could see a rare Asian face. Like I would take my son out for a
walk and any English woman would say, "Ah isn't he lovely," just thinking he's a
different color and all that. And just stick a shilling in his hand or something, like
some sweets. Now they just look at you and say, "Oh no, not another one."
Things are different.

With these words, Aunty Krishna echoes a general contention asserted by
many of the migrant generation: racism was not rampant when they first

arrived. Their understandings of racism and being different have changed dramatically since their migration.[7] How can we account for these perceived changes?

Unlike other topics, racism was a difficult subject to broach with parents. They were willing to speak to me about their lives when they first arrived in Britain and about changes in Hinduism and marriage, but they were noticeably silent on racism. During interviews I would approach the topic indirectly by asking people to reflect on a recent newspaper report of a racist killing or beating. Once they began to speak about the news story, I would enquire about their initial personal experiences of racism in Britain. Once they indicated a willingness to speak to these issues, I would ask about the connections between their past experiences with the present. Pressed in this way, people would be more candid about their own experiences and perceptions.

Uncle Prem

Uncle Prem came to Britain in 1952. He is now retired from his management job with a major multinational industrial company. He has been active in local Hindu temples for the last twenty years and is economically successful, but he remembers the days when he worked "on the shop floor."

At the time when I came, only four [or] five people were here, like me only a few people were here. From Tilbury to Aldgate maybe four, five people. So hardly see any Indians around here. And that was really a very tough time. You can't get accommodation at that time to live somewhere else. I become lucky; for three months it was a hell of a time. Then, after that, I had my own house, which was good for me.

Uncle Prem and other men of his generation (many now entering retirement) would recount incidents of racism they had experienced when trying to find a house or their first job. Housing was their first concern and, like Uncle Prem, many of these men, even though not "sponsored" or part of a chain migration, knew someone, often a distant family friend, in the United Kingdom (although not necessarily in London). Some were able to find accommodation through their networks, but for others like Uncle Prem, the connections were tenuous and distant, and they wanted to move out and establish themselves. Renting accommodation was difficult since many advertisements would clearly state, "No Blacks allowed." "People would shut the door on your face and tell you that the bedsit had been let," but then allow a "white bloke in to see the place." Consequently, it became their first goal to own their own homes.

Men also recounted their concern to find employment, often a daunting task. Uncle Prem spoke of his initial search for employment: "I don't know which way to put it. It was very difficult and I thought, 'Well, oh if this is not the way, I'm out from my country now; my parents didn't want me to go out' [of India, implying that despite racism he had to prove himself]." Uncle also spoke of initial difficulties in securing a job because his Indian qualifications were not recognized.[8] One manager, after hiring him, had said, "I didn't think Asians could do that kind of work." Like others, Uncle Prem remembered instances of name-calling and job discrimination as characteristic of racism.

Eventually Uncle Prem found stable employment and stayed in the same company until his retirement. Despite his long service, he remembers the difficulties he encountered. He was aware, for example, that the personnel manager was hostile:

I mean when I first joined them I knew that he didn't like me. But I still asked that man, "Would you like a cup of tea?" . . . I think I was treated like a boy for the first few months, that I am nothing. I spoke to my boss, "Can you tell me what job I am employed for, what am I going to do? Am I a tea boy or just picking up the telephone when everybody is gone, or keeping the message?" And he said, "No, no, no you are not like this." And I said, "It looks to me that I'm like that."

He recalled that:

After six months there was a redundancy that came into our company but my boss he said to me, "No, you're fine," and some of the people that had been working there for such a long time, they got the redundancy. And the one [personnel manager] he passed a few nasty remarks. And I said to him, "Look if you came to India and we treat you like this, or you go to a different country and they misbehave with you like that how would you feel?" And he said, "Oh, I would punch their nose. Why don't you do that because I tease you?" I say [to him] "that I consider you an idiot that you have no brain and psychologically you are a madman so I just ignore you. I mean if I come down to your level I will be the same madman like you are now." So he gone home and he spoke to his wife and his wife said, "He's right because you're a madman; you should not misbehave with anybody." He came to me, he apologized to me and he said, "Yes, you're right," and he never done anything wrong with me after that time. But then, within that three months, I know how much this man knows. How much the rest of them knows.

Uncle Prem was ready to speak objectively about his experiences with racism in terms of housing and employment. These were experiences of the distant past, recounted in a style similar to stories of migration, that is, in terms of conquering adversity and eventually personal success. However their experiences of racism outside of employment and housing were more difficult for the migrant generation to talk about.

In fact, only one other Uncle was prepared to do so openly, and he spoke about his successful rebuttal to racism. Uncle Madan recounted an incident during the height of the 1970s "Paki-bashing" period in which he had been attacked at the local tube station. He punched his attacker back and people learned of the incident, which "changed the neighborhood." He lived in Ilford, in an area that has since the early 1990s become increasingly Asian, as people establish themselves in lower-middle-class housing. The rows of Victorian terraced houses all seem identical, but somehow individual at the same time: each has different colored trim and doors; some have front garden flowers, some do not. I never did meet anyone from his immediate neighborhood when I had visited him; it is uncertain how Uncle Madan's assertiveness might have changed the neighborhood. Certainly, the news of this would have spread quickly, but this had occurred in the 1970s. Since then, more subtle forms of racism have permeated everyday life. Nevertheless, in recounting this story, he inadvertently pointed to the fact that I met very few among the parental generation willing to speak about their responses to racism.

Women's experiences were rather different: boasting and violence were not part of their accounts. Women such as Aunty Krishna initially had limited experiences of racism, because they rarely were directly involved with securing housing and their own employment followed later. Once employed, the women also encountered racism. Aunty Rani's story exemplifies the experiences of these migrant women, especially those who began to work in the 1970s.

Aunty Rani

Aunty Rani was married to a doctor and lived in an affluent middle-class neighborhood in West London where no other South Asians lived. She was a teacher and was one of the three women I had met during my research who had migrated as single women. Her views of racism were unequivocal: "Oh yeah, it's everywhere, racism. It happened when I worked in the bank as well as when I was teaching in the 1970s in the East End. Often children's parents don't like you — they would come and say, even Asian parents say, 'I don't want my child to be taught by a Black teacher.'"

"They can call you 'Paki,' yeah they called you 'Paki.' Or they say, 'I don't want to listen to a Paki teacher.' It's not so bad now that the equal opps racial rule has come in. It's much better now. Well, it's getting better. Somebody calls you Paki and then I say 'I'm not Paki.' Then they would say, 'Well to us you are all same,' and I would say, 'Well to me you and the Irish are the same — I can't differentiate.' Things like that." The parental experience of racism changed their ethnicity to force them to think in terms of the distinction between white and nonwhite.

When I asked Aunty Rani if things had changed since the 1970s, she continued:

Oh, it is always there; only white people will get the promotion. You see, I took one of my head teachers to the tribunal [equal opps]. She didn't let me go to this course, she would prefer white people, so I took her to the tribunal. Nothing much happened, but they said that she was wrong not to let me go and that I was wrong to take her to the tribunal, that it would have been sorted in the school. It was in the school that I am working at now, but you know the equal opps. I think it's a bloody joke [laughing]. It's just for the sake of paper; in reality it's not implemented.

But it's become a deterrent in a way that there's a set of procedures that we have to follow. So in that way that is a really big deterrent in the sense that they won't do much, but now they give more the body language and the movement, but there is no verbal abuse. I mean, not too many people are like that, but there are a few. There are some very nice people too.

Aunty continued her reflections on multiculturalism in her school:

I keep a fast at Karva Chauth [in the autumn]. I get the day off from school for that, for religion. You know in London, where I teach we have quite a lot of ethnic minority people so we have Diwali, Guru Nanak, and Eid.[9] Three ethnic holidays a year, all the schools are closed. But there is a lot of problem going on; it looks like in the next couple of years that they will stop . . . because it [non-Christian religious holidays] affects the Christmas holidays, which nobody likes. You see at the moment by law we have Diwali, Eid, and Guru Nanak off [all three] for everybody. And those affect the three days at Christmas. So they make the Christmas holidays shorter for schools and for everything related to the council. And the trouble is if the school wants unanimously, without one person [dissenting], then they can remain open; if everyone agrees they can do training days. And the head teacher said, "If you have a training day we will give you that day off." But I said, "No, you are depriving me of my training rights. It's a violation of equal opps; I mean you can't do that." And so because we [Aunty and a Muslim colleague] both said this, there was no way that they could open the school and have training days. It doesn't worry me, but I want to be on the defensive side. I mean if the council has given that day off what right do you have as the head to tell me to not take the day off? . . . Well, I like having a day off, but I do mind

Christmas holidays being cut short. Because now we can't go to India. It's only two weeks' holiday; it used to be three weeks.

Multiculturalism in my school? Well, you can do an Eid party, Diwali party. I used to but I don't bother now. That was my responsibility, multicultural education, at one point, but then they changed that because they thought it should be an ongoing thing that should be implemented all the time for the education, not just on Diwali and Eid. So they got away with it that they are implementing at every curriculum area and I got the provision that I could arrange a party, but why should I arrange a party on that day because it's a lot of extra work for me. So I got out of the party. It's just lip service. They do implement in home economics, because the English, they like our food — they want us to cook; they want us to cook and feed them and then call it multicultural education. I don't bother. Tokenism, I call it.

If parents were prepared to speak of racism as part of their experiences of the early days of migration, enveloped in the larger stories of hardship outcome, it is significant that many also asserted that racism had become worse. In fact, many reiterated, "It never used to be like this," or "When we first came there was no racism." What, then, has changed? In one sense what has changed is the sense that racism is now "out in the open," part of a pattern of antagonism that cannot be dismissed, reframed, or discounted. Yet there was also a sense, if pressed, that patterns of disclosure had changed. For example, when I referred to the newspaper reports of young Asians being beaten in the streets, Aunty Krishna began by saying, "As far as I can remember I haven't seen anything like that and I haven't heard anything about it, not really." After a pause, she continued:

Well, before it never used to come into the open, people never used to talk about it, but since the last few years, all that come into the open and people talk about it. And then, you know, oh yes, this is happening and that is happening. It has changed because we were poor people, at that time the Indian population was poor. I don't think it had changed but that, the only thing is that people never used to talk about it.

I return to Uncle Prem's reflections here because, like Aunty Krishna and others, he believes racism has become more prevalent since his arrival in the early 1950s. In speaking of this increase, he draws on ideas and assumptions shared with white conservatives, namely, that it is a "natural instinct" to stick to one's own kind and that visible economic success among Asians breeds hostility. But this is given a specific twist in which Asian virtues and British failures play a part. Uncle Prem stated:

Oh yes, it's worse now because the unemployment. See now if you are an English person and I am Asian and you are equally qualified with me and you haven't got a job and I've got a job, this is the natural instinct, or feeling, "Oh the foreigners come to this country and they're getting my jobs and I am getting no jobs." It's a natural thing. You can't change it. The majority of the English people are not very well educated, they go to the O levels [GCSE] and be done with it, they work in a bank or some office. But the Asians, their children are working, studying hard for higher education, so they get there [implying getting higher positions because of educational qualifications].

In these accounts, it is significant that individuals draw on terms that relate to broad ethnic or racial categories to describe their experiences: "You are an English person and I am an Asian"; "She would prefer white people"; even the Asian parents say, "I don't want my child to be taught by a Black teacher"; "Only white people will get the promotion"; "At that time the Indian population was poor." And indeed some informants, like Uncle Prem, would draw on stereotypical ideas of "Asian success" in their explanations of racial antagonism.[10] At the same time, some informants, Uncle Prem or Aunty Rani, for example, would point to differences that placed them outside the stigmatized group, leaving others as a legitimate target of hostility. The implication is that some ethnic groups (the Irish, the Pakistanis) may be inferior; others are not and should not be grouped with them. Aunty Rani does this in her comments on "Pakis" and the Irish; Uncle Prem too engaged in a straightforward "splitting" between "good" and "bad" migrants. He continued by emphasizing skin color as the main factor:

You see, you're going on the street and I'm going on the street — you're an English girl and I'm an Indian fellow. I may be living here since fifty years and some other Indian on the road maybe he came only two years back. How you're going to differentiate between me and him? That I am here even since before you were born. So they take you in the same category; we're not different to one another. I mean I put forty-two years into the system — all my efforts. I worked with them; I contributed towards the society. I am not living on national assistance; I am not living on their help.

It is easy to see how this splitting may be linked to a strategic rejection of a shared "Indian" or "Asian" identity in favor of ethnic particularism, to Modood's "mode of being" rather than "mode of oppression." Indeed this is one area where racism and the development of ethnic consciousness clearly intersect. At the same time, this did not mean an unawareness or denial of racial hostility. As Uncle Prem explained:

I have earned the money. I am enjoying myself, so I have got a nice car. You will feel, "Oh I haven't got even a car, I've got an old banger with me. How did this

BECOMING BRITISH ASIAN   149

man get it? He only came yesterday." See the feeling? It's a natural thing. But when I retired I had a brand new car, this one [pointing out his front-room window]. Couple of them [his neighbors] said to me, "Oh, a new car." And he doesn't have a new car; he always buys the old [secondhand] ones. I said, "Well, I bought it on loan. It took me twelve years to save £5,000 so now everything is on HP [hire purchase], and I have to pay slowly, slowly for so many years. It's very hard, it's very difficult to live on pension." So if you boast, that "I bought this, I paid cash," straight away the reaction will be "Oh, they are the one's who are picking up the jobs." Instead I show that I am one of them, as they are hard up, I am hard up. I don't say that I've got money, I've got a post office, and I've got this and that, that I've got money in India. Oh no, "I'm a poor man like you brother." So they are happy. So they think, "Oh, he's also hard up, he hasn't got the money." They are happy that way. Why boast? You don't have to boast. I don't make too much in front of my house; you can inside make what you like, a comfortable place. See you're in line with them. It's the way you want to make yourself comfortable.

Uncle was concerned, like others, to attribute racism to increased numbers of migrant groups and changing economic conditions. While emphasizing that people migrated in different years, he understood that, to the host society, being a migrant of almost fifty years "doesn't mean a thing." Uncle Prem's concern in not revealing his wealth to his non-Asian neighbors (that he paid cash for his car, that he owned a post office, or had landholdings in India) was less marked in the accounts of affluent and established Asian professionals. Regardless of their position, however, all of the migrants explained increased racism in terms of economic antagonism.

Other nonofficial reactions to racism include "telling tales," retelling a racist incident or experience to others. These are not personal tales, but "news" items. However, the people may reflect on a news item by including personal details, sometimes boasting of a person's own capacities to handle a racist incident. Like Gillespie, I noted that although people do not discuss racism regularly at social gatherings or at home, media reports of racism affecting Asians offered people an opportunity to talk about their personal experiences. More importantly, some parents used the news item to speak to their children about discrimination.

Parents spoke about racism in economic terms. But for this generation, racism was also about creating silence and the parental generation's "Just ignore it" attitude. Some like Uncle Prem and Aunty Rani spoke directly, but as middle-class individuals for whom racism is not usually a threat of physical violence, my interlocutors often preferred alternative explanations for antagonism or discrimination. This, of course, is only possible when the discrimination experienced is not overt and verbal, but rather

is part of the subtlety of racism. Class achievements factor into the subtlety by providing those Asians who experience "racism" with more
pleasant alternative explanations. For example, when I asked Aunty
Aggarwal about her experiences with racism, she mentioned that after
moving into her new home she would often find rubbish strewn across
her front lawn. She confided that she did not really know if it was racism,
or just children leaving rubbish behind on their way home from school,
or perhaps one of the pitfalls of owning a corner plot. She had considered
racism as only one of many explanations. When I enquired if it continued,
she said it had stopped after a few weeks. Perhaps whoever was littering
her lawn had caught a glimpse of her elderly white gardener picking it up.
Since Aunty did not know the cause, the reasons for the cessation were
also a mystery; racism was only one of many other possible reasons.

The silences, excuses, economic explanations, as well as the coping
strategies combine to reveal the migrant generation's experience of racism
in Britain. In this way, their experience of racism changed their "ethnicity." This does not indicate some sort of communal effort, or a consensus,
but rather a long-term shift that certain families articulated: an emphasis
on the need for their children to think strategically. Thus, repeatedly the
second generation hears variations of the phrase, "You have to be stronger,
smarter, better, and work harder to get anywhere in this country." (These
were one father's direct words recounted during an interview.) It could
be argued that simply telling one's children to do well is not an "antiracist
strategy"; for one, it does not address the systemic problems of society.
As a strategy it accepts the experience of race, but turns, as a solution, to
individualism. It is a strategy that does not see systemic change as prob-
able and instead attempts to apply immediately pragmatic solutions. In
this way, it echoes migrants' earlier strategies in dealing with bureaucracy,
passports, and the problems of migration. I would argue that this links
to the ways in which the post-Partition experiences of Hindu Punjabis
have served to make them flexible, adaptable, and mobile, to fit in wherever they are. So part of what could, on one level, be seen as "ethnic," a
"mode of being," in fact, on another level, could be read as a response to
historically specific conditions of exclusion.

Tales of initial racism included day-to-day events, such as shopping for
groceries, when differences based on color were articulated and experienced. One Aunty told me, "Oh yeah, like they will do the packing for the
white people but they would not do the packing for us. Things like that,
just a small thing like that." A "small thing like that" experienced in everyday life is "small" precisely because it is subtle and unexpected. Its mean-

ing only becomes clear on reflection. Other accounts, however, emphasized structural disadvantages that had to be overcome.

The man who told his children to "do better than the whites" also spoke to me about his eldest son's difficulties in procuring a hospital consultancy. For him, this "glass ceiling" smacked of racism.[11] Among the parental generation, concerns of racism have changed from their own beginnings "on the factory floor" to their children being denied top professional positions. Although parents were able to speak about economic biases and resulting financial difficulties, they could do little to combat racism directly. Instead, they just hoped it would disappear. More importantly, however, they did not feel comfortable talking about it. Attributions of racism involve a "projection of intentionality."[12] Attributing purposeful intention to others by using racism as one of many explanations becomes an interpretative tool used by people to explain other people's behaviors. Parents preferred not to use this conceptual tool when thinking about their children. As Aunty Kalia said, "For me it is OK, but for my kids, they are British."

A number of "small thing[s] like that" also featured in accounts offered by the second generation; but unlike their parents, they did not see racism as a "small thing." Racially motivated incidents were easier to discuss with the children of migrants, probably because most young people interpreted their experiences within the discourse of "racism," about which they held firm opinions. Young people, moreover, spontaneously wove racism into their life stories and reflections during interviews and fieldwork. Thus, when my friend Nishma (aged twenty-seven) was telling me about her recent business trip to India — her first visit in eight years — she spoke of how it made her unexpectedly aware of her life in Britain: "I never really realized the pressure of constantly knowing that I was a different color than everyone else until then." She went on to reflect on her thoughts of potentially living in India and "how cool it would be." Yet even for young people, as for their parents, racism was something shaming, hurtful, and, if speaking of personal experiences, difficult to discuss. But the children are facing racism at a different level, and, unlike their parents, they will not indulge in a collusion of silence.

The children's reactions to their parents' strategy of silence are connected to their understandings of racism, xenophobia, nationality, and belonging. Youths experiment with "fighting" racism at many different levels, particularly because they have taken on board their parents' admonitions to be "overachievers" (reflecting their belief in a "liberal," "democratic," and "tolerant" Britain). One ethnographic instance of such understandings between parents and children is particularly illustrative. One evening I was with the Kapurs and Arti began to tell me about her friend's brother who was physically assaulted in Surrey while at college. This was not the first attack. In the last few months seven of his friends had also been attacked. When his assailants were kicking him, they yelled, "PAKI!" so in his mind there was no question that it was racially motivated. At the time of the beating he had his mobile phone and had called the police immediately. He was able to identify some of the people involved and also to give some names, since some of his attackers were people on his course and the others he recognized from his "uni." A few "arrests" were made, but after three weeks, no charges had been made. "He wants to do something about it," Arti told me, "and I was wondering if you could tell me what he could do." On hearing these words, her mother, who had been in the room, listening to our conversation said, "No, you should just ignore it, not fight back. Just ignore it." Arti replied to Aunty Kapur who kept repeating "just ignore it." The exchange became heated and Arti raised her voice: "How can we just ignore it? No, you guys ignored it, but we are not going to. The young generation was born here and we are not just going to ignore it. It is wrong. The next time if I get raped on the street because of these people, are you just going to ignore it?" The reference to her own sexuality and its violation seemed to appall her mother. In the end Aunty just said, "Who knows why it happened — maybe he did something — you don't know." My friend was obviously deeply frustrated by her mother's attitude and looked at her in amazement. Then she turned to me and asked, "Who can we contact aside from the police? Do you have any numbers that I can give to his sister?"

This fieldwork incident indicates the change in attitude between the first and second generation; there is no longer a "just ignore it" attitude. Another Aunty reflected on the change:

It's worse for my children [fifteen and eighteen years old] in the sense that I can cope with it [racism] coming from India. They are born with equal rights and they can't accept it, whereas I can accept it and get on with it. They'll answer back one day because they think that they are equal and know what is right and wrong. They are very Indian at home; once they are out they are English. They are like coconuts, isn't it? Brown on the outside and white inside.

Not all think of their children in color terms, but what this quotation reveals is the difference in generation that the parents recognize, differences that produce distinct reactions to living in a racist environment. One friend told me about an incident at a large supermarket involving her boyfriend. He had been knocked over by an elderly lady who, despite the wide aisles, ran into him with her shopping cart. Under his breath he called her "a stupid cow," which she heard. Instead of the usual charge of being "an insolent young man," she responded with "How dare you foreigners, so rude, go back to where you came from." Her boyfriend had his response ready: "You came to our countries for many years and took everything we had. Now we are here and you better deal with it."

The British-born and -raised are "dealing with it" and are more ready to admit racism. Nevertheless, there are those who remain uncertain about how to respond, thanks to the combined result of (a) the buffering effect of their middle-class upbringing; (b) relatedly, their belief in the individualistic ethos of their parents and the liberalism of the nation-state; and (c) the subtlety of racism. However, there is some shift in attitudes, as evidenced in recent attempts to push awareness to a "community" level, one characteristically articulated around the identity "Asian." During fieldwork this happened at live theatre performances. The Asian comedy "D'yer Eat with Your Fingers?" playing at Theatre Royal, Stratford, reflected and articulated young people's experiences of being "Asian" in Britain (or rather, the funding explicitly tied them to "Asian" identity as minority identity). It was a deliberate attempt to "laugh at ourselves" — a theatrical piece consisting of a series of short, sharp sketches, many of which made fun of "our parents," "arranged marriage," "bhangra gigs," and being chatted up by an Orientalist at a night club. The final skit of "D'yer Eat With Your Fingers II" was more political and addressed racism. The skit began with a song, an easy rap in which the whole troupe recited place names (such as boroughs around London and cities around England) and names of young Asians who had been beaten in the streets (such as Muktar Ahmed). The chanting voices were harrowing and then a loud voice began, "On Vallance road, white men, surrounded him in 1992. . . . They say 47,000 cases of racial incidents are reported in London, but there is suspected underreporting and perhaps the actual figure is as high as 1 million." This powerful piece brought together the experiences of race along with their own reactions: "Quudas Ali, Sher Singh Thagoo, Sitaram, Manor Park, this land is still my home." Significantly, the names on the list span Britain's "mosaic of communities": Bengali Muslim, Sikh, and Hindu.

In addition to the play's admission of and overt reaction to racism, there was a tension between the terms of reference and the experiences of difference. This difficult articulation is perhaps an indication of how racism has changed. Skin pigmentation is no longer the only issue. The racialization of ethnicity and the difficulties of difference are equally part of the youth's experiences of Britain. Thus, parents were alluding to their sense of living in an era of "new ethnicity" when they said "things had changed." What are the limits of "new racism"? How has the British-born generation responded to its assumptions?

Brah's comprehensive review of cultural intersections and difference explores the debates of the applicability of "Black" identity to Asians (1996: 96–102).[13] Detailing its rise as a political term in the United States, and the specific critiques rejecting it as a valid term for Asians in Britain (she cites Hazareesingh 1986; Modood 1988), she argues that the Black political identity debate reveals how semiotic constructions of difference are determined by wider debates concerning political communities and identity (Brah 1996: 102). Brah addresses people's own use of these terms with the example "*kale*" ("Black") as a phrase used by Asians to describe themselves (Brah 1996: 99). Her main contention is that the term "Black" is important because of its implications for political solidarity. It flags what all colonial migrants from Africa, the Caribbean, and South Asia come to share in Britain, a common position of exclusion and difference (which are different). I do not accept or reject "Black" as applied to the Asian experience. Indeed, I knew people who called themselves Black. However, as Baumann argues for Southall, it must be recognized that this term generally is used in South Asian populations primarily as an index of solidarity by activists and community leaders, that is, by relatively few members of the so-called Black Asian community.

I had been curious about the use of the term "Black" and its relation to Asian identity. Consequently I asked many of my informants if they considered themselves Black. The term "Black" was rejected by most of the parental migrant generation. Aunty Rani, who worked in the state school system and had taken her head teacher to the Equal Opps Tribunal, said to me:

"Black" is mostly used for African, isn't it? I am not Black, no, brown [laughing]. I don't like to be called a Black woman. People do call me Black but I correct them, "I'm not Black. I'm brown." But they use this language like "the needs of Black people and this and all that." They just say that anyone who is not white is Black. They have not got any little bit of understanding, have they? They think if you are not white you are Black. You can't be any other color; for them you're Black. They can't think in-between, can they? It's either white or Black that's it. For them, OK. But not for us.

Most interesting is Aunty Rani's attribution of Black identity, not to the activists of the 1970s and 1980s who attempted to claim Black identity as a positive unification, but to another negative misperception of white society. Again, her strategy is one of differentiation: "They are Black; I am not."

Those likely to use the term "Black" were exceptional, usually young, and were often involved in antiracist work, or work that depended on government multicultural funding (Asian women's organizations, for example). It, therefore, surprised me when one Aunty, Anu's mother, said to me during her interview, "We are Black." I later learned that her daughter had actively encouraged her parents to think of themselves as Black and all Asians as politically Black.

As Anu explained:

They didn't [use it] before, but it is a recent thing. When they came here they really believed if you work hard you can make it. But now all the illusions are being shattered. It is a hard thing really for them; they have to accept that they will never be accepted. They do now say that they are Black, but I am not sure if that is not because of me and my work and constantly telling them what is happening. But then again, they see their friends, who are doctors, or whatever, and who have been stopped by the police and checked. My parents just thought that it was the *gundās* before who this was happening to, but when it happened to their friends then they realized that it was true.

This young woman had been concerned from a young age in issues of antiracism. Her family, although now living in a more salubrious area, had lived in Newham, and she had known some of the Newham Seven and had been involved in the trial campaigns and the marches (her current work also involved antiracism).[14] However, those who were not active in antiracist work rarely used the term "Black" about themselves. But what of the term "Asian"?

As we have seen, individuals of the migrant generation sometimes used the term "Asian" in contrast to terms such as "white" or "English" when talking about their experiences of racism and exclusion. Individuals were, however, less clear about accepting "Asian" as an identity for themselves. When I asked Aunty Rani, for example, "Are you Asian?" she responded, "Well, we do come from Asia." She continued:

"Indian Asian," or "British Indian," they classify in two nowadays, or "Black." Like my daughters will be "British Indian" because they are born in Britain, but I'll be "Asian Indian." I changed my passport from Indian to British a long time ago. But my kids, because they are born here, they are British Asian. All of us are British passports, because by birth, they are British, but not by blood. We are by birth and by blood Indian and changed to British. You see, we live here, we pay our taxes here, and we change our identity, our views, our living.

In this passage, ideas of citizenship ("All of us are British passports"), ideas of birthplace ("British Asian" versus "British Indian"), and ideas of blood ("by blood Indian") are all entangled. They suggest multiple and over-lapping possibilities of identity. Yet it was clear to me that one important element in people's unease with these labels was a search for an authentic, workable identity that is fixed and easy to comprehend.

One important anthropological approach to the question of identity is a focus on the boundary, which, in some important respects, defines differences between "us" and "them" (see, for example, Talai 1986; Wallman 1978; P. Werbner 1990b). In this section two examples of such boundaries and implications for identity are examined. The interaction of my informants with non-Asians was the most difficult aspect of partici-pant-observation. Although meetings occurred daily, I did not have easy access to the places where they occurred — work places or schools — or during the evenings because such meetings occurred outside of the home, or at planned parties for which invitations were required. This is not to imply that relationships do not exist or extend beyond the Asian community for dispersed Punjabi Hindus. They often did. For example, one man living in Havering told me, "My neighbors are great, lovely peo-ple. They are always bringing cakes and biscuits over and when we go out we leave our keys with them. Of course they also come over for tea and my wife takes things that she makes to them; they are good people." Yet, aside from Hindu Punjabis speaking of their non-Asian friends and neighbors, coupled with my own experiences with the English, there were few regular and sustained sites for participant observation between Hindu Punjabis and other ethnic and religious groups (English, Gujaratis, Punjabi Sikhs, or Muslims). Below I offer two reflections on such encounters: the first is an account of one woman's involvement in an "English" women's organization, and the second is a conversation with two Hindu Punjabi friends involved in the media

Aunty Sangeeta is a member of the Women's Institute (WI). She infor-mally spoke to various WI meetings about Indian cookery and sari tying. In the four WI meetings I attended, we were the only "Asians" present. Initially she chastised other Asians who did not perform duties of cross-cultural bridging:

They [Hindu Punjabi women of her social circle] wonder why I do it, taking time going around for WI. It is not for the money. Look at my house — I don't need money, but these people [the British women's group where she speaks] are interest-ed in Indian things; they eat Indian food. When they were in India [during the Brit-ish Raj] they did not learn all these things; they need to learn about these things.

To see how "these things" were presented to an English audience I accompanied Aunty Sangeeta to the WI meetings. When initially she asked about my interest in attending, I hinted at a curiosity about how "Asian" culture was being presented to an all English audience through her talks. On a trip out to Essex she asked again about my interest. I elaborated that the talks and meetings allowed me to observe at least one setting where "our people" interacted with the English. I explained that I had no access to other places and was glad to be able to accompany her. She accepted this and was proud of her work and the new light I threw on it.

Unforeseen, however, was her inclusion of this knowledge in that afternoon's introductions to WI members. She said, "This is my friend. She is studying Asians, you know, how we came here, what life was like. She's come to see how whites and Asians get along, how whites treat Asians." I was surprised and hurt by this introduction; it allied me with some other agenda, her agenda, and prevented me from speaking to the others in any nonthreatening manner. To blatantly speak of racism at a WI meeting was to invite trouble, if only at the level of a fieldwork casualty. The casualty was clear: after her talk, the English women's questions and comments were restrained. At the previous talks when this introduction was not offered, misunderstandings and perceptions of Asian culture would surface in the discussions.[15] My discomfort regarding her introduction remained unexpressed; I did not want to offend her by voicing dissent. Since then, I have realized how this introduction allowed her to further her own agenda, that is, informing non-Asians about "Asians." Through my introduction she could present tensions, problems, and apprehensions while remaining detached. Using me in this way precipitated the contentious issues lurking beneath the gentle tea-sipping, craft-making facade. As the self-fashioned cultural broker she viewed herself in battle: her weapons were anecdotes and history used to advance her views; her enemy was the pervasive misunderstanding of "Asian life."

One memorable and slightly confrontational moment occurred at a WI craft fair. The tables of the community hall were full of "Egg Art," crochet, and calligraphy demonstrations, while Aunty made samosas (donating all profit to her local WI chapter). While she was bringing out her ingredients, one of the women asked, "Sangeeta, will you be making curry for us then?" It was a loaded question, and Aunty Sangeeta launched into an unexpected tirade. She recounted the recent VE Day celebrations she watched on TV. Prince Charles had met some Asian girls and greeted them with the words, "Do you eat curry?" or "I like curry" (the exact statement was vague). Telling the story allowed her to rant against the word "curry."

We don't eat curry, such a knowledgeable man, the future King saying things like this — someone should tell him: we don't eat curry. Ask any Asian family, they don't eat curry at home; they eat vegetables with spices and chappati or rice. But never curry, that is from Britain, from the restaurants. We don't even order curry when we go to the restaurant. I had never heard of curry until I came to this country.

The second example involves a complex rejection of the term "Asian" and reveals how young Hindu Punjabis both make use of and question this identity. Below I include a transcription from a spontaneous conversation with two friends who are involved in the "Asian media" and are trying to "go mainstream."[16] My friend, a woman, said to me:

This country and to a certain extent the Asian music scene is something which we have created for ourselves and it is a voice for us to say, "Yes, this is us," and there are all these other offshoots, which have come off of it like production, the other kind of music. And it is really an overused term. I don't know, you should come to the Asian comedian night, because what they do is not just Asian comedy; at a slapstick level there is a lot of underlying things in there. They go on stage and they talk about how we are in such a difficult position being Asians and how we've suffered. You know, take the piss out of it, which makes it positive rather than the depression thing that it is. You know, everyone's around them saying, "Oh you are so hard done by." Bollocks, you've got to go out there and just do it like every single other human being.

Here her male friend interrupted: "There's not been enough of people getting off their ass." "Yeah," she continued, "and we're luckier. Instead of twisting it around and saying we are so hard done by, they should say, 'We have two cultures.'"
He said:

We have turned it around and used it to our advantage and completely turned it around and said, "Listen we talk very much in English and we are giving you an Asian product but it is not aimed at the Asian market." . . . We've actually gone out and said, "Right we are going to target this audience" and we know we are going to get older people going "you can't do this; this is very wrong" [imitating an Indian accent]. We tell them, it is not for you to watch, we are quite happy for them to turn the channel over and watch something else. "This is not aimed at you, this is aimed at people who are between 18 upwards to 30 who not only listen to the Asian music, but also Rap and right across the board."
A lot of people don't realize that Asian music is not the be all and end all of Asian music. I mean, bhangra is not the be all and end all. There are groups which we have known about for five or six years who are suddenly hitting the market.

They have actually jumped over the Asian market because they've just not given them the plug and because there is a hypocrisy in the Asian media, and enough is enough. I mean you simply can't say that you are Asian and that's an excuse to just go in and make a program or go in and make a record, and say, "Listen here's a record — we are Asian; we've got it, let's do it." It just doesn't work that way. You have to now say, "Listen *we're Asian second.* Here's a good idea, why don't you push it?" That's what we are doing. We've never actually gone in and said, "We're Asian first," and yet we consciously made the programs to be specifically aimed at young Asians. Again it's not to go out and say, Bang! Here's Asians, but Bang! Here's a couple of Asians with some good ideas. I bet you didn't know about this, it is simply that. Asian people have created a stereotype — the *gora,* the English, they haven't gone out and done it; it's the Asians who have gone out and filled and perpetuating the stereotype. We should be going out and saying there was never a stereotype — you just made a mistake. We are going to put it right.

My friends' attempt to say "look we're Asian second" and to reject the "Asian stereotype" related especially to national television where representations of "Asians and their culture" perpetuate stereotypes that exist. These friends understand Asians as perpetuating the stereotypes, which are constituted by the constant references of difference and exotica that young Asians then need to explain to a non-Asian audience.

Underlying the culture and color collusion is a sense of the need to separate, define, and clarify terms and categories of reference. Racism, self-naming, and reactions to nominal categories were significant topics that were often discussed between young people. On the one hand, as above, individuals might argue that they wish to be seen as talented individuals first and "Asians second." For others, on the other hand, the need for separation is powerfully argued in a rejection of the label "Asian" in favor of other "communal" identities. To reveal one such articulation of young people's reactions to "naming," I quote from a talk given to a "Hindu Soc" by a young Gujarati male who heads an organization that promotes separate "Hindu Socs" and organizes events around "Hindu identity" aimed at young people in universities and colleges around the country.[17] Some of the young Hindu Punjabis in his audience were moved by his words, so much so that in a few months they had established their own Hindu society separate from the Asian society. The young man's words, attempting to inspire people and to organize a nationwide body, appeal to the general feelings and reflections of young Hindus in Britain. He seeks to question and discredit the various labels that Hindus are known by, all of which ignore their "Hinduness" as a primary aspect of their identity. The labels "Asian" and "Black" are rejected outright. "Black" is seen as an "external" label, useful as an umbrella, but not reflecting self-identification. A further "identity" label that is in use (indeed it was the 1991 census ethnicity indicator), "Indian," during my fieldwork was also rejected by the young people. Being "Indian" is about "roots," but for the children of migrants it cannot be a meaningful label in the British context (it has significance for a notion of homeland, but not for community, for living in Britain, or for an individual's own sense of identity). Throughout these many rejections of labels with the interconnected implications for community, identity, and ethnicity is a desire for an identity that is fixed, which seems not to contain as much variation within the category. In the young man's speech, he proposed being "Hindu" as an authentic response to racism in Britain. He argues, "It is up to us to be able to educate the communities in this country, the so-called British community in this country, about what we mean to be Hindu and through education we can eradicate these so-called racist tendencies." Aside from the implications of the pro-Hindu sentiment expressed (this connects to the experiences of religion and the overt globalization of Hinduism discussed earlier), the young man clearly employs xenophobia and assumptions of cultural difference to play out issues of identity and to encourage the young people in their Hinduism. It is a reaction that takes into account the experiences and reactions to new racism by young people and is specifically a reaction that attempts to demarcate boundaries. The engagement, however, is of an essentializing variety, perhaps inevitable given the current climate when cultural difference and peculiarities matter.

The goal has become to distinguish oneself from other Asians and gain political representation as a religious interest group. He strongly wishes to set his group apart from Muslims, particularly the Bangladeshis. In the adult generation, the creation of "pan" organizations — organizations such as the Muslim Parliament and the Hindu Council UK were similar gestures based on religion. These organizations have formed with the explicit intent of political organization and representation of "community" views and reveal a solidification of identification around a "basic" common denominator — religion. The assertion of religious communities is both an insistence on an adequate basis for "cultural" identity, which is not skin color, as well as a strategy of differentiation from others who share the same skin color. On the one hand, these requirements challenge "new racism" by rejecting the premise of skin color. On the other hand, the assertion of a religious identity "Hindu" over a homogenizing one such as "Asian" inevitably takes on the same difficulties, difficulties that arise in any attempt to found an identity on a nominal category.

Furthermore, differences in class and achievement in Britain factor into the assertion of religion. While, for Hindu Punjabis, the distinct Muslim *other* is carried from the parental generation as a result of Partition and the Sikh "other" has been reinforced by events in India, especially since the 1980s, the impact of the employment and education differences between Hindus and Muslims in Britain cannot be discounted (Andrews 1996; T. Jones 1993; Modood 1992). This process of splitting has strategic implications: certain migrants or communities are "bad," and "we are good." The young Hindu activist indicates, "If we look throughout Britain, Hindus have been a boon to this country, not a burden. If you look through the achievements of our accountants, our doctors, our businesses we come up on top of the table and therefore we should make it clear to these people that yes we are British and yes we are making a very active contribution." The discussion for this young man is to prove that "yes we are British," by revealing their Hindu contributions to Britain.

One of the most startling moments of my fieldwork occurred when Manoj complained about the Bangladeshis coming into Britain, "taking up council housing, being on the dole, having eight or ten kids." When I suggested that these same complaints were used by the English when migrants arrived from India during the 1960s, he did not believe me and claimed that the migrants of his father's generation had come to make money and build a better life, that they were hardworking and honest. Instead, he continued, because of the favorable exchange rate, the Bangladeshis siphoned funds from benefits back into Bangladesh. The validity of this statement is not the issue, but it reveals the differences fracturing the Asian identity. Yet another impetus comes from the politics of ethnicity in urban Britain and the mobilization of "communities" around religious identities. While it may be the most obvious in ethnic ghettos (Baumann 1996), the turn to religious identification has thus had a broader impact.

The move is toward increasing fixity and rigidity in defining nominal identities by smaller units that require homogeneity. What is specific to the British context that has allowed for these changes? The requirement of fixity is the result of having to define oneself, to be defined in terms of meaningful and accessible categories. The ruptures, differences, distinctions, and subtleties do not matter. The young man quoted above is attempting to relate to one such common experience: what it means to be a Hindu to a non-Hindu audience. The HP youth related to this constant awareness of difference and the burden of diversity.

There are various reasons for this. One is television. In the spring of

1995, the BBC aired a documentary on arranged marriages. The next day Nishma asked if I had seen it and we discussed it. She was highly critical of it, adding, "I remember when I was in school and there was this crap Asian program on Black families. I had to go to school the next day when kids would say, 'Oh you do that' and have to explain to them that it wasn't like that and spend the whole day explaining how it was not like that for us!" Television documentaries, aimed at exploring diversity end up creating incommensurate gaps of difference in everyday experience.[18] British-born youth have had to face these gaps repeatedly in different situations from the school playground to university. The experience for this generation, moreover, is to be distinguished from that of their parents who, as adult migrants, entered into a workforce and adult world where such differences may not have been discussed, but rather assumed, or not known. The children of migrants, therefore, are required to become cultural brokers or ambassadors of difference, speaking for a whole Asian population constructed by difference but not differentiated until recently into various religions. These roles of negotiating difference and understanding are foisted on the unsuspected and the unprepared. Many lack the skills, knowledge, and diversity of experience to speak about "being Asian" and to explain the various practices they are involved in, leaving aside the problems of speaking for being Hindu and Hinduism. The result, then, is a rising need for homogeneity, reification, and a substantivist definition of Hinduism (thus returning us to our question, "What is a Hindu?").

In Britain, the Hindu Punjabi diaspora is in the process of becoming, defining itself as a minority within a minority, an ethnic "community" in the British landscape, and as part of the Sanatan Dharm (Eternal Religion) whose members are found in more than sixty-five countries.[19] The example of the Hindu Punjabis dealing with new racism reveals a contradictory trend in global identity formations. On the one hand, their Punjabi identity has changed over time. On the other hand, their religious identity has come to have certain fixity of meaning. Thus, the "noncommunity" in the perpetual state of becoming can also articulate itself as a rigid community with fixed boundaries of being. This trend is part of the perpetual reform of Hinduism found and espoused by political cum religious reformers within the Subcontinent, but not entirely a result of it (see, inter alia, Knott 1987). It is also a requirement of living in Britain and having to explain religious identity on the school grounds after a BBC documentary on Hinduism is aired or when religious education teachers explain Hinduism to their pupils (Raj 2000). Multiculturalism's unsuspected by-product is the increasing fixity and reification of religious identities. Liberal rhetoric celebrates multiculturalism but simultaneously denies the syncretism of Hindu Punjabis by defining them as part of a larger "Hindu tradition," which is glossed as orthodox and uniform in practice. The requirement for a substantive identity results in Hinduism being understood on its own or in opposition to (and comparison with) other "faiths" (with a belief system, a liturgy, a canon). This process, begun by the British in India and now encouraged by religious expressions in Britain itself, establishes a politics of minority religious identity, which is both divisive and destructive.[20]

Similar questions of identity are being forged in other areas, such as Europe and the United States. In fact, even the question of the British entry into the European Union and public media discussions of Britain's support for the ECU both reveal recent ways in which identity politics are simultaneously about being and becoming for those who are not minorities. For visible minorities, the discussion of cultural identity cannot be separated from the discussion of new racism. The pervasiveness of the question opening this book, "Where are you from?" reveals how new racism subtly translates sensory markers of difference, notably sound (accent) and sight (skin color or dress), into epistemological cultural differences.

I have attempted to unpack the questions of "new racism" and the ways that race has become a part of everyday community cum culture cum ethnicity cum identity connections. For Hindu Punjabis in London, the identity politics of new racism are played out in their challenges to the category and images of the "Asian." Such pernicious identity politics result from their experience of being ethnic in Britain. Yet their everyday conversations and observations reveal how ethnicity is made through specific notions of difference and belonging premised on movement. It is surprising to note that while cultural difference has become officiated by the nation-state in the form of multicultural policies, the parental generation has nevertheless felt that racism has increased, because it is now "out in the open." More so than any other category of identification, "Asian" has become the primary trope in which to understand minority cultural experiences. The parents seem to reflect that being in the "middle of difference" has changed from absolute otherness to an overt otherness embroiled in the nation-state.

Multiculturalism has become a crux of difference and reveals the ways globalization effects the imagination of the nation. Opening up discussions of difference in the arena of the nation-state has affected the ways in which people negotiate their own sense of their identification, based on a reformulation of community, culture within a specific matrix of power and representation. The young Hindu Punjabis, in response to the question "Where are you from?" can only reply with their sense of belonging — they are not Asians but Hindu and they can never be "English." Moreover, they can only claim being "British" with clarification or hyphenation. These nominal categories reveal the interplay of new racism and people's sense of identification; instead of opening up the category of the nation to include its minorities, the minorities' sense of belonging to the nation is fractured, thus solidifying the equation of community, identity, ethnicity, and, implicitly, location. The migrations of people, such as Aunty Rani, Aunty Krishna, Aunty Kapur, Aunty Aggarwal, Aunty Kalia, Aunty Sangeeta, Uncle Madan, or Uncle Prem, their movements in the modern world, have simultaneously opened up the world for questioning how difference is ascribed and also reinscribed a conviction of who can constitute the nation-state. When can Hindu Punjabis claim to be British?

CHAPTER 7

Being British, Becoming
a Person of Indian Origin

Hindu Punjabis experience and think about who they are in relation to varied concepts of themselves (historically through Partition memories and through migration), in relation to each other (through religion, marriage, and intergenerational changes), as well as in relation to contemporary Britain (experiences with racism). By highlighting the processual negotiations of each potential identification I have indicated how ethnic minorities not only are the products of globalization but also create the cultural changes inherent to those very global processes of the "ethnoscape" (Appadurai 1991). During the course of their lives, the migrants and their children have moved from being marked as outsiders from the lands of emigration and immigration, to being deeply implicated by each (as exemplified in their experiences with race). In doing so their lives disrupt the place-contingent narratives that highlight the nostalgia for culture based on place. I wish to develop further the complicated ways in which they experience the disconnections between and refigurations of culture, community, identity, and ethnicity, using the two place-based national terms of identification: "British" and "Person of Indian Origin." Each term indicates how transnational connections are being created and fostered in specific ways because of the reimagination of the nation-state with respect to a particular location. Thus far I have explored how Hindu Punjabis create various aspects of their identity in a transnational terrain. Here I wish to examine how South Asians explicitly perceive and make transnational links. In particular, I demonstrate the complexities of national belonging in a transnational world and expose how these people can conceive of themselves as British and as "Non-Resident Indians," for these are not de facto identifications, but ones that have been created and changed.

I want to begin with a reexamination of the idea of diaspora and how some researchers share the collusion for the nostalgia for culture. Earlier, I critiqued the perspective that homelands function as framing devices to understand immigration and movement in the sense of a cultural prior. This understanding of the immigrant as forever connected to a cultural prior creates a chasm of difference, into which the second generation is seductively pulled, or into which they sometimes simply fall. Instead, I explore the migrants' material and symbolic experiences of the Indian homeland. In doing so, I sketch out a different cartography of belonging. Having destabilized the homeland and the notion that migrant ethnic minorities are on a permanent sojourn, I illustrate how transnationalism plays out in people's lives by questioning how the homeland has been framed and created by the Hindu Punjabi migrants and the Indian nation. To fully sketch how ethnic minorities are constantly involved in the production of globalization, I focus on how and why the migrants and their children are being framed as "Persons of Indian Origin" by the Indian nation-state. By moving the discussion into the ways migrants imagine national belonging and establish their transnational connections, I return to the central questions of the book now looking through a different lens, namely, how ethnicity has become a product of globalization and how difference is the primary trope of signification for migration.

Migration places "the global" into the anthropological toolkit, but there are many debates around what we should understand this to mean. Currently, with respect to South Asian migrants and other groups, diaspora and transnationalism dominate. There is, however, an inability to offer a concise definition of diaspora: "It is not possible to define diaspora sharply, either by recourse to essential features or to private oppositions. But it is possible to perceive a loosely coherent, adaptive constellation of responses to dwelling-in-displacement" (Clifford 1994: 310). Tölölyan suggests a plethora of terms that refer to people "dwelling-in-displacement," such as "immigrant, expatriate, refugee, guest worker, exile community, overseas community, ethnic community" (1991: 4–5). Each term describes a different migration experience characteristic of late-twentieth-century life, and most of them have been used to describe the different migrations forming the South Asian global population of approximately

twenty million people in sixty-five different countries.[1] Researchers studying the global ethnicity have different understandings of the group being
studied: some emphasize the migrants as an "encapsulated" minority,
while others emphasize "core-periphery"-type relations (the migrants'
sending country as peripheral to the receiving nation-state); still others
are more concerned with issues of assimilation, integration, and social
cohesion; and some have asked, "What makes a certain people a 'diaspora?' " (Axel 2001: 8).[2]

A number of studies in recent years have sought to explore precisely
the complexity of the South Asian diaspora (cf. Barrier and Dusenberry
1989; Clarke, Peach, and Vertovec 1990; van der Veer 1995). These works
look to the trajectory of migration from the Subcontinent and wrestle
with how transnationalism affects ethnicity as a manifestation of a transplanted culture. By being studied as a particular group in a particular
place, the ethnic community becomes an exemplar of diaspora. As a
result, diaspora itself simply becomes a framing device for ethnicity.
Researchers have also challenged the long-held assumptions of Asian cultural stability and attempt to move beyond the ethnicity framework. For
instance, van der Veer points up a conundrum of research on South Asian
minorities in his introduction to *Nation and Migration:*

This present volume is concerned with the ways in which the South Asian diaspora produces a politics of space that has diverse forms and dynamics in different
historical contexts. The contributors certainly do not want to unify and homog-
enize these differences into "Indian culture overseas." . . . The differences are real
and important and should be taken seriously; on the other hand, we do not want
to deconstruct the South Asian diaspora to the point of dissolution. (1995: 7–8)

One question continues to inform research on the South Asian diaspora: How can difference be researched while recognizing commonalties,
especially a shared global immigration dimension? Researchers are thus
grappling with "unity and diversity," disunity, and "naming and identity
politics" at both local and global levels. As van der Veer argues, part of recognizing the dissolution of "South Asian" as a meaningful category
means ensuring that the term is not deconstructed out of existence. At the
same time diaspora processes cannot solely account for the experiences of
South Asian migrants to Britain; local dynamics are also important. Two
full explorations of South Asians in Britain include such an approach,
Baumann's *Contesting Culture* (1996) and Marie Gillespie's *Television,
Ethnicity and Cultural Change* (1995). These works are innovative, push-
ing forward questions about ethnicity, in line with the existing literature,

the majority of which comprises geographically defined "community studies" — (both conducted their fieldwork in Southall, which is also called "Chota Punjab").

On one level, it may be argued that the "global" aspect of researching South Asians "overseas" has always been present in British ethnicity research. A number of studies on South Asians outside of the Subcontinent have indeed focused on the connections between the overseas population and "the motherland" as well as on cultural change: working "at *both* ends of the migration chain" (Watson 1977: 2). This wider perspective, especially that of the South Asianists, would expand "race relation" studies (this is claimed by Watson 1977; see also Jeffrey 1976; E. Kelly 1990; Saifullah-Khan 1977). An abundance of "Little India" or "Chota Punjab"-type studies proliferated in the United Kingdom and were concerned with the disarticulation of South Asian-ness in the local milieu. These works studied "culture" through a comparison between British Asians and "their counterparts" whom they left behind in South Asia.[3] Yet the research involves specific spatiotemporal assumptions about the who, where, and what of research subjects. In such work, Britain's South Asian migrant communities were understood as outposts of tradition, as keepers of tradition, or the researchers, informed by specific understandings of culture, gauged their putative loss of tradition (critiqued by Axel 2001; Shukla 2001). This is not to state that the Subcontinent is not important, but that the manner through which it is assumed to provide a de facto connection has limited the ways we can understand migration and cultural change. As argued above, researchers often share in the nostalgia for culture.

Does diaspora allow a study to be conceptualized beyond the here and now? Diaspora has become a key concept for recent research on South Asians outside of the Subcontinent, but one which spans differing histories, migrations, and experiences (van der Veer 1995). The term "diaspora" has been accused of "being analytically vacuous but because of this lack of utility has no serious limitations of use" (Norman Buchignani, personal communication).[4] Peter van der Veer questions the validity of the term "diaspora" for South Asians because of "the complexities and contradictions of the South Asian diasporic experience," referring explicitly to the "fragmented nature of these contexts and experiences that complicates the use of 'the South Asian diaspora' as a transparent category" (van der Veer 1995: 1). Certainly, "diaspora" entails certain limitations that may be problematic if attempting to speak conclusively of the South Asian experience. Does the term necessarily eclipse experiences by nominally equating the "descendants" of nineteenth-century indentured laborers who moved to Guyana or Trinidad, known as East Indians, with those "East Indians" who constituted the "brain drain" migration to Canada in the 1960s?[5]

At the center of the many criticisms of the term "diaspora" is the implied connection with, or longing for, the "homeland" and its perceived role for the migrant. South Asian diaspora research has focused on the "dialectics of 'belonging' and 'longing' " (van der Veer 1995: 4). This focus inevitably evokes the image and place of the homeland. Similarly, Roger Ballard sees homeland as central for the South Asian experience. The title (of his edited volume) *Desh Pardesh* immediately implicates homeland, as "Desh" simultaneously evokes "home," "homeland," and "nation." Ballard translates his title thus: "*Desh Pardesh* has a double meaning, for it can equally well be translated both as 'home from home' and as 'at home abroad'" (R. Ballard 1994a: 5). In both senses consideration of homeland is a focal point that renders diaspora as an act of negation of those on the inside, in which those outside the "homeland" are somehow inferior to those inside who remained in the Subcontinent. Yet "part of the post-colonial predicament is its Moebius-strip-like character, whereby categories of 'inside' and 'outside' are in a state of interchangeability" (Radhakrishnan 1996: xxiv).[6] By emphasizing "homeland," diaspora clearly marks insiders and outsiders, and the interchangeability and complexity of how these terms come to have meaning are erased. Furthermore, the term "diaspora," owing to its specific etymology, presupposes exile, reinforcing the notion that those on the outside are the unfortunate outsiders.

These limitations are too great and there is an ongoing debate as to the utility of diaspora (Anthias 1998; Axel 1996; R. Werbner 1998). Important questions are being asked: What does diaspora explain? What does it leave out? These questions must, of course, be asked of all analytical tools, and currently it is unclear what theoretical work diaspora allows beyond an ethnicity writ global (Anthias 1998). For an anthropologist researching Asians in Britain, diaspora is useful because it invokes global relations, yet it allows one to research a local population. Unlike the "two ends of the migration process" that underpinned much 1970s research, diaspora enables us to think of South Asians in Britain beyond the local community, simultaneously implicated, as others, in the local and the global. The "global" dimension is important but the concept of diaspora does not enable us to question our conceptualization of culture spatially and temporally. Instead, it assumes a spatial and temporal constancy and the research focus must be sensitive to the changes in the transplanted culture. Culture itself is seen as changing, but this change is ascribed to the movement alone, moving from being an insider to an outsider. The change is not thought of as ongoing processes of interaction and experience. Moreover, hierarchy and asymmetry are ignored in diaspora: diaspora is like a flattened plane through which people move, and the equation between culture, ethnicity, and community remains in tact. Diaspora highlights ethnicity but emphasizes a changing essence that is not implicated by concerns of class or gender but rather focuses on generation. This further ignores the complications of the migration itself, particularly the importance of the nation-state and its roles at both ends of the migration chain. The state is seen as a perfunctory bureaucratic arm, but its policies determine the types of migration, the experience of the move, the experiences once people arrive, as well as the development of the society. Diaspora allows for multiple centers of culture with problematic boundaries. For South Asian migrants and other large-scale migrant groups with historically different reasons for migration (both voluntary and involuntary), diaspora fails to account for connections beyond that of "longing and belonging," beyond the locally shifting, globally connected ethnic. This approach is entirely unsatisfactory.

However, there is also much to gain in infusing the local places that we study with an overt notion of the global. Accordingly, I examine people's lives not as exemplar of diaspora but as indications for the changing notions of national identification. In my research, the parents' plans for retirement, specifically, provide closure, a reversal or a way of dealing with and reflecting on the questions of how they create their South Asian identity and how they see themselves, especially in relation to "longing and belonging" (van der Veer 1995: 4) or as "Vilayati" or "Asian." During the 1970s, ethnicity research in Britain concentrated on the role of South Asia for the migrants. Certain research agendas informed this period. Were South Asians in Britain sojourners or long-term migrants? What were the specific connections between the migrant and South Asia? Underpinning these questions were concerns over the migrants' allegiance to Britain — were they in fact proper Britons at all? The role of the homeland also features strongly in these questions. Moreover, these questions are framed by the assumption that "home" can only be in one place, "here *or* there." In suggesting that the issue is more complicated, I am arguing with an assumption that India is an inevitable homeland for migrants. I seek to understand how it is being constructed as one. To do this, I explore the tensions of a specific example previously known as the "myth of return."[7]

The phrase "myth of return" developed and is used in response to specific circumstances (see Dahya 1974, Robinson 1981). It referred initially to the unfulfilled intentions of migrants (male) to return home (to Pakistan). The phrase also implied that the migrants had taken a more permanent residence in Britain, and that their return to a homeland was a myth. Research from the period, notably Anwar (1979) and Jeffrey (1976), revealed how the myth affected migrants' lives in Britain (in the form of remittances, social networks, leisure and friendships, language spoken at home, and economic practices in Britain). For these migrants, then, "home" was always "back home," an unproblematic prior. Anwar and Jeffrey's groundbreaking studies shifted the allegiance to Britain and showed how the migrants' plans to return were myths.

But the "myth of return" is not entirely a myth. Over time, it has become a plan for some migrants to return to South Asia. The original return — the gold rush-type of return envisioned by early migrants and academics, whereby migrants came to Britain to make a lot of money quickly and then return to South Asia to establish themselves securely — never actually occurred. That myth of return indeed was a myth, as Anwar and Jeffrey rightly argued. It was fostered by the immigration policies and recruitment drives of the time. After living in Britain for some time many men and families realized they could not go back to the Subcontinent. There were instances of people attempting to return. I met families who during the 1970s had gone to India when their children were young so that they would not "*lose* their children." But they found that they did not "fit in" there and often would come back to resettle in Britain. These cases were exceptional; most did not have the means to reestablish a whole family. Migration, or rather, return migration always somehow implied a one-way movement from and to a putative homeland. For the migrant generation, then, the question of belonging in Britain was always about allegiances to elsewhere. After scholars established and challenged the myth that migrant's allegiance did not lie elsewhere, the complexity of the relationships between migrants and their putative homelands has only been briefly explored.[8]

How has the "myth of return" itself become a myth? For the adult generation, at least, the myth to return to India has been resurrected in a different form. It involves exploring the possibilities of returning to India after retirement. The plans that they are making to return bring forth interesting and important questions about how the question of belonging is framed for the migrant generation. An example of one couple's plans for return help to explain the formation of this neomyth. Uncle and Aunty are both doctors with very successful medical careers. They have established themselves nicely in Britain with the accoutrements of a well-settled life — three children who are all university educated, a Jaguar in the garage, a BMW for her, as well as a gardener who visits weekly to take care of the large garden and miniature apple and pear trees they had recently planted. Yet despite this sense of prosperity and full participation in the benefits of life in England, at our first meeting they revealed their retirement plans for India. It was a shock to hear them talk about their preparations. As far as I was concerned, Anwar's "myth of return" had finally put to rest the idea that migrants were sojourners. I was expecting that there to be no desire to return because they had left India for a "better life" for themselves and their children.[9] Yet there I was sipping tea out of what was sure to be fine china, with people who had realized the migrant's dream (their streets were practically paved with gold), but still they planned "to go back." They described the flat that they recently bought in India, a "Non-Resident Indian" (NRI) flat built on the outskirts of Delhi. During the afternoon Uncle repeatedly accused Aunty of being an Indophile, not only did she love all things Indian, but also she was unable to muster a harsh word about the place. I suspect that it was a strategy used by Aunty to ensure that India was always a topic of conversation. The plans for return and the building of the flat were her own, as she later told me on the telephone: "It is a different life there. Here, coming to this country, what have we done? Just worked our whole lives, nothing else. We have given the best years to Britain and I don't want them to take my golden years as well. India is fun, and because of the exchange [referring to the rate of exchange, which at the time would give them approximately 50 rupees to the pound] we will live well there; we really work too hard here. And then there are all of our families that are there; there is always something happening."[10] Many others who were making retirement plans for India gave similar statements. These plans, which involve financial commitments (such as building a flat in India), render *the myth of return itself a myth*. The migrant generation is returning but the phenomenon is not identical.

Instead of the myth of return, it should perhaps be called the "six-months mantra." Repeatedly during fieldwork I heard the same mantra, *"six months here, six months there,"* from those who had purchased built flats, land, or flats not yet built in Delhi. This simple phrase contains the knowledge that this desire to "return" to India (and indeed it is called a return) was not a plan of permanent resettlement (unlike individuals from the Caribbean communities who left Britain after retirement to settle back in Jamaica and Barbados). A number of factors keep these migrants from permanently returning to India. These reasons were never explicit but were articulated only by those who were *not* planning a return.

One man who did not want to return stated in an interview what I had heard more casually stated at dinner parties and other gatherings.

They're doing it because they feel that their money here is not secure and they should invest in India [referring to his friends making preparations to return to India]. I doubt it if they can go there and live there after living for so many years with all the facilities the way of life that they are used to. I know about five or six people who have went [to India] and come back [to Britain]. It was a bloody disaster. My brother-in-law, they were here for twenty years, they went back, lost everything and now they are back again. It's not practicable. You may say, "I'm going, I'm going, I'm building my property over there, buying a house and making this bungalow" and all that. Fine. But at the end of the day you will not go there. My attitude is different because you are living in this country, you've got to live in this country, invest in this country and make the life easier here. Either move from a three thousand pound house to a five thousand pound house from five to fifty, fifty to two hundred and fifty thousand pound and have a luxurious life here rather than investing over there.

My two children, they are born here, they are used to this country, they can't speak Hindi or Urdu or whatever it is, they can't understand it. Do you think that they will go back? No. So why do I invest over there? They are not going to go. After my death the property [if bought in India] would just go to my brothers and sisters [in India] or someone who will take over. So what I earned is gone to them rather than to my children. If I have a property here, if I have invested here, then at least there is a property that they can look after.

I think that they are crazy to go back. I think that talking about going and staying there is very different. They won't. I won't. Nobody would. Anyway I got a daughter and I have to think about my son.

Despite being a narration of nonreturn, Uncle's account reveals that those who are buying property in India justify their "six months here, six months there" plan in terms of their children. The main reason given for not wanting to settle permanently in India was that their British-born or British-raised children would never relocate to India. Indeed this was not even expected. Parents realized that they would need to maintain a flat at the very least in England because their children were not interested in living in India, or even regularly visiting. Moreover, as Uncle's narration reveals, people are conscious of not fitting into India, of being different, of having changed. This is perhaps where van der Veer's "dialectics of longing and belonging" (1995: 4) play themselves out; they know that they will not fit into India, but they want to return to what they remember as India. Some who are not planning to return claim that life there is too different because of the economic, political, and social changes in India. In this recognition there is no pretense of belonging in India. This is why most are purchasing NRI flats where other diasporic individuals will be living.[11] But just as they do not belong in India, they feel that they do not belong in Britain either. Moreover, difficulties of belonging in Britain do not refer to relationships outside the "ethnic group" since even relations with other Hindu Punjabis prove difficult for some. For example, one Aunty complained that in Britain "you're limited in choice with who your [Asian] friends are. It's so superficial and people always say, 'This is what we do' [referring to money and jobs]. They are so superficial and nouveau riche." Within the Asian minority, there is the Hindu Punjabi minority, and within them, only a few in the potential social circle with whom one may have an affinity or friendship.

The remainder of Aunty's narrative is worth exploring at length, because it further illustrates the distinctive elements of this neomyth of return. Referring to plans to move to India after retirement, Aunty said:

This was my brain child in 1990. I booked the property and we have been building ever since. My cousin [MZ's daughter] is different. She has a different attitude than I have, loves the life here. And her husband, he'd really like to go back to India. You see Indian women even through docile and calm we always get our way [with a laugh]. That's why even though my husband does not want to go to India, we are building a flat there and her husband who desperately wants to go back [but they] are staying here. I'm so pro-India, if my husband had married my cousin they would have lived happily ever after here.

I asked, "But Aunty, why go to India?" She began responding with her cousin's husband's reasons:

For one thing his mother is there [her cousin's husband]; he likes the relaxed attitude — meeting one another. Over here you are chasing your shadow. My attraction is that it's so much fun there — my brothers are there; it's a holiday. Here you're limited in choice with who your friends are. It's so superficial and people always say, "This is what we do" [referring to money and jobs]. They are so superficial and nouveau riche. The Brits are cold like the climate; the weather here is awful. I can't stand the weather. I have lived up and down this country and you never get to know them, I mean really inside. And do we go to the pub?

She trailed off, perhaps remembering a visit to the pub, or an incident when the decision was made not to go in, or a request to her husband. I can only conjecture about what her change in voice and tone meant. We were speaking on the telephone, and I had no other signals to indicate what she had meant by the oblique reference to the pub. I assume that she was referring to her perception of the main way of socializing in Britain. She continued, "We moved back to India in 1970, for the children and the life. We went for eight months and could have stayed our lives. But we thought that the working standards were poor and that there was loads of corruption. We decided against it and took the sale sign off the notice-board. We were back here. We didn't belong there."

They may have realized that they did not belong in India more than twenty years ago, but now they are making retirement plans in India with the *six months here, six months there* "clause" firmly repeated. Furthermore, Aunty's narrative reveals that the myth of return is not a lifelong dream of return. This return was toyed with, reconsidered, attempted, forgotten, and then pursued.

What has allowed the myth to return? Transformations in economic and political factors precipitated the myth during the migrants' working lifetime in Britain. Political and economic changes have encouraged the migrant's to modify their perceptions. Most migrants with whom I worked did not expect to be treated as differently as they had been when they arrived in Britain. Most were from "good" families and had previously only experienced "the best" of the British. Perhaps one of the most significant events, which focused this realization, was Amin's forced exodus of Asians from East Africa. Of those with whom I did my research a few had either been expelled from East Africa, or had friends or relatives who had come to Britain after the crisis, or have become friends with those who had left. Nevertheless, the knowledge of Asian exile from Uganda, of the forced removal of economically well-established households like the Madhvanis, has become a part of people's experience of Britain. The exodus of East African Asians had not only an effect on the refugees but also on the Asians who were already resident in England, especially those in London where the arrivals first landed and were covered extensively on the media. Although Britain helped the East African Asian refugees get settled, for those already in Britain watching the exodus changed their sense of Britain. In the sense that, the view of the refugees made them question their security in their passports, in their citizenship, and diminish their belief in their rights. The undercurrent of not belonging was brought forth by the knowledge that people who for a century had called East Africa home were being forced to leave. This is perhaps not surprising since calls for "Asian" repatriation continued until the early 1980s. In oblique references to the exodus, some of the parental generation would state, "If we have to leave this country, India is the only place that we can go."[12] The Hindu Punjabi migrant generation's reference to the exodus are founded on their experiences of being a minority in Britain. Their words reflect their negotiation of their space of difference by reference to specific places. This is not a question of a specific response to racism, but rather a fear being British, and yet of not belonging in Britain, which makes India the de facto homeland.

My response is to a specific construction of India as the unquestioned homeland. Instead of inferring that the act of leaving India inevitably constitutes India as the homeland for the migrants, I suggest that it is only in the context of their specific histories that India has become the homeland. Or perhaps it is still in the process of becoming the homeland. Part of this transformation lies in how India itself imagined its migrants. The majority of the migrant generation left India shortly after the country gained independence from Britain. After their migration, two parallel processes occurred simultaneously: the process of making India into the homeland, and the process of making India a nation. These two processes are parallel, yet the homeland and the nation are different, a difference partially set in motion by their migration. The making of India into a homeland for these migrants therefore is not caused only their experiences in Britain of negation (of feeling not British) and rejection (anxieties of belonging), for there have been changes in India regarding those who leave "her shores."

Before independence, attitudes toward those who left India were generally hostile. Those who were co-opted into the indentured labor system were shipped around the world, including to places like South Africa, Fiji, and Guyana. Their return to India provided the first opportunity for those who lead the nation into independence to clarify their views on "Overseas Indians."[13] Mahatma Gandhi, referring to the South African returnees to Calcutta, stated:

These men are neither Indians nor colonial[s]. They have no Indian culture in the foreign land they go to, save what they pick up from their uncultured, half-disindianized parents. They are not colonial in that they are debarred access to the colonial [that is] Western culture. They are therefore out of the frying pan into the fire. There they at least had some money and a kind of home. Here they are social lepers not even knowing the language of the people. (qtd. in Mohapatra 1996)

After India gained independence, the nation explicitly did not create itself as a homeland. For instance, Pundit Nehru, Prime Minister of India, "was afraid that any attempt by his government to cultivate overseas Indians or even to take a keen interest in their affairs might be seen as an inter-ference in the internal affairs of another country. He was also worried that it might expose the precariously positioned Indians to the charge of divided loyalty" (Parekh 1992: 147). But economic reforms in India and the establishment of the migrants and their children have changed these terms of reference. The once dreaded "overseas Indian" has become the coveted "Non-Resident Indian."[14] The term "NRI" is loaded with con-notations of longing and belonging, albeit initiated because of the Indian government's need for foreign investments.[15] The creation of the non-resident Indian has been called the "prototype for transnational capital-ist classes" (Shukla 2001: 565). A category with its basis in material con-cerns, it is also a category fostering the idea of an imaginary link. To be a non-resident Indian is to be an "Indian" away from home. The new "People of Indian Origins" card and the ten-year visas granted to "NRIs" both reveal the ways in which the governance of this new identification is implicated in the nation-state. India has transformed itself into the homeland. The transformation makes national identities like "Indian" normative. The change also brings back the underlying metaphor of the migrant as a permanent sojourner. In this instance, however, the cause is not rejection by the putative host country but instead the changed poli-cies of the "sending country." This change in status, moreover, moves beyond economic concerns. For example, Hindu revivalism and com-munal politics have also begun to posit India as a sacred homeland, the "*pitra-bhumi*" for diasporic Hindus.

The shift was not sudden. When the Indian government realized that there were problems for Indians in Africa it set up consultative commit-tees regarding its overseas population. The Indian High Commissioner to London at the time of my fieldwork, Dr. L. M. Singhvi, graciously granted me a telephone interview. As the chair of the High-Level Com-mittee on the Indian Diaspora, he has observed and petitioned for changes regarding official Government of India policy. We discussed the terms and official responses to "Overseas Indians." As High Commis-sioner his duties included events that involved many British Asians.[16] As an officiate of the government in a key posting, his role was to be the icon for India in Britain. He recounted some of the debates taking place when he served as member of Parliament in India, particularly the ways in which India became concerned with its émigrés. During the period of which we spoke, many who migrated to Britain still held Indian passports and thus fell under the "care" of the international Indian embassies and commissions. He explains:

When I was a cross bencher in 1962 there was an enormous issue of what was happening as far as our people were concerned. I was the vice-chairman of the Africa Centre. . . . I came to the conclusion that the Government of India had legal and moral obligations to relate to people, Indians, in Africa. We owed it to them, they had gone as indentured labor, they were sent under arrangement with the Government of India [GOI], from Bihar, from Calcutta, from the South, and the GOI was obliged to look after them . . . but there was no sympathetic considerations from the bureaucracy. Punditji [referring to Nehru] as an internationalist wondered how could GOI have interventionist view in overseas community? He thought they must integrate, a very romantic view, and they should not look to the GOI for support. . . . There was a change in reception during the time of Lal Bhadur Shastri, and he said this was important, but he died during the Indo-Pak war [1965–67]. Then I took up this matter with Indira Gandhi. On this I must say she was truly on the uptake and very supportive. . . . She sent me abroad, going to these parts where Indians were to give reports. That's when I went to Trinidad, Guyana, and Africa. . . . This started a whole new chapter in our thinking about overseas Indians.

During the early period, India had no official interest in those who had left India. His words reveal the changed perceptions of those running the nation. Dr. Singhvi continued and elaborated on the phrase "NRI."

NRI is a concept which has to be defined by law. It is one with an Indian passport but nonresident — for more than 179 days or there will be problems with taxation at home. In Indian law you may be and may not be an NRI; there's great chaos and confusion. When we were selling bonds, it was a very loose definition, but for tax benefits it was used in a restricted sense. Every law has its own reference of NRI; it's a very open term. . . . I've given it a more positive connotation as the National Reserve of India.

Dr. Singhvi's positive connotation reveals how the government wishes to fete the migrants, some of whom departed India thirty years ago. The interest in the NRI is not met with enthusiasm on the ground in India. In Delhi at least, there is a joke circulating that NRI is an acronym for Not Required Indians.

In any case, Dr. Singhvi himself indicated that he did not like the implications of the term "NRI." Instead of a negative connotation he wanted to institute a positive one. He had thought of "'Persons of Indian Origin,' and identity by referring to origin, but it was too long." He continued:

Indogenic came naturally to me — I thought it already existed — I looked into the ten-volume *Oxford Dictionary,* but it said that those people who produce Indigo. Nevertheless, I began using the word 'Indogenic,' in a sense of Indian origin. It was a term that came naturally to me. Prakash Shastri [MP], a Hindi speaker, and myself as a Sanskritist and Hindi speaker coined "Bharat Vanshi," a racial concept implying "in origin," "personal genealogy," and it also implied cultural pedigree.

The many phrases that were being discussed highlight the different attempts to position and centralize India as "homeland." The play with creating new terms for those who left would inextricably bind the migrants to India. With the large numbers of second-, third-, and fourth-generation Indians around the world, the ideal term needed to be expandable and flexible and inclusive. The concern with terminology reveals the changes in the nation-state and the conscious shifts that have created India as the "homeland." Moreover, that people were moving back and forth to India for visits revealed how the Indian nation-state also had to imagine these people anew in political ways.

In 1999 the "People of Indian Origin" card (PIO) was introduced. Overseen by the Ministry of External Affairs, the card is issued by the Indian embassies at a cost of $1,000 USD for a period of twenty years. In a parliamentary address by the President of India on February 22, 1999, the NRI were stated to be "part of the great global Indian family. Their emotional, cultural, social and economic links with India are a source of great strength to us. The Government has approved the Persons of Indian Origin [PIO] Card Scheme. This permits visa-free entry and offers other facilities to persons of Indian origin who are citizens of other countries."[17] By March 31, 1999, the PIO scheme was finalized in an official announcement by the Union Home Minister: "Under this Scheme, Persons of Indian Origin up to the fourth generation (great grand parents) settled throughout the world, except for a few specified countries, would be eligible."[18] The PIO benefits wave the visa requirement for entry and permit a stay of 180 days, 30 days after which registration with the Foreigners Registration Officer is required. Also, in economic terms, the scheme provides for:

Acquisition, holding, transfer and disposal of immovable properties in India except of agricultural/plantation properties; Admission of children in educational institutions in India under the general category quota for NRIs — including medical/engineering colleges, IITs, IIMs etc. Various housing schemes of Life Insurance Corporation of India, State Governments and other Government agencies.[19]

It is clearly stated that PIO card holders "shall not enjoy political rights in India."[20] This card indicates the ways India, as a homeland, has changed with respect to imagining its emigrants. Far from the earlier understandings, the PIO card is a clear attempt by the government to "renewing and strengthening the emotional bond amongst PIOs with the land of their origin . . . [to] exhort them to play an increasingly constructive role in the socio-economic and cultural development of the country of their origin." The PIO card revitalizes the connections between community, culture, identity, and belonging.

Additional reforms in India are also enabling these reconnections. External Affairs has dedicated a portal to the diaspora (Indiandiaspora .nic.in), which functions as a novel attempt at a sustained interface on culture, trade, and citizenship. The Ministry appointed R.C. Sharma as the "Additional Secretary in charge of NRIs" and convened a government-appointed Diaspora Committee, chaired by Dr. Singhvi, which conducted a global fact-finding mission. Beyond PIO cards and websites, the Government of India has actively responded to the Report produced by the High Level Committee on the Indian Diaspora. In January 2003, the Indian PM, Atal Bihari Vajpayee, announced dual-citizenship rights to nationals of seven select countries (including the U.S., the U.K., Canada, and Australia). Significantly, the declaration was made at the first annual Pravasi Bharatiya Divas, held January 9–13. This initiative of the Government of India was "the largest gathering of the global Indian Family . . . to engage with all NRIs/PIOs to understand their sentiment about India, their expectations from India, and to propose a policy framework for creating a more conducive environment for their sustained and productive interaction with India and her people" (http://www.indiaday .org/nri/index1.htm). These recent developments indicate a changed relationship between India and its émigrés.

These recent changes are part of a longer history established by such instrumental figures as Dr. Singhvi, R.C. Sharma, and others. It is the most recent imagination of the Indian nation that now constructs itself as the homeland for those up to the fourth generation, which, taking each generation to be 30 years, includes the last 120 years of migration out of India. In effect, what counts as India comes from the 1935 British Government of India Act. The current PIO application form clearly states that India can be "any other territories which His Majesty in Council may . . . declare to be a part of India."[21] This reveals the cartographic imaginary inherent in disapora, and one can only assume that His Majesty, long deceased, is no longer in the habit of declaring territories.

For the migrants to Britain who left India up to forty years ago, to which India and to which "home" are they returning? Many know and recognize the changes in India and in Britain, which have allowed for the plans of return. I asked one woman in the temple if she would return to India, a question prompted by her candid statement: "I hate this country! We should have never left India. I am too used to the life there; it's an easy life, I am used to servants — here you have to do everything yourself." Despite this seeming pining for the putative "good life" her response to my question was, "Oh no, we couldn't go back to settle there; we are not used to the life. No we are here" (as if to be somehow trapped in this pining imaginary). She was a later migrant, arriving to Britain in the 1970s after she married a man who had migrated to Britain from Iran (his grandparents had settled there from India). Despite her own definite rejection of return, there are people from the same temple who, reciting their the six-month mantra, are going to India. On their return to Britain they glorify the lifestyle in India, while keeping a watchful eye on the favorable rate of exchange, for this is what transforms them into kings and queens. The memories of their home in India are for a home that has come to exist in specific ways because of the work of the Indian nation. Before the decision to return, or to buy property, in India, they have had ongoing connections. Of the core-research families, all the parents had been to India for a visit within the last two years, and they had visited many times. Others, too, spoke of their vacations and holidays in India. Sometimes this was for a family wedding or ceremony, other times just to meet with their relations.

How is India being constructed as the homeland? One significant clue is the location to which people eventually return. The neomyth of return incorporates a reformulated homeland: when Hindu Punjabis speak of home they often mean Delhi.[22] Hindu Punjabi migrants who want to return "home" buy property in *Delhi,* which is not in present-day Punjab. Some, of course, had come from families who had moved to Delhi after the Partition. They had then migrated to the United Kingdom; for the others, those who migrated to the United Kingdom from Punjab (that is, who were not from refugee families), some of their families or spouse's families have since established themselves in Delhi. Moreover, many of the migrant's siblings have also migrated outside of India around the world. There was a clear division between those who wished to return and those who did not; notably, those who had siblings around the world really had no desire to resettle in India.

The plan for return is not an indication that migrants' allegiances have been permanently elsewhere, as implied by the assumptions of former conservative MPs infamous "cricket test" of allegiance to Britain, in which one's allegiance to Britain could be tested based on the team one supported in a cricket match. Rather, the neomyth of return suggests that there have been structural social changes that have allowed the possibilities of a return to India. New in its desires and potentials, old in its use of memory, this myth is not going to fade away as an aberration or stage in the migrant's establishment in Britain. The Aunty who was branded an Indophile by her husband was preparing to go "home" to an NRI flat in Delhi. The fact that she plans to stay for "six months here and there" reveals they will be transnational sojourners and perhaps also that a permanent "home" is lost for the migrant: after she leaves Britain her only permanent home will be that of memory.

What then are the implications for diaspora? It should be clear by now that the "jostling of terms" (Clifford 1994) for what to call those living in various states of displacement or movement is not restricted to academics trying to specify various experiences of movement across borders. As Dr. Singhvi's quotations reveal, the postcolonial governments are also reconsidering their terminology. The Indian nation is differently imagining its emigrants. Coupled with the specifically national definitions of ethnicity assumed in Britain (and here I again emphasize how in the British census national terms such as "Indian," "Pakistani," and "Bangladeshi" are used as distinct ethnic categories) have made belonging to the Subcontinent a *natural* assumption. But, in fact, there are no easy identifications for these people, as Indians or Britons. For Hindu Punjabis who plan to enjoy part of their retirement in India, they are not "Indian" but "British" NRIs. The same holds true of their children who become British when they leave India. One of my interlocutors was asked in an interview with the British press if he felt British or Indian, or if the question itself missed the point. His response was telling: "It's salient. . . . What I've had to realize is that I am who I am. I'm not defined by concepts of nationality or religion, or anything else that anyone wants to apply to me. The BJP would probably want to define me through religion, and the BNP would probably want to define me by the colour of my skin."[23] The youth experience being Indian as a changing claim on their identity, just as their parents no doubt have experienced being Indian. Each becomes British in certain ways and responds accordingly. The jostling of terms in the diaspora is a jostling of identifications and claims to their identity based on shifting notions of what it means to be an insider and an outsider: at first the migrants were simultaneously Vilayati and Asian, now they are British and NRI.[24]

The implications of the parental return to India for six-month sojourns are yet to be realized. The NRI subdivisions are relatively recent developments; these are quite new areas in Delhi. During my fieldwork, peo-

ple were only buying these planned properties; as Britons they were buying into changed understandings of themselves constructed by both
nation-states. Their "six-months" mantra as well as the changing policies
of the Indian and British governments have lead them to complex notions
of identification based on belonging. Such a vision fundamentally revises
the paradigm that premises ethnicity as an end product of globalization,
by seeing the Indian nation-state as actively *creating* its diaspora. I have
shown how the production of difference is contingent on national agendas, which are not de facto identities, but ones that are in constant active
construction.

In the end, these people do not constitute a "community" going (or
not going) "home": they are a people who have complex ties to who they
are and, "since history has intervened, who they have become" (S. Hall
1990: 225). Their children live in Britain and only occasionally visit India.
The children have cousins in Canada and the United States. For now, they
will face an equally complex future of belonging, implicated by their parent's decision to "return" and by the new constructions of belonging
advanced by India and Britain. Being British precisely at the moment of
departure from Britain is a telling symptom of how community, identity,
and ethnicity are constructed around issues of difference premised on
movement. The circulation of themselves, capital, and consumer items
takes their relationships beyond a homeward orientation to also be connected to the United States, Canada, Hong Kong, and so on. What is
emerging in the experiences of difference is a sense of South Asian con-
nectedness across the global terrain, premised not on a homeward orientation, but one in which the nostalgia for culture is being produced or
shattered. Interactions and sharing of cultural change, discussions of
belonging, and experiences of complex cultural citizenship all are working to construct India as a homeland, but as the fact-finding activities of
the high-level committee of the Indian diaspora reveals, there is no de
facto equation between culture, community, and identity. Rather, there
is a constant refashioning of various primordial and circumstantial
identifications as coalesced or questioned by the changing nation-state
policies. The migrants move to India is not a return home, but a result of
the reconstructing and refashioning of home as a result of official policy
changes in which India attempts to position itself as the homeland. This
response is a result of the experiences of exclusion felt by the migrants and
their children in Britain. To continue to see their "return" and fascination
for India in terms of a "natural" turn to home leaves unquestioned the
role of the nation-state in creating and sustaining the nostalgia for culture.

CHAPTER 8

"Where Are You *Originally* From?"

Multiculturalism, Citizenship,
and Transnational Differences

Is ethnicity nothing but . . . what ethnicity does? Is ethnic selfhood
an end in itself, or is it a necessary but deterministic phase to be left
behind when the time is right to inaugurate the "post ethnic"?

Radhakrishnan, *Diasporic Mediations*

I have explored ethnographically how Punjabi, Hindu, Asian, Black, Indian, and British identifications are produced by people. In focusing on the spaces of difference that make being and becoming Vilayati, Asian, Punjabi, Hindu, Black, British, NRI, and PIO potential identifications for people, I have highlighted the role of claims to cultural knowledge and agency that create specific constructions of collective agency within the transnational frame. Transnationalism is a modality of lived experience in which migrants constantly and subtlety (re-)create globalization through their choices and negotiations of identification. The articulation of a "third space" (Bhabha 1990a, 1990b) disrupts any easy understandings of HP identity and instead emphasizes analytical framework of the play between constructions of *being British* and *becoming South Asian*. The individual and collective formations of HP knowledge and agency challenge the idea that ethnic minorities are merely the products of globalization. Instead, opening up the discussion that identity, community, and ethnicity are equated within the notion of culture reveals how London HPs are deeply implicated by the cultural changes inherent in globalization in their everyday lives. The disruptions and negotiations, the possibilities of being and becoming HP, form in the spaces of difference between ethnicity, identity, community culture, and nation for minorities. Without that space of difference, South Asian migrants are extensions of a prior culture, displaced and yet forever connected to the nation of their emigration. Instead of a framework based on a rearticulation of the tension between the homeland and land of adoption, in which cultural change and cultural clash remain the main analytic concepts for connecting people across the transnational terrain, I have instead argued that time and space rework identity, ethnicity, and community as changing, constantly negotiated, and existing in moments. Below, I reexamine the role of the nation-state — in this case, that of the so-called receiving society — to explore one final aspect of how and why the nostalgia for culture flourishes. By way of a conclusion, I wish to examine how difference plays out in the lives of those we study as a result of the processes of transnationalism as inscribed through the nation via multiculturalism.

Difference and the British Nation-State

Unlike nations that have a relatively recent history of migration, such as Canada, Australia, or America, the British nation and indeed the nations of the European Union define themselves in terms of internal homogeneity and an imagined autochthonous citizenship. For the case of England, this is ironic

since the English cannot — and indeed have never tried to — trace their heritage back to a single homogeneous linguistic, cultural and biological source. However distinctive English traditions may be, they are by common consent the outcome of a complex admixture of Norman, Scandinavian, Saxon traditions with yet more ancient Celtic elements. Nevertheless a more or less homogeneous set of social, cultural, linguistic and religious conventions which could be categorically labelled as "English" gradually began to crystallise out from these strongly creole origins, and in that process two events appear to have been of critical importance: firstly Henry VIII's break with papal authority 1533, and secondly his daughter Elizabeth's construction of an explicitly Protestant English state in the aftermath of her sister's Mary's brief pro-Catholic reign. (R. Ballard 1999: 3)

Ballard indicates that there was

a newly crystallized sense of Englishness [which] played a crucial role in stabiliz-
ing this whole enterprise. First of all it played a key role in establishing the external boundary of the English state, on the grounds that the one thing that an
Englishman could not be was the subject of a foreign potentate or power — and
most notably of the Pope; secondly, and perhaps yet more importantly still, this
same imagery was used to secure a sense of national homogeneity — and hence of
ethnic solidarity — amongst those included within that boundary. (R. Ballard
1999: 3)

The shifting sense of English identity has variously encouraged a solidarity around the people, church, Parliament, and crown. Class identity
also played a large role in shaping British identity, a term with origins
designed to unite the aristocracy (Cannadine 1990). Importantly, Britain
has had a history, through its Acts of Exclusion of dealing with those who
did not come under the umbrella of purported solidarity. These minorities, particularly religious minorities such as the Catholics, the Hugue-
nots, and the Jews, variously experienced being "second-class citizens" (R.
Ballard 1999). The imaged autochthony of the nation is crucial to understanding the history of a sense of internal homogeneity and previous ways
of dealing with minorities through official exclusion.

Leaving aside historical notions of hegemonic definitions of identity,
the modern concern with immigration in the United Kingdom and the
resulting policies address an underlying assumption of how to define the
nation-state (Fryer 1984; Yuval-Davis and Anthias 1992). The repeated
mainstream concerns claimed by politicians are the concerns of a "host
society" — the need to restrict numbers and control borders. The fact that
Britain has one of the most restrictive immigration policies in Europe did
not hinder the push for an asylum-seekers–oriented Immigration Bill,
which sought to restrict refugees attempting to escape hardship and was
not aimed at curtailing economic immigrants (previous policies had
diminished immigration to a trickle) and in September 2000 the Department of Employment announced revisions in the work permit scheme
that "aimed to speed up the system to meet skill shortages while 'pro-
tecting' the jobs of UK citizens."[1] "Political debates and media coverage
of 'economic migrants' and 'asylum-seekers' during the late 1990s has
served to reinforce the view that minorities who are perceived as not sharing the dominant political and social values of British society pose a threat
to social stability and cohesion" (Schuster and Solomos 2001: 8). The government rallies around the connection between immigration and economics, creating a specific ideology of belonging that perpetually rejects
migrants and their children (as the talk of migrant repatriation, that is, of
sending immigrants home, during the 1970s and 1980s reveals).

The voices of what constitutes Britain have always been diverse. From the (Northern) Irish to the Scots and the Welsh with their new assemblies, from the various gendered voices, the flippantly labeled Blair's Babes, to the class distinctions that continue to operate in many different ways. In England, there is a call to rethink the nation-state itself.

We need a new England. The old one is no good. It is made up of half-remembered war stories, imperial guilt, disappeared green acres and the cringe, snobbery and xenophobia left behind from the glory days like a scummy chemical residue. The old England is the England whose nationalism makes liberals flinch. It is a fake, mis-remembered place, the Home Counties without the North, the Royals but not the radicals, the imperialism but not the passionate non-conformism. That England has lost the faith and now stands by, watching the Scots do their thing and the damned continentals do theirs. For the real English, the people of today's country, it [the image of jolly ol' England] has got in the way.[2]

The nation imagined as jolly ol' England is being challenged for many social and economic reasons.[3] A letter to *The London Times* in 1993 offered that schools teach children a notion of British culture that "is dominated by the values of the British Empire in its heyday." There has been a recent spate of books, the products of public intellectual outcry tempered with academic treatises, which reveal the deep-seated anxiety of the demise of Britain (these works include *After Britain: The Abolition of Britain* [Hitchens 2000], *The Day Britain Died* [Marr 2000], *In Memory of England* [Vansittart 1998], *"There Ain't no Black in the Union Jack"* [Gilroy 1987], *The Channel Tunnel and English Identity* [Darian-Smith 1999], and the British Council Report *Looking into England* [2000][4]). Each of these tomes brings forth a complex of genealogies that highlights various aspects of the passing of "traditional" British values and freedoms. The role of immigration and demographic changes are noted in these ideas.

Immigration, one of the key aspects of these public debates about national identity, remains a touchstone for the British press to be symbolic of a direct assault on jolly ol' England. This is fostered by allusions to the potential flood of illegal immigrants, refugee asylum seekers, and recent changes to work permits. The modified public image of the nation-state was not only due to straightforward immigration. The British Parliament has passed increasingly restrictive immigration policies throughout the last thirty years. Rather, the demographic growth of the minority populations has occurred because of the birth of second and third generations. Demographically this has changed the character of the Asian minority population to be younger and British born. Thus, the nature of who constitutes the Asian minority has also shifted since the postwar migration.

Currently, it consists of a large number of British-born youths who are changing and challenging the public face of Britain in various ways. As minority populations have grown, one official response to the diversity was to take up a policy of multiculturalism.

The migration of people such as Aunty Rani and Uncle Prem and the birth of their children have made cultural diversity an issue for modern liberal nation-states such as Britain, the United States, and Canada.[5] Each of these democracies has conceived of differences in a fashion that makes a problem of their internal heterogeneity. The implementations and understandings of "multiculturalism" vary between individual nation-states.[6] In Britain, multiculturalism has developed into a concern for disadvantage and advocating a pluralist model of democracy that is *tolerant* of minorities.[7] The British conceptualization of multiculturalism is based on a model of fair benevolence and assumption of assimilation, which characterized the nation's colonial history. This concern for minority diversity has a double-edged quality; it is simultaneously a source of celebration and concern.

Multiculturalism is the official policy for minorities, and immigration policies affect those seeking entry into Britain. These are very different sets of issues, yet the debates on immigration in Britain, as elsewhere, are de facto tied to the issue of the existing minorities and the composition of society. The press, local and national governments, policymakers, and elected officials conflate them and connect these issues as they attempt to comprehend and represent diversity. The liberal democratic framework is on a political continuum with respect to minority issues. On the one end are those who press for group rights, and on the other are those who see the individual as the basis for any political action (Appiah 1994; I. Young 1990; Habermas 1994; C. Taylor 1994). As such, the debates on minority issues run to the core of the nature of the democratic nation-state. The whole spectrum of dealing with diversity has involved a specific spotlight on cultural difference. Some scholars have indicated the dangers of making diversity a matter of public policy: "At best, it transfers some of the practice of oppression into the political realm. . . . A system, which recognizes difference politically or publicly, does not necessarily confer advantages on the differentiated group. It may make the group more visible, but it does not make it more powerful- particularly if it is a small minority" (Kukathas 1997: 133). The policies and attempts to grapple with minorities, in other words, do not erase differences, but rather solidify them and in specific ways enshrine them within the nation-state.

The co-option of culture into the sociopolitical realm has "officialize[d] difference as a matter of individual's a priori membership in collective groups" (Greenhouse 1998: 13). The sense of identity as being constantly constructed and negotiated and reconstructed is completely missed. Multiculturalism, as adopted by many nation-states, has amplified the sense of difference felt by ethnic minorities. Recalling Aunty Krishna's observation that she sensed things had changed and "are worst now," I would suggest this is her response to the combined effect of multiculturalism that has been to "singularize difference" (Greenhouse 1998: 14) and conflate difference with issues of immigration. Or perhaps it is her sense that these discussions are much more public, that diversity is in the open and therefore limits her "self identification in other terms" (Greenhouse 1998: 13). Other parents also alluded to their sense of change, but they could not indicate to me how or why things had changed, just that they also sensed that "things are worse now." Their understandings of change for the worse is a discontent with overt difference in which they are more visible as a minority group, though they are not any more powerful. In other words, I trace their response to a constant accountability of difference encouraged by multiculturalism. This becomes a "pressure to choose an identity prefigured in official discourse that constitutes the hegemonic aspect of liberalism" (Greenhouse 1998: 15). The sense of identity that gets constructed in multiculturalism limits the potential identity that is possible, which constitutes a liberal hegemony of identification whereby ethnic identity is possible only under terms that give a certainty to ethnicity.

The people I worked with in Britain, both the parental migrant generation and the children, lived through and experienced the development of "multicultural" Britain, which began in earnest during the 1980s. The specific history of its evolution in the United Kingdom can be connected with the earlier context of race relations. During the 1970s the liberal voice was overshadowed by Powellism, which questioned the allegiance of people like Aunty Rani and her children to Britain (the often quoted "cricket match test" is a case in point).[8] The concern was *when were migrants going to stop being different and assimilate,* when were they were going to become *British?* Migrants during this period were generally characterized as inassimilable or in a perpetual state of assimilation. During the iron-fisted rule of Thatcher in Britain, this concern with assimilation transformed into a concern for multiculturalism. The construction of two separate spheres and the stress on assimilation continues as a muted public obsession with the putative culture clash between children and parents (a topic that elicited considerable media interest during my fieldwork). During the

1980s Black and Asian activists for equal opportunity fought for "separate but equal" platforms. For the migrants and their children, these decades solidified their sense that pure difference was the starting point for cultural understanding, reinscribed with a notion that two separate cultures existed and could meet. The 1990s signaled a shift in general perceptions of cultural difference, suggesting a move away from a clash of two dominant ideologies: thinking about identity as fluid and constructed as opposed to imagining it as rigid and fixed.[9]

These two poles have also characterized the trajectory of Asian community development in Britain. This is especially apparent in the lives of young Asians who form the second and third generation in Britain. On the one hand, for youths there is a popular culture scene that includes the music of the "Asian underground" in London, or the BBC television comedy serial that feature Asian and non-Asian characters in dialogue about cultural difference, such as "Goodness Gracious Me," as well as various artists who fuse and mix music, acting, language, and genre to create the ultimate cultural hybrid. On the other hand, there is a tendency for notions of fixed identity, such as evidenced in the Hindu student's movement, that has thoroughly gripped the postsecondary institutions in the United Kingdom (Raj 2000).[10] The two forms of identity politics are played out by Asian minority youths; many of the young Hindu Punjabis I met moved between these two notions of identity as becoming or being in their responses to their experiences in a multiracial multicultural state, one that requires minorities to define their own minority status by managing their difference.

Making Multicultural Citizens — Auditing Difference Through Tolerance

Multiculturalism is the product of a sociocultural environment in which "otherness" is an overt policy concern. Multiculturalism, as adopted by Britain, renders minority cultural difference as a problem to be overcome. To take one example of how this otherness is framed in modern Britain, let me turn to the final report of the United Kingdom's Advisory Group on "Education for Citizenship" and the "Teaching of Democracy in Schools" presented to the Secretary of State for Education and Employment in September 1998. This report is a recent example of how governments bureaucratize difference. The authors aim to promote active citizenship in the primary- and secondary-education system by shaping responsible young Britons with certain key qualities. The report outlines the main required qualities to be taught by the end of compulsory schooling. These include, but are not limited to, the following:

· equality and diversity as key concepts;

· a disposition to work with and for others with sympathetic understanding;

· the practice of tolerance; and

· the commitment of equal opportunities and gender equality and an ability to tolerate other viewpoints.[11]

These goals advocate, among other things, an acceptance of difference and even a sympathetic understanding of difference. At first glance the call for sympathetic treatment of cultural minorities indicates a changed official view, that it is important for citizenship issues that all members of the nation are taught how to understand others. As all such documents with specific policy overtones, it outlines the ideals worth striving for and lays bare the expectations of teaching citizenship and democracy in schools. This teaching is becoming a required aspect of British compulsory education and part of this curriculum will include the rhetoric of tolerance. However, what that tolerance involves is not clear. The development of multiculturalism in Britain and elsewhere has entailed the official recognition of minorities, the development has solidified notions of discreet cultural boundaries with absolute differences that perpetually need to be tolerated.

The concern for tolerance in citizenship education returns us full circle to Lord Paul's quotation from Chapter 1: "I want to see the word 'Asian' dropped out; we need to be British." His terminology invokes the complexities of modern understandings of identity that are intertwined with measures of accountability.[12] By calling for the absence of an ethnic qualification, Lord Paul's words indicate that some of those I studied, perhaps not all, want to move away from the focus on the rhetoric of difference as tolerance. However, the concern for accountability has pervaded everyday life. Tolerance, difference, and accountability are a potent Molotov cocktail, creating a sense of identity that is constantly from elsewhere and that has to perpetually account for and justify its own difference.

The collusion of the concepts of nation-state and ethnicity make clear how the ethnic is the perpetual other. The last census in Britain includes an "ethnicity" question. Yet it uses a very confusing set of categories, which understands national boundaries as part of the ethnic culture (thereby reproducing British understanding of both ethnicity and nationality).[13] The use of "Indian" as an ethnic category assumes an immutable connection to another nation-state despite immigration, a changed passport, or a British birth. "Indian" refers to a geopolitical entity and a relatively recent nation-state that gained independence only in 1947. However, the use of "Indian" as a nationalistic adjective for the migrant creates a constant immigrant syndrome, which perpetually assumes allegiance to another place. This was a common belief that was finally enshrined in law in the 1981 British Nationality Act that substituted *jus sangium* for *jus patrias*. In using Indian, Pakistani, and Bangladeshi as "ethnic" categories, the subtleties of distinctions that South Asians themselves profess are washed away in the tide to understand ethnicity in Britain. As Axel and others have noted, this way of thinking originated in an earlier period when the "colonial discourse generated a shifting theory of peoplehood, race, sect and caste for which the term *nation* was often a synonym" (Axel 2001: 5). With origins in the colonial period, this imagination of difference predicated on the (assumed to be homogenous) nation erases certain differences while stressing others. In other words, where are the Sindhis, Tamils, Punjabis, Bengalis, Sylhettis, or Gujaratis in these accounts?[14] Although each of these regional ethnic groups may not constitute statistically significant quantifiable entities in Britain, "Indian" for these people eclipses these boundaries and introduces another that is based on a difference constituted by a national imaginary, one imagined just as actively by India as by Britain. The differences within the category "Indian" are much greater than between "Indian" and "British."

The April 2001 census includes ethnic and religious terms that indicate some of the complexity. The possible answers to the question "What is your ethnic group" include: (a) White, (b) Mixed, and (c) Asian or Asian British, which is broken down further into the more familiar national imaginaries of ethnicity, namely, Indian, Pakistani, and Bangladeshi. This sense of national identity as conflated with ethnic identity is not limited to the Asian groups, for "(a) White" one may check mark "British" or "Irish" or "Any other White background" (with space to write in and indicate one's cultural background). Similarly, Section D on "Black British" contains the following boxes: "Caribbean," "African," and "Any other Black background" (again, with space to write in the details). In the collusion of the nation-state, locality is a clear indication for belonging in

Britain. What distinguishes Asian and Asian British? Those I worked with in London would most often use the phrases "British Asian" and "HP" to refer to themselves.

The politics of the accountable ethnic, that is, the official constitution of an ethnic group, are clear in the British census ethnic categories for Asian and Asian British — Indian, Pakistani, and Bangladeshi. As categories of "self-identification" these labels create a dangerous tautology of difference as natural and inherent. In Britain, it is clear that the categories of ethnic difference are marked by the ways the nation imagines its other in terms of a collection of distinct nationalities — the Scots, the Welsh (who are not marked as distinct), and the Irish (from Northern Ireland). In such a framework, the boxes "Indian," "Pakistani," and "Bangladeshi" are categories of *sedition* that permanently define ethnics in terms of their affiliation to a different nation-state. In the census, the individual self-identifies by checking off a box of identity. This is an act of accountability that forces one to accept a certain ethnic identification and glosses over the specific notions of ethnic identification as created by the myth of the multicultural nation. The need for such accountability is a question of governance in the colonial imagination (see Cohn 1996). This particular demarcation of identity is constituted by the nation-state. The use of the nation as a marker of identity frames ethnicity in terms of a "minority" status, which will never belong to the British state. In the long term, these are dangerous categorizations. While the "Asian community" is fracturing into "communities" of religious difference and calling for recognition of such distinctions, the nation-state readily identifies other differences by emphasizing ethnicity.[15] The specific forms of this emphasis highlight an alternative national identity (Indian, Pakistani, Bangladeshi) and thereby keep Asians distinct as a perpetual "other" in which ethnicity is first judged by phenotypic racial category.[16]

I should be clear here that I am not calling for more accurate census categories, nor am I reiterating the "familiar thought that the bureaucratic categories of identity must come up short before the vagaries of actual people's lives" (Appiah 1994: 163).[17] Instead I am exposing the specific construction of identity that is enshrined in an ethos of audit culture, how identity is thought of in terms of a management control in which people become agents for accounting for their difference. The census categories reveal much about the British imagination of itself as a multicultural nation. In this form of multiculturalism, the audit of difference produces an accountable ethnic. The Hindu Punjabis in Britain can only check off the box marked "Indian." The category implicitly suggests that one is not from

Britain; however, perhaps "Asian British" is meant to mark some sort of inclusion. Moreover, by using nation-states as categories of ethnic difference assumes that there is no change in ethnic identity over time. An absolute notion of cultural difference is perpetuated through the generations. According to the census, Aunty Rani is Indian and so are her children.

These census categories read alongside the call for citizenship make for a perpetuation of difference based on nostalgia for culture. The rhetoric of tolerance being institutionalized in the curriculum in the United Kingdom is worrying and reveals the ironic solipsism inherent in national policies that officiate difference. It has been argued that "liberal politics, in pursuing the ideals of an individualist egalitarianism, is essentially assimilationist in spirit" (Kukathas 1997: 133). In light of its liberal idealism the key goals of the citizenship report has less to do with ethnic minorities and more to do with the British imagination of itself as a nation-state. Part of this imagination reinscribes notions of Britain as a group of islands bound together by people's fine art of demarcating differences based on locality (for those who claim to be from "up north" or the "Southeast" or "London," all of which are infused with local complex meanings and allegiances). Within this constant engagement with difference based on place, British minorities experience an alterity that combines ethnicity, belonging, and transnationalism. These are the chess pieces in the game of multicultural representation. The concern for tolerance, as stated in the citizenship report, shows how overcoming ethnic difference will always be something that the British nation-state needs to strive for, a goal, rather than something that can be achieved. As such, difference can never be erased unless it becomes an inherent aspect of the imagination of the British nation-state itself.

Impressions of Multiculturalism: Karnal Bhandari on Being British and the European Identity Crisis

During fieldwork, a friend offered his own impressions of how the British nation has changed during his lifetime. Karnal Bhandari offered his reflections on the complexity of categorizing members of the Asian diaspora because of the identity crisis Britons were facing in light of the formation of the European Union:

There are other pressures that are worrying the diasporic Asians. Particularly amongst Asians a lot of those pressures are to do with the fact that we are in a country, which in itself is having a massive problem of what it is. . . . And the big question is, especially in relation to Europe, what are the English? English as a tool has been a synonym for Great Britain. But by now it is clear that the Scots do not think of themselves as English, the Welsh don't think of themselves as English; they are Welsh. There is a clarity of that; there is a clarity in Irish.

These words reveal how the use of national categories for ethnic groups is not new for Great Britain, in fact, this is the way in which they have historically understood their "minorities" such as the Welsh, the Scots, and the Irish. In such a framework, Asians were simply co-opted into this scheme. He continued speaking about challenges the European Union posed for the English, a label he claimed for himself in interesting ways, and then clearly indicated how the challenges of European unification for Britain, influenced his choice of identities.

The demand of Europe is, clearly, do we become a monolith? Or do we assert our distinction? That's what every country is doing, its distinction. Now where does that distinction actually lie? What is English? What is it to become English? Recently on a discussion program where they were asking in what sense do you see yourself as English, British and European? [For] the Scots and the Welsh their answer initially was "OK first of all I am British, then I am a Welshman"; English is to be resisted. Now the Englishman is different seeing the cultures as synonymous, seeing English as British. [The Englishman interviewed on the program said:] "So I would say that I am an Englishman first, a British person second, and a European third." Then they asked this Black man who was from the Caribbean, whose parents were from the Caribbean but [he] was from here, and they asked him, "How do you see yourself?" [His] kind of assumption of Englishness, now is carrying a whole other wave. . . . See, when the Englishman said "Englishman" prior to this particular predicament [of Europe], he meant Britain and that's a direct result of empire.

His quotation establishes that identification with being British has had to change because of the European "predicament" and a seeming engagement with the question "Is European Citizenship possible?" (Balibar 1996). Karnal goes on to reveal how the Asian sense of Britain has changed, how migration has changed Britain. His challenge lies in how people from the former colonies have come to claim Britain.

You see, now when we [Asians] came over, the sense of Britain was not of Wales. No one knew where the hell Wales was. London in fact stood for the whole country — "*o London ja reya*" [he's going to London]. Vilayat [variably translatable as "Outside," "England," or "London"]. It was that sense of England. That was kind of a colonial legacy — shaped that colonial legacy and that is what I find kind of interesting now. Today a West Indian is not apart from the Englishman in

Europe. That's almost like taking on the territory of empire but you know in a way reversing it. . . . At the moment I actually assume a Saxoness in a real sense more than Anglo-Saxons do.

He paints a rosy picture of a changed inclusive identity. He attributes the European "question" with changing the power dynamics of naming and categorization so much so that he and other minorities can claim to be the "Englishman in Europe." I challenged his inclusive vision of Europe, which would categorize him as British. In fact, I pointed out to him, the best retort for his vision came from the ways in which Hindu Punjabis and other Asians used "English" and "British" as a gloss for "white" and multicultural was a gloss for nonwhite. I argued that this gloss indicated that the young people and their parents did not envision themselves as ever being British, but forever being non-British. In Britain the only identification open to them was either "Asian," which many young people were rejecting, or "Indian," which seemed to smack of allegiance to a different nation-state. He conceded, "I think you are absolutely right," and continued to tell me more about his own experience of being a minority in a place where many different cultures meet. He said, "That's absolutely true and in a way I find that even reflecting in myself, in my own thinking that I have had to have a pause. I am absolutely convinced now that there actually is no meeting of the races, the cultures; there are only encounters across the borders. The most I can hope for is a good handshake but what you are more likely to get than anything else is a wave." When I asked if his cynicism for multiculturalism was related to growing up Hindu Punjabi in Britain, he continued:

Part of that is, I think, the difference in a sense to here from the Americas. For all the effective purposes, the Americas have been created [where] there is no culture, there is no history; it's fine to talk about the North American Indians. . . . And if there was, it was erased by the Europeans and they reinvented themselves. So you have a different soil. [When Asians arrived in Britain], we entered into a world which was not capable of a drastic reinvention. In other words, it was an intact world. Our first job was to learn to somehow negotiate with the native and that goes back to the business of multiculturalism and the kind of policies to integrate and so forth.

He paused and then asked, "How do you fit in?" It was a question that he had asked himself before. He articulated a main question Asians seemed to ask themselves, without ever indicating that this is what they were trying to do. His response to that rhetorical question indicates how "fitting in" involved change.

Only as we fit in did we actually begin to open up space and reinvent, we couldn't just do whatever we wanted. And it is only as we became more confident that we reinvented and, in effect, we have reinvented the country. Like when they talk about diet, I know in my own lifetime here the diet has fundamentally changed. Who were the engines of that? Was it us? Now to talk about eating a curry or biryani or a samosa or kebab is passé — any English household at least once a week will have that and make it in their home; they know about spices, it is a known, something has happened already to the country. It didn't happen at the beginning in that sense it was a time to negotiate within ourselves, that's one sort of thing. The other one (and this is how it came to me) is Bosnia, is what is going on in Europe. It is too close to us; we are all too conscious of the fact. I am convinced now that for politicians as much as ordinary people it doesn't really work. Here is a nation which was put together and for 450 years or more of intermarriage and stuff has just been an absolute failure. When push comes to shove the tribalistic response came out.

To make his point clear, he returned to his own experience. His words reflect the sense of belonging that Hindu Punjabis feel in Britain. He recounts his own challenges to his cousin, who seemed to be saying "don't kid yourself man, we will never belong here." His sense of belonging implicates belonging to Britain, the nation-state. He told me:

I remember last year I was talking to a kind of relative, a cousin, and the guy was born here who has as much an interest as I have in India. He's an accountant with one of the big firms, but he said to me, "I have no illusions at all as to what I am. I am an Indian. I have no illusions about being British. We never will be. Look at Bosnia — don't kid yourself, we never will be. I have no problems with that; I think it is perfectly well to live here. I know I will probably die here, but that doesn't mean that my soul is silly as to be locked here." I was taken aback because it made me question what am I actually posing as an alternative? It is really just a hope or a wish. But that bullshit is no good based on reality, a lot of running around and bullshit. But now when I am faced with those kind of questions [I respond], I know where I am going to die: it is here, if for some that means that "this is my country" well so be it. If you ask me all I can say is that "this is where I am going to die, that's it." I am different things in different places but the only thing I have, which I think is consistent, is being a nomad, of being a foreigner everywhere.

So from that point of view I can connect with lots of different countries and situations in different countries and I find that a more comfortable position. That is my invention; it's my myth, it's my territory. In that community I feel very happy, and comfortable in a way but I know that community does not correspond to a physical geography now. I think that now, talking about your own focus on HPs, I think that's the seed. It is because of the nature of that community which has died here and which has had that kind of restraint.

His lengthy quotation addresses questions of belonging and, by implication, homeland. In the poetic turn that he knows that he would die in
Britain, and that would perhaps make it his home, he is also indicating
how only the passage of time can determine belonging to the nation-state.
Karnal Bhandhari's reflections complicate the possible answers to the
question, "Where are you from?" The question could be used to promote
a sense of community within a community, or within an imagined community that feels threatened. The specific identity politics invoked in posing this question ignore the negotiations and complications, or the many
ways these migrants and their lives and their children's lives have changed
as they produce their transnational identification. The qualification,
"Where are you *originally* from?" clarifies that the intention behind this
everyday question is to mark their identity as non-British. This question
is a first move in the identity game of open public multiculturalism in
which the individual is responsible for accounting for his or her difference
through representation. Such a constant engagement with difference
requires a strategic response to address the nostalgia for culture produced
by multicultural transnational politics.

The question of belonging is asked by the Hindu Punjabis of themselves in different ways. The fact that Karnal had a conversation with his
cousin about it indicates how it comes into conversations at different
moments. The comfort with being a nomad everywhere seems to indicate
a comfort with the constant engagement with the many spaces of
difference he has had to negotiate during his lifetime. In any place, he is
a foreigner; claiming to become a nomad erases the question of belonging. He relates to my typification of Hindu Punjabis as an a-community,
one that does not correspond to a physical geography in India or in
Britain. But not everyone has these romantic ideas about belonging
nowhere, although this does echo that "we are nowhere people," as one
Uncle declared. After thirty or forty years in Britain, the migrant generation has moved from being Vilayati to becoming an Asian box with a
subheading "Indian" in the rhetoric of the multicultural British state. At
one level, adopting the "Indian" label allows an easy response to the question "Where are you from?" For London's Hindu Punjabis, some of
whom have origins in Punjab, Africa, and even Pakistan, their multiple
and overlapping possibilities of identity are silenced in the label "Indian."
Recalling the words of Uncle Ram that "I am from nowhere," and Karnal
Bhandari's reflection that Hindu Punjabis "are nomads" reveals how
uneasy the people I worked with are with labels of identity that implicate
a specific place. By contrast, with the active imagination of homeland and

their sense of exclusion in Britain, their place has become India. This is one potential response to this official need to predicate difference on a fixed location, which has been a subtle reformulation of an authentic, workable identity that is fixed and easy to comprehend (see Raj 2000). This is the "zero sum" of multiculturalism: the accountability of difference, in fact, creates the need for an easy way to assume the creation of a displaced "Other," to be able to respond quickly to cultural difference, without any complications, without qualifications.[18]

Imagined Autochthony, Belonging, and Imaginative Difference

British multiculturalism officializes cultural difference and encourages a specific sociocultural construction of an ethnic identity as a national identity, connected to a far-off place, a spatialized difference. With the British example, as evinced elsewhere, national identity is based on "fictive ethnicity" (Balibar 1991b: 96) in which people constitute a "unity" whether that be "British" or "Indian." In doing so, "national ideology does much more than justify the strategies employed by the state to control populations. It inscribes their demands in advance in a sense of belonging in the double sense of the term — both what it is that makes one belong to oneself and also what makes one belong to other fellow human beings" (Balibar 1991b: 96). Projecting outward, Britain has constructed a nation made from various national identities in which the sense of belonging is assumed to be located elsewhere. Such an understanding is not confined to government census bureau administrators or peers debating identity labels. The question of spatialized difference based on "fictive ethnicity" occurs in everyday life, everyday experience, the media, shops, museums, airplanes, and hospitals. In a world of hybrids, cosmopolitans, lamented disjunctures, and celebrated differences people live through increasingly complicated life experiences and histories. However, all this complexity is reduced at certain moments when identity comes into question as an inevitable difference, tied to a different locality. Of course, when people ask, "Where are you from?" it is a question of identity, which could potentially be read as an act of curiosity or even friendship. However, when that question is clarified and posed as "Where are you from originally?" or "Where are you really from?" or even "Where is your family from?" these evoke responses based on extemporaneous spatialized difference. In other words, each question simultaneously acknowledges movement as part of globalization and fixes identification in time and space; these questions are founded on the principles of autochthonous foreignness. Children of migrants from South Asia who attempt to respond with a local referent to the question, "Where are you from?" are often met with the clarification, "Where are you *originally* from?"[19] The question returns me to the issue of how the anthropological focus on "self" and "other" highlights alterity and renegates individual identities as being subsumed to cultural identities. By focusing on people's negotiations and using the metaphor of space I have called into question how cultural and national belonging subsumes an individual's everyday interaction and agency with respect to difference. The question, "Where are you *originally* from?" as an everyday act of transnationalism, makes apparent that ethnic identity is a "zero-sum" game of difference. This question interrogates belonging and assumes a fundamental alterity; the implication of "Where are you *really* from?" is that one is not really from here. For migrants, the question behind the question is "When are you going back?"[20] The implication is that the migrant is a perpetual sojourner and that the children of migrants can never be anything but a child of an immigrant. The movement is never erased, but rather is constantly being reinscribed.

At the level of everyday interaction the question "Where are you from *originally*?" lays bare the assumed coalescence of nation, language, religion, territory, and blood. It is clear that in the perpetual concern with tolerance, people will never belong, but will always be seen as different. The second-generation Hindu Punjabis, like my friend who commented to me that he was not from Britain in the same way that I was from Canada, are at the crossroads of what being British means. A change in the way belonging is constituted in Britain will be reflected in two terms: "British" and "English." "British" and "English" continue to be a popular and official (as per the 2001 census) glosses for "white Briton."[21] The ideal is the tolerant liberal white, who is savvy with the ways of the world, but quintessentially polite and undramatic about his or her own sense of belonging. The cultural traits of the essentially British may involve anything from Radio 4 and regular rambling through the countryside to body piercing and shopping at Sh!, the women-only sex shop in London. But general parlance does not acknowledge nonwhiteness as British or English, except in a strategic political sense of Black British.[22] Part of this specific sense of the nation comes from the technologies of the British nation-state that instituted a sense of white Britain through restrictive immigration policies during the 1970s that, in addition to a "grandfather clause," aimed blatantly to keep Asians and Blacks out and allowed white migrants into Britain. The idiom of place as identity minus any complications all play out conveniently in national identities, such as British and English. By using British and English for those who are white, questions of representation become questions of belonging. Qualified Britishness is claimed as Black British, British Asian, Asian British (on the 2001 census) or even "Brasian" (Kahlon and Kalra 1994). This is not an identity politics of hyphenation; on their own English and an unqualified British are not open to identification despite citizenship. The construction of English identity is a particularly closed category, as the words of one Asian journalist make clear: "I don't feel myself to be English, I never will" (Yasmin Alibhai-Brown, qtd. in Marr 2000: 157).

The nationhood categories used to refer to migrants connects them as an ethnic minority group to far-off places, forever non-British and never belonging. In creating a state of perpetual difference, it is perhaps therefore unsurprising to have tolerance as a concern for the citizenship report. Of course, in the citizenship report, teaching young people to interact civilly with minority groups is only one of many concerns of teaching British identity. Nevertheless, by including a multicultural entry, the report espouses a liberal ideal of individuals who are tolerant of difference. The report does not imply that the very definition of British identity itself could be expanded, as it was to include the Scots and Welsh but not the Irish (this construction is clear from the 2001 census forms whereby the "ethnic category" white is divided into British and Irish). There are fundamental notions of the British nation, which render certain differences as subsumable and certain others to be perpetually foreign because they are made to inhabit a space of difference. The writers and consultants of the citizenship report assume a priori difference; difference is not a construction, a process, or a negotiation. The certainty of such a nominalized conceptualization of difference as absolute, poses no challenge to the ways in which Britain imagines its citizenship as autochthonous, albeit reconciled with its own history peppered with Celtic, Roman, German, and Viking invasions and the 1066 Norman conquest. The report does contain a hint of changing attitudes; in the end, there is a call for *imaginative* ways to manage difference.

India itself is seeking imaginative ways to administer difference. The 2003 example is the decision to allow dual citizenship. The People of Indian Origin card (PIO) with its hefty $1,000 USD price tag has only attracted about 200 people worldwide. According to an *Express India* article, the cost is likely to drop. Apparently, one of the suggestions is to have

$1,000 apply to a whole family of five, rather than a single individual. More likely is a reduction to $750 and $500.[23] India is creating itself as the homeland and is going through the bureaucratic maneuvers to think creatively about difference among its supposed diaspora where those from Britain, the United States, Fiji, South Africa, and the Persian Gulf region may be variously disposed to think of India as the homeland, because of their own experiences of postmigration settlement. Fundamentally, India as a homeland is not a de facto position, but something that is being actively fostered. This is clear from India's external affairs minister, Mr. Jaswant Singh, who is quoted as saying, "There is evidently something wrong with the concept which needs earliest ratification and must be sorted out."[24] The concept of the PIO is one in which the various migrants, their children (up to four generations), and partners are encouraged to endorse a view of India as a homeland, but what that means to each of these groups is very different because of their spatial and temporal experiences of difference in the putative diaspora. This complexity is not lost on the Indian government officials. As Mr. J. C. Sharma, Additional Secretary in charge of Non-Resident Indians, has reported, "Most of these PIOs are old timers, and each family has a different story to tell, depending on the period of time they have been away from India."[25]

HPs' lives, lived in a local context, constantly reference the transnational when people evoke their migrations whether that be partition or their move to England, when they seek marriage alliances and during the course of their lifetimes when they visit relatives around the world, or when parents plan to retire in India. In their everyday lives they experience connections across the transnational terrain. It is this constant awareness of the transnational that was most striking. This has passed into the second generation, but as can be expected, in ways distinct from their parents'. For example, Arun and Pamela Aggarwal were showing pictures of their Victorian home in Boston, Massachusetts, to Arun's parents in London, England. This was the young couple's first visit to England after their marriage and purchase of their home. One photo was of four identical modern clocks displayed in a straight line on the wall. Arun explained that they were arranged geographically and represented the local time for various members of his family around the world. Each clock had a city name underneath — Boston for Arun and his wife, London for his parents in England, Delhi for his grandparents in India, and Tokyo for his sister and brother-in-law in Japan. Arun and Pamela had created in their everyday lives a secular shrine of their personal transnational connections. Examples such as this, and the other ruptures and negotiations that I have outlined, open up the possibility of thinking about globalization outside of the putative local-global dynamic and into that of everyday life. Hindu Punjabis in London, like migrants families elsewhere, reveal how everyday minority knowledge and collective agency produce a transnational terrain in which difference is a key to understanding concepts such as ethnicity, identity, and culture.

Researchers have been grappling with how to imagine the transnational aspect of South Asian migrants. Some have recognized that there is a wide diversity of experience subsumed under the label "South Asian" (R. Ballard 1994b). Others have warned that this insight concerning the wide range of South Asian difference should not result in dissolving the category itself (van der Veer 1995). Walking a tightrope between difference and the danger of dissolution, scholars need to analyze how differences are conceptualized in terms of transnationalism. One effect of globalization is that "people everywhere are showing a new level of self consciousness about culture" (Hannerz 1996: 52). Wallerstein argues that culture has turned into an "ideological battleground of the modern world system" (1990). Difference and diversity run to the core of this debate. Difference is a crucial modality of Hindu Punjabi identification because of the changes involved in the global politics of culture and ethnic identity. I now want to connect this to globalization. As social scientists we see the complexities of transnationalism and the intricate inflections and refractions of globalization in our (multi)local field sites. Hannerz cogently argues:

Today's cosmopolitans and locals have common interests in the survival of cultural diversity. For the latter, diversity itself, as a matter of personal access to varied cultures may be of little intrinsic interest. It just so happens that it is the survival of diversity that allows all locals to stick to their respective cultures. For the cosmopolitans, in contrast, there is value in diversity as such, but they are not likely to get it, in anything like the present form, unless other people are allowed to carve out special niches for their cultures, and keep them. Which is to say that there can be no cosmopolitans without locals. (Hannerz 1996: 111)

In other words, displacement alone does not constitute a concern with difference and globalization. Rather, the locals and the cosmopolitans are equally invested in thinking about diversity and identity. On the surface, people's understandings of what these terms mean may seem similar. However, identity and diversity may actually mean different things to different groups. Baumann has argued for this dynamic of diversity in his book based on South Asians in Southhall, in which he contrasts the majority discourse and "demotic" local understandings to speak about community and culture. I would push this further to argue that the making and remaking of meanings and cultural practices of communities in local spaces, as infused by global dynamics, involves reconceptualizing the "the ethnic group" as inherently implicated by ongoing transnational experiences.

Turning away from the vagaries of the meaning of culture, many are now considering how difference and identity are brought forward by the global trend of multiculturalism.[26] As Schuster and Solomos indicate, "There is little agreement about the meaning attached to 'multiculturalism' from either a conceptual or an empirical perspective" (2001: 4). The term nevertheless conveys that "not one but multiple cultures co-exist within a limited, state-bounded territory" (Schuster and Solomos 2001: 4). As such, "Multiculturalism has become a global credo" (Samad 1997: 258). The globalization of multiculturalism has been reviewed in America (Gordon and Newfield 1996; Schlesinger 1992) and Britain, and critiqued for reifying cultural identities (Caglar 1997; Vertovec 1996; Werbner and Modood 1997). The second important critique is, as Samad points out, that multiculturalism "has different implications and impacts in different locales" (Samad 1997: 258; see also Modood and Werbner 1997). The self-consciousness of culture across the globe plays out in terms of a particular sense of what cultural identity and difference mean: these terms are understood uniquely in individual nation-states.

A necessary caveat is that multicultural nation-states and the minority group may also construct difference and identity in ways that seem to be similar either as an indexical marker, or as a representation of self, but they have multiple significations with no single organizing principle or commonality in the ways in which they speak about these terms. Public debates over assimilation, identity politics, or the goals of a possibility of a nonracial society (as espoused differently by the right and left) are highly informative on how nation-states and their ethnic minorities are implicated by transnationalism. Both the United States and Britain have developed multiculturalism to address issues of inequality arising from diversity. While each nation has specific notions of diversity, there is a certain focus on place of origin. In this vision of multiculturalism, diversity is caused by immigration, a movement from a prior whole, the movement from a place of unquestioned origin and uncomplicated identities, and people have come together to form a mosaic, a garden, a melting pot, a "*pot-au-feu*" (Geertz 1973: 4).[27]

Anthropologists, like national policy makers, are also seeking imaginative ways to deal with difference. And yet, as the letter to *Anthropology Today* (August 2000) discussed in the introduction revealed, the debate about identity, assimilation, and multiculturalism tends to conflate difference with a set of constructions around national identification. In such an understanding the ethnic minority simultaneously creates and benefits from multicultural nations such as Britain. And thus, multiculturalism must aim "not only to allow national, ethnic and immigrant minorities a voice, but to protect them from offensive symbolic as well as civic and material exclusions and violations" (P. Werbner 1997: 263). Multiculturalism is understood by the researcher to aim laudably to recognize "the rights of minorities to demand restitution for historical racialisations which disempowered them and suppressed their voice in the national sphere" (P. Werbner 1997: 263). The national sphere must be multicultural to redress past injustice. But as Samad (1997) and others have indicated, multiculturalism is the political rhetoric of identity politics writ large on the global stage. It is curious to understand how and why this specific understanding of the politics of difference is playing out in the transnational arena. As a corollary, multiculturalism itself needs to be seen as a part of the flows of democracy and capitalism and to be understood as a national project to manage difference and inequity. Transnationalism and difference complicate multicultural identities, by questioning how "the other" can be incorporated into the nation-state while reinscribing the "narration of the nation" (Bhabha 1990b).

Important but neglected aspects of the conceptualization of difference are the metaphors of spatiality and temporality that pervade current social science understandings of naming, belonging, ethnic group, and identity.[28] To recognize spatiality implicates our tools for understanding cultural change by moving from the taxonomical accountable notions of difference to the "interactive" (King 1988: 47; Collins 1990; Mohanty 1998) and "intersecting" (Frankenberg and Mani 1996: 359) in which the power dynamics that constitute difference are made apparent. The transnational flow of people, goods, capital, and ideas has reworked how we think of everyday life (Appadurai 1991). Moreover, place as a defining aspect of our concepts of culture has been challenged (Ferguson and Gupta 1992; Gupta and Ferguson 1997; Lavie and Swedenburg 1996; Rodman 1992), and yet it is constantly assumed in everyday understandings of difference, power, and representation. "Where are you from?" is a question of place — a location elsewhere that gives meaning of social identity, one that presupposes movement but does not allow for change. Spaces of difference, not in the sense of the (dis)locality of place, but in

the sense of the interstices of identification, reflect the further complications of transnationalism, beyond here and there, to include class, gender,
generation, and the various reinscriptions of the nation-state. Negotiations of identification, of what it means to be Asian, Punjabi, Hindu,
HP, Black, British, and Indian, reveal the spaces of difference inherent to
notions of culture cum ethnicity cum identity cum community. Attention
to these spaces complicates the presumed transformative effects of the
transnational (Smith and Guarnizo 1998) and focuses on the subject
knowledge and agency formation of individuals who live complicated
lives. There are those for whom, for example, "Where are you from?" or
"Where are you originally from?" are problematic questions of identification, premised on the nostalgia for culture. Each question is based on
place and ignores time and change, a perspective that is entirely sanc-
tioned in the politics of multiculturalism.

Homi Bhabha suggests that transnational migrants also have the
power to disrupt the singular narratives of the nation (1994). Displacement is a powerful aspect of transnationalism (Ferguson and Gupta
1992; Gupta and Ferguson 1997), which is inherently implicated by the
local population (Hannerz 1987, 1989, 1996). The local politics of belonging get variously reinscribed and reterritoritialized because of transnationalism. Great Britain is facing its own specific set of politics with the
simultaneous devolution of Scotland and changing sense of Europe,
each altering what it means to be British (cf. MacDonald 1993). Transnationalism challenges our understandings of culture and difference as
played out in and through the nation-state. To recognize fully people's
lived transnationalism allows a historicization of their movement, allows
for disjuncture as well as connections (thereby allowing for comparison
without presupposing that the cultures should be alike); it is not dismis-
sive about the nation-state, but deeply implicated by it.

One precondition for true multiculturalism, that is, an official policy
that teeters on the fine line between recognizing differences without
insisting on assimilated sameness (or one that imaginatively deals with the
other without constantly seeking to tolerate the other) is that we address
the spaces of difference alongside the questions of time and place as used
by people to relate to each other. In opening up the anthropological
toolkit to examine "the experience of what it means to be 'in the middle
of difference' " (Bhabha 1998a: 130), I have reviewed identity, ethnicity,
and community as the tools social scientists have to understand the various constructions of otherness; the nostalgia for culture can be undone

by focusing on the negotiations and interrupting the links between ethnicity, community, culture identity, and location. The spaces of difference, the claims for culture knowledge, are always represented and reflexive. Yet they are organized to create specific constructions of collective agency.

The investments of nation-states and minorities in these constructions demonstrate how each constantly produces the nostalgia for culture. At one level, using the lives of London's Hindu Punjabis, I have de-exoticized the complex interpellations of theoretical abstractions such as ethnicity, identity, community, and difference as variously lived by people in their everyday environs living in a particular nation-state. By stressing negotiations of what constitutes cultural knowledge, I have shown that difference, as experienced differently across race, class, and gender and at the level of the nation-state, differently brings the complexities of thinking through the implications of time and space for the conceptualization of "the Indian Diaspora." "Punjabi," "Hindu," "Asian," "Black," "Indian," and "British" as referents of identity are fraught with various interpretations, and at times one meaning gains ascendancy over another. The analytical utility of the terms "community," "culture," "ethnicity," and "identity" are brought into sharp relief when thinking through the complex negotiations and specific articulations that connect the Punjabi/ Asian/ Black/Indian aspect of British-born Hindu Punjabis to a specific history. The danger is always about stuffing people into prescribed categories without an understanding of how each comes to have salience and why. By taking seriously the people's constructions of cultural knowledge of their identifications, this book has addressed the many sites in which these various identifications attain meaning, sites in which there are multiple and overlapping boundaries of community, ethnicity, and culture that de-essentialize and essentialize anew various modalities of identification. Such an approach, which calls for thinking about ethnicity not as a product but as a part of the production of transnationalism, inevitably raises further questions of how identity is made for others who are products and producers of transnationalism, such as migrants, refugees, and expatriates. How has displacement also created a jet set, unlike the older elite global nomads, the members of which are able to be at ease in many places around the globe and yet are operating with a varied sense of what it means to be a part of a sociocultural group? Are there others for whom the nostalgia for culture is not a factor? If so, why? And, of course, why and how do certain forms or ideologies of identity, particularly religious identity, gain ascendancy when and where they do?

The migration of English-speaking, degree-educated, middle-class workers from India continues in the form of technology and Internet workers who are moving to the United States, England, and Japan. In the United States, the increase of H1B visa workers to the United States (600,000 are allowed to enter between 2000–2003) show how tenuously immigration has been thought out in terms of long-term social consequences. The creation (in the United Kingdom) or expansion (in the United States and Japan) of technology workers will create a whole underclass of urban educated migrants whose belonging is tied to a corporation, and who initially have no recourse to state citizenship. Often it is these very workers who are responding to the demands of the high-tech workplace, in terms of long hours and extreme mobility. Creating this underclass of workers solidifies an understanding that migrants function only as itinerant workers who are perpetually from elsewhere. When this is considered alongside emerging demographic trends, there is a cause for concern as to how the nation imagines itself and is imagining coexistence. Recent statistics reveal that "according to the US Census Bureau, 83 countries and territories are now thought to experience below-replacement fertility" (Eberstadt 2001: 45). This trend is projected to have a *depopulation* effect, already evidenced in Europe and Japan. The most striking effect will be that "in Europe, immigration must nearly quadruple — to an average of almost 4 million net entrants a year — to prevent a decline in the size of the 15- to 64-year-old 'working age' population over the next 50 years" (Eberstadt 2001: 48). The inevitable choice is either depopulation and a graying of the existing population, or increased immigration and further ethnic shifts of the nation-state. In light of these trends, Lord Paul's quotation on the "need to be British" and Andrew Marr's claim that "we need a new England" reveal the crucial rethinking that needs to take place around issues of belonging, transnationalism, citizenship, and multiculturalism. Yet it seems that whenever the debates occur, there is fierce backlash involved in rethinking what precisely it means to be part of a nation (the negative press in 2000 surrounding the Parekh Report — "The Future of Multi-Ethnic Britain" — is an interesting case in point).

The response of the British state, like other nation-states, to the complexities of transnationalism has been to construct an absolute notion of difference in which the individual is accountable for his or her own diversity, but that diversity had no effect on the identity of the nation. This typology of difference began in the colonial period, but there are specificities to the current sociohistoric situation.[29] Prior British understandings of difference use ethnicity, identity, community, and culture as empirical realities that were devoid of negotiations and tensions and presented a unified collective agency. In the earlier colonial period, this meant that one was never required to ask when the "Indian" would become British because the difference was contained; it always existed outside of the nation-state. In fact, during the colonial period, a whole new supra-category of diversity, the Commonwealth, allowed for the differences to exist across the empire, while stressing the centrality of Britain. The post-colonial turn made the Commonwealth into a collection of independent nation-states, marking an ongoing salience for the former empire. Nevertheless, difference remained constructed outside of the national boundary. With migrations throughout the Commonwealth, these notions of difference outside of the nation have become highly problematic and somewhat untenable. The development of multiculturalism in the United Kingdom has roots in this way of thinking and was a response to the demands for recognition by minority activists. The new rhetoric of multiculturalism stresses constant bridge building, a perpetual concern with how to overcome difference, by inadvertently stressing it. The reticent British response, entirely in keeping with its own history is one of liberal fairness and tolerance.

Is it unfair to ask when the bridge across difference will be built? Constant bridge building further exacerbates the very need to solidify collective unity around the coalescence of ethnicity, identity, community, and culture. Multiculturalism invests the nostalgia for culture with legitimacy. In such an understanding there are perpetually two very separate shores of identity, one that the migrant left behind, and the other to which the migrant has traveled. While the second generation unravels that web of understanding, the perpetuation of ethnic identity through time, for example, based in popular questions of what sports team will be supported by the ethnic group, reveals how little we have learned and implemented in public policy. The ideal of the nostalgia for culture remains central to nation-states policies.

It remains incumbent on minority individuals, whether migrant or of subsequent generations, to do all the bridge building, because they are the ones accountable for their difference. Lord Paul, Manoj, Aunty Rani, Karnal Bhandhari, Uncle Ram, Nishma, and others all evoke aspects of this when they speak; they indicate the sense that HPs as South Asians are inconsolably different and constantly need to be included. They are the Ambassadors of Difference and yet they are trying to break out of the constant reference to their ethnicity. They are calling for the postethnic in which the individual is not first and foremost a product only of ethnicity. This is why Lord Paul makes his claim to be British. He does not call for bridge building across Asian and British; this would reinforce the very sense of the constant awareness of difference. Instead, he embraces the British nation as his own. Problematic though it may be — at one level his call seems to reinforce the notion of an exchange of one separate sphere of identity for another — his construction shows that for all the rhetoric of multiculturalism, the one thing that the accountability and management of cultural difference has not produced is the changed sense of a national identity, a sense in which all the citizens of a country can equally claim national identification. If such a change had occurred, qualifications of identity such as Asian British, Black British, British Asian, or Brasian, would not be necessary, because the term "British" itself would be understood to include all people forming the nation. Also, if such a change had occurred, Lord Paul's call to be British would not be a startling statement. The imagination of the nation is implicated by the nostalgia for culture. The current possible models of difference are limited to questions of assimilation. Subsuming ethnicity, community, and identity under culture categories circumscribes the ways in which people can attribute and claim subjective and collective agency; individual agency has become a negotiation across difference. For Hindu Punjabis and other minority groups, agency and difference are constantly at play within the framework of a nostalgia for culture. Until this dilemma is addressed, migrant minorities and those that create public policies will be battling constantly against the idea of a "clash of civilizations." The clash is not one of civilizations, but rather of ideological imaginary played out within the larger forces of history, which seek to fix the place from which migrants come, circumscribe where they belong, and limit all future possibilities of their identification.

Glossary

Ana-jana (ānā-jānā)	Literally, coming and going, or a social visit.
Arti	"Wavering a lighted lamp before a revered object [including a picture of a deity] as part of an act of worship" (Carrithers and Humphrey 1991: 296). The term often also refers to the song that is sung when the flame is circled in front of the deity.
Arya Samaj	Nineteenth-century Hindu reform movement established by Swami Dayananda Saraswati. Movement was most prominent in Punjab.
Azadi (azādī)	A person who has freedom, independence (in the political sense).
Bhabi	Kinship term, refers to brother's wife.
Bhagavad Gita	"'Song of Krishna', Krishna's sermon to Arjuna on the battle field, exhorting him to carry out his duty. For many Hindus this is the holiest scripture" (Jackson and Nesbitt 1992: 207).
Bhajan	Hindu religious hymn.
Bhog	Precedes *arti*, the ritual of offering the food that is to be served communally to the deities and the invitation of the deities' blessings.
Beti	Kinship term for daughter.
Biradari (birādārī)	A brotherhood, kinship community, fraternity, or caste.

Bua (būā)	Kinship term for paternal aunt, that is, one's father's sister.
Darshan (daršan)	Seeing, observing, making an appearance before, or having a glimpse of the gods.
Desi	From Hindi *desh,* which means country. It is a colloquial self-referent used by migrants and their children to refer to those who originate in South Asia. Sengupta reveals that term refers to a "Hindi version of homeboy or homegirl" (*The New York Times,* June 30, 1996, "To Be Young, Indian and Hip").
Diwali (divālī)	"Festival of light" held in the autumn (exact date depends on lunar calendar). Celebrates the return of Lord Ram from exile. Laxmi (goddess of wealth) and Ganesh (deity of good beginnings) are worshipped on this day. "Diwali" is also transliterated as "Divali," "Dipavali," or "Deepawali" in temple publications by Hindu Punjabis.
Doab (doāb)	Confluence of a river from two different sources, specifically refers to the area in Punjab where the Ganges and Yamnuna Rivers converge.
Dusshera (dašahrā)	Festival marking Lord Ram's defeat of the demon Ravana, held in the autumn between Navratri and Diwali.
Gayatri Mantra	"Ancient Sanskrit prayer of enlightenment" (Jackson and Nesbitt 1992: 210). Translation: "Oh Lord, the protector of all, life giver, destroyer of all sorrow, source and embodiment of all joy, I focus my thought on that power of yours which gave form to the entire universe and which can cleanse all sins and surrender myself to you. Lord bestow upon me the consciousness to make me think and do what is right at all times."
Gora (gorā, plural gore)	White person. Can also be used as "gore log," meaning white people.
Gundā	Derogatory term for young male hoodlum.
Gurdwara	Literally, doorway to the guru, refers to a Sikh place of worship.
Ish-devta (iṣhṭdevta)	An individual or family's favorite deity.
Izzat (izzat)	Honor, family honor.

Janmashtami (janmaṣṭmī)	The birth of Lord Krishna celebrated in late summer/early autumn; the exact date depends on the lunar calendar.
Jot (jyot)	Oil lamp in small earthenware or brass container, made with cotton and ghee.
Jyotshi (jyotiṣī)	Astrological pundit.
Kāle log	Literally, black people.
Kanyadaan (kanyādān)	Literally, gift of a virgin. The first rite of a marriage ceremony when the bride's family gives her away.
Kara (kaṛa)	The steel bangle that is one of the five Ks of Sikhism, also worn by Khattri Hindus.
Karva Chauth (karvā-cauth)	A one-day fast and ritual that occurs before Diwali in the autumn (the exact date depends on the lunar calendar, especially as this fast is held on the fourth day of the waning moon) where married women pray for the health and well-being of their husbands. Women who keep this fast drink only water until after the moon is sighted, then they have a large meal. Often groups of women will keep the fast together. Also it is a time when gifts of clothing or jewelry are given to the women.
Khattri (khattrī, also spelled khatri)	The mercantile subgroup in the traditional caste hierarchy.
Kirtan	Devotional singing, collective singing, hymns, refers to an event for singing praises of the deities that may be held in the temple or home.
Kshatriya (ksatriya)	One of four Hindu caste distinctions (the others are Brahman, Vaisya, and Sudra).
Mahabharat	Ancient epic recounting the story of a great battle between two lineages.
Matha tek (mathā tek)	The full action is prostration in front of the deity by touching one's forehead to the ground. The action usually performed, however, is the bowing of the head with hands joined together in prayer, or first touching the deity's feet and then touching one's forehead.
Mauli	Red thread tied around the wrist after a religious ceremony, or a visit to the Hindu temple.
Mela (melā)	A religious or secular fair, a festival, gathering of people, often held outdoors. A *Dusshera mela* is a

	celebration of Lord Ram's victory over the demon Ravana. The exact date is based on the lunar calendar, but it occurs in the autumn, before Divali.
Mithai (miṭhāī)	Sweet food or dish, general reference for various sweet snacks.
Murti (mūrti)	Form, the representation of the deity, a Hindu statue. May be a picture or a statue
Nam (nām)	Literally, name. Family name
Namaskar (namaskār)	Greeting, sign of respect when meeting someone. One joins his or her hands with palms together. In the temple, used when people are bowing to the deities. When meeting other people, they may also say "namaskar," or "namaste."
Navratri (navratre)	Literally, nine nights; the term refers to the festival for the goddess, which occurs in spring and autumn. The final day of the festival is called Astmi.
OM (ॐ)	"OM is the root mantra and the soundless sound from which all creation issues forth . . . . Its three syllables stand at the beginning and end of every sacred verse" (Samabhav Festival of Spiritual Unity Programme Booklet 1994: 60).
Om Jai Jagdish Hare	North Indian devotional hymn, in the Vaishnavite tradition.
Pardeshi (pardeşi)	Home; from the homeland.
Parshad (pra-sād)	Food offered to the deity; the blessed offerings of fruit, dried fruits, halva, or Indian sweets dispersed after Hindu prayers.
Pitra-bhumi (pitṛ-bhūmi)	Land of one's ancestors; ancestral homeland.
Pooja (pūjā)	"The act of showing reverence to a god, a spirit, or another aspect of the divine through invocations, prayers, songs, and rituals" (from Smithsonian Arthur Sackler Website, http://www.asia.si.edu/devi/text1.htm).
Pran pratishtha (prān pratishtha)	The giving of "life" to the murti, when the deity comes into the stone.
Preeti bhojan (prīti bhojan)	A food banquet, communal food offering sponsored by an individual or family after a temple service.

Ramayan	"Ancient epic whose hero, [Lord] Rama, endures unjust exile before returning to his kingdom" (Jackson and Nesbitt 1992: 217).
Ramlila (rāmlīlā)	The dramatized performance of a portion of the epic story *Ramayan*.
Ramlila Chalisa	Mythological story that is a portion of the *Ramayan* based on the two Sunder Kand and Lanka Kand chapters relating to Lord Ram's triumph over the demon Ravana.
Ravan (rāvaṇ)	Mythological ruler of Lanka who kidnapped Sita and was defeated by Ram; the story is found in the *Ramayan*.
Rishta (riśtā)	Literally, relation, but used also to refer to marriage proposal.
Rokna	Family preengagement ceremony when both parties agree to stop looking at other prospects.
Salvar-kameez	A Punjabi "suit," a matched trouser and tunic outfit.
Sanskar (sanskar)	Rituals that govern the life stages such as marriage, death, and so forth.
Sari (sarī)	Women's garment; usually six yards of fabric worn by women in India.
Sharnarthi (Śaraṇthī)	Refugee; one seeking shelter, refuge.
Shivratri (also known as Maha-Shivratri)	Celebrates the birth of Lord Shiva (the destroyer in the Shiva-Vishnu-Brahma triad). It is celebrated in the autumn, usually in November.
Videshi	Person from outside of *desh;* a foreigner.
Vilayati (vilāyātī)	Foreigner, often English, British, European; refers colloquially to those emigrants to these lands. Could also be used as an adjective to refer to a foreign-made article.
Wala (vālā)	Person (masculine); also *wallah*. Important person in a particular field or organization.

Notes

Chapter 1: Questions of Ethnicity

1. The terms "minority" and "minorities" are found throughout the book without quotation marks, because they are being used in the sense of numerical minority (that is, each term is not used in a pejorative sense as an ethnic marker of perpetual difference). Nor are these terms being used in contrast to majority, an unhelpful term in that it does not mark the differences inherent in the dominant society. As for further analysis of sport and nation, and specifically of the critical use of Bhabha's *Nation and Narration* to understand Australian soccer, see Danforth 2001.

2. *The Guardian,* May 29, 2001, 7.

3. The assumptions are that Asians should be cheering for the "right" team, the one representing the nation of their residence, and that young Asians should become British in specified ways, namely, by waving the correct flag at a cricket match. Hussain added, "Following England has got to be the way ahead" (*The Guardian,* May 29, 2001, 7). This way of thinking implies that there is a unidirectional change, from being culturally Indian to culturally British.

4. For further discussion of class, see Chapter 2.

5. Difference is a necessary aspect of ethnicity, identity, and community; it can be conceptualized as fundamental otherness (that is, you are not like me) or humanist alterity (that is, we are similar in our differences). In both senses, difference is reified and assumed. In fact, the assumption of difference in this oppositional way allows anthropologists to equate and exchange ethnicity, identity, and community. For a call to counter this trend, see Baumann 1996.

6. The parental generation and others who have actually moved can claim to be from somewhere. For them, their movement or sojourns create certain places as "home," even a prior one that has changed. However, for the children of move-

ment, their experiences and assumptions of homeland are challenged on a day-to-day level.

7. As quoted in *The Observer Magazine,* September 19, 1999, 17.

8. See Appadurai's distinction between "marked" and "unmarked" culture (Appadurai 1996: 13–14).

9. Lord Paul was awarded a life peerage and elevated to the House of Lords in November 1996. He continues to work as an industrialist with CAPARO, his steel business.

10. In Britain, "Asian" commonly refers to people from the Indian Subcontinent, including those who have origins in India, Pakistan, Bangladesh, Sri Lanka, and Nepal.

11. As argued by Lavie and Swedenburg, the "theoretical examination of third time-spaces . . . involves a guerilla warfare of the interstices, where minorities rupture categories of race, gender, sexuality, class, nation and empire in the center as well as on the margins" (1996: 13).

12. Of course, his quote could be read in other ways as well, such as the putative abandonment of ethnicity (cf. Rattansi 2000). This reinscribes the notion of the divide between the two groups. See my critique of the abandonment of ethnicity in Chapter 2.

13. In Merleau Ponty's view, "Myself and the other are like two nearly concentric circles which can be distinguished only by a slight and mysterious slippage" (1973: 134). In this ethnographic exegesis the 'slight and mysterious slippage' occurs because of difference. It is this slippage, moreover, which gives the query "Where are you from?" an insidious quality.

14. See the proceedings of "Integration Pressures: Lessons from around the World," a symposium held in Cambridge, Massachusetts, on March 29–30, 2001. The event brought together senior government policy officials, practitioners, and academics to explore policies addressing integration across the globe. It was cosponsored by the Canadian Policy Research Initiative (PRI), the OECD Local Economic and Employment Development (LEED) Programme, and the Weatherhead Center for International Affairs at Harvard University.

15. On identity as being and becoming, see S. Hall 1990: 225.

16. Gregory has noted, "Community describes not a static, place-based social collective but power-laden field of social relations whose meanings, structures, and frontiers are continually produced, contested, and reworked in relation to a complex range of sociopolitical attachments and antagonisms" (1999: 11).

17. In focusing on negotiation I am not advocating an account of ultra-agency that ethnic minorities are free to be hybrid as the ultimate rational actors who negotiate and manipulate their identities, but instead for the intersection of process, agency, and structure (see Holland et al. 1998).

18. Time is implicit in scholars' discussions; they have framed identity as something that "keeps happening" (Fox 1985: 198), or as "a matter of 'becoming' as well as of 'being'" (S. Hall 1990: 225).

19. Whereas "diaspora" is a cultural term, transnationalism is social network term that recognizes "the new and increasingly significant place of globe-spanning

social networks in labour, business and commodity markets, political movements and cultural flows" (http://www.transcomm.ox.ac.uk/).

20. P. Werber explicitly engages with Gluckman's conflict theory (1990b: 241) and "situational behavior," as well as Cohen's "political ethnicity" (1990b: 5).

21. For a full exegesis on the development of ethnicity as a concept in the British context, see Banks 1996.

22. An example can be found in the work of Muhammad Anwar, who argued: "The more objectively distinguished characteristics, such as race, nationality, language and religion, a minority ethnic group has the more distinctive and visible it is to the wider society. The majority [of Pakistanis] are migrants, they are of Indo-Aryan origin, and have Pakistani nationality. Their mother tongue in the main is Punjabi or Urdu and they follow the Islamic faith. All these characteristics and other cultural values make Pakistanis in Britain an ethnic minority" (1979: 13). Anwar examines kinship, friendship, and economic networks using a transactionalist approach arguably informed by primordialism.

23. The instrumentalists view ethnicity essentially as a weapon in the pursuit of collective advantage. They stress the situational and circumstantial nature of ethnic solidarity and focus on competition and interaction. The primordialists stress the assumed givens of shared culture as the heart of the ethnic matter (Young 1983: 660).

24. On this see for example Tinker 1977. For a critique of this approach see Khan 1994. For recent challenges to this way of thinking about South Asians in the United States, see Prashad 2000, Maira 1999.

25. Much of the research on Asian migrants by U.S. scholars is engaged by questions of identity choices and changes in culture and ethnicity. See, for example, Lal 1999; Srikanth and Maira 1996; Ganguly 1992, 2001; Maira 2002; K. Hall 2002; Shukla 2001; Prashad 2000; Leonard 1992, 1997; Siu 2001, forthcoming; and Lowe 1996. Research on religious practice in the United States is more often focused on community (for example, see Eck 2000; Singh Mann 2000; and Williams 1988).

26. Many have attempted to revise the research agendas that have informed anthropological conceptualizations of British Asians (Baumann 1996; Gillespie 1995, 2000; Hutnyk 2000; Sharma, Hutnyk, and Sharma 1996). Much of the literature pertaining to the complications and shifts of identity as a result of living in Britain is informed by research on Afro-Caribbean minorities (S. Hall 1990, 1991b; Gilroy 1993). Some works challenge the community studies tradition by introducing transnationalism (Brah 1996).

27. August 2000 letter signed by well-established researchers of South Asians in Britain in response to commentary on the state of British anthropology, *Anthropology Today* 16, no. 4: 25.

28. Others have argued against thinking in these prosaic terms of home or insider outsiders. For example, Kumar in *Friends, Brothers and Informants* (1992) declares that her fieldwork in Benares is not fieldwork "at home" (even though she is from Benares) because of class and power differences that create a culture gap between herself and her own upbringing and the lives of her informants.

Moreover, Kiran Narayan's *Storytellers, Saints and Scoundrels* queries her place in anthropology's studying of "the other." She relates an uneasy relationship "as shifting between distance and identifications" (1989: 7) and connects this uneasy relationship to the complexity in being identified as a postcolonial indigenous or native anthropologist (because of her parentage, a Gujarati father and German-American mother, and because of her previous visits to the village in the Gujarat where she conducted her research). In her clarifications, she seeks to dismiss the easy assignment of "insider" research to her work. In fact, both these authors, although working in India, are not "insiders." An option, which has been pursued to undo the dichotomy, is to characterize oneself as both insider and outsider (see, for example, Abu-Lughod 1988: 158, who states she is a partial insider, or see also El-Solh 1988: 111, who states that she is both insider and outsider). This strategy complicates any straightforward understanding of both terms and in doing so serves to highlight the problems with the false dichotomy.

29. The rhetoric of accountability inevitably transforms this debate into an argument of the pros and cons of each position. Marilyn Strathern sees a cultural ease for insider research that leads to "greater reflexivity and enhanced critical awareness." The insider researcher's "processing of knowledge draws on concepts which also belong to the society and culture under study" (Strathern 1987: 18).

30. Under "insider-outsider," I have subsumed "home and away studies" (Jackson 1987; Messerchmidt 1981), which overlap in a significant respect: those at home study as "insiders," and those away as "outsiders."

31. Many have spoken of academic training as a process of "othering" or have viewed the mainstay of anthropology as outsider research (see Altorki 1988; D. J. Jones 1970; Morsy 1988; Nakhleh 1979; Narayan 1989). I am thankful to Patricia Evans, of the Commission on Minority Issues in Anthropology, American Anthropological Association, for her stimulating e-mail discussions on Anthro-L.

32. For a critique of this way of thinking about diaspora, see Shukla 2001.

33. People would mention cousins or aunts and uncles who lived in Toronto, Vancouver, or the United States.

34. This distinction was perhaps more accurate when speaking of white researchers who moved into Asian or African settings.

35. As I previously indicated, the term "minority" is generally found throughout the book without quotation marks, because it is being used in the sense of a numerical minority (that is, it is not used in a pejorative sense as an ethnic marker of perpetual difference).

36. The title for this section, "This, My People," comes from Madanjeet Singh's photographic book of India (1989). By referring to "my people," I invoke the reference common in anthropology to refer to one's group of study; to be clear, this is not a reference to diasporic commonalities.

37. At the time they were only known to me through the Punjabi Hindu referent; I had not yet been corrected by Manoj. My interlocutors, especially Manoj, had not yet been explicit about this.

38. Tabla are two small drums, the main accompanying percussion instrument in Hindustani music. Zakir Hussain, son of Allah Rakha, is one of the world's

foremost tabla players, trained in the Punjab school. Hussain is known for his innovative experiments with the tabla (such as the jazz instrumentalist pieces fusing tabla with guitar).

39. "Uncle" and "Aunty" are fictive kinship terms of respect and connection; they do not refer to any familial relationship between me and those I studied.

40. Pratt (1986) critiques the mythology of the anthropologist's first contact.

41. See also Bashram 1978; Green 1997; Hannerz 1980; Harding and Jenkins 1989; and Toulis 1994.

42. See Introduction regarding the difficulties of estimating the Hindu Punjabi population.

43. The total number, 203, includes religious temples, societies, meeting groups, and youth groups (derived from Weller 1993). This total includes some groups that are categorized as part of "South East England" in Weller's directory (but fall within the Greater London area, such as Harrow, Hounslow, and Ilford).

44. Grillo (1985) used a different sort of strategy. His research turned to organizations that catered to an ethnic clientele to overcome the problems of locating a group. This strategy, although explored in my research, was less effective, because many agencies worked with the category of "Asian" or "Hindu" without language or caste-group affiliations. Defining and locating a community in any prescribed fashion was problematic and unproductive.

45. International Society of Krishna Consciousness (ISKON) main temple in Europe, in an idyllic setting in Hertfordshire, donated by ex-Beatle George Harrison. The connections between ISKON as a new religious movement and the Hinduism of migrants has been detailed in "The Iskonisation of British Hinduisms" (Nye 1996) and "The Indianisation of the Hare Krishna Movement in Britain" (Carey 1987).

46. Hertsmere Council did not give planning permission for public worship and charged the Manor for illegal use of its facilities. The activities and events of the temple received much attention from the media (a BBC documentary, "My Sweet Lord," was also produced). Illegal public worship at the largest temple in Europe (and the dispute) continued until the Department of the Environment granted planning permission to the Manor for building a private road off the motorway. There is only one festival a year (Janmashtami), when a substantial number of people actually attend the temple (twenty to thirty thousand). Diwali is celebrated on a much smaller scale and attracts upward of perhaps five thousand people.

47. Time constraints have factored significantly in field research in Britain. For example, Pocock's (1976) work on a Swaminarayan sect occurred during evenings and weekends with certain Swaminarayan families. Elizabeth Bott (1971 [1957]) also conducted a majority of her participant observation on English couples in the evening. Jackson and Nesbitt (1992) also confirm evening and weekend participant observation.

48. I am grateful to Dr. Leo Howe for the phrase "empirical bricolage."

49. Interviews were conducted with eight women migrants and thirteen male migrants. For the children of migrants, five interviews were with females and six with males.

50. The phrase "cultural broker" has some pejorative connotations, because these individuals are seen as those who have learned both systems and exploit those less powerful. Alternatively, they exploit their minority status to speak for, rather than to open a space for others to speak through. However, when I use the term cultural broker I am referring only to an individual who is able to negotiate the gaps.

51. It is notable that it was primarily women who would introduce me in this manner.

52. "Black," in Britain, has been used to signify African, Caribbean, and South Asian ethnicities. For the politics surrounding the shifting of Black identity in Britain, see Fisher 2001.

53. Homi Bhabha has argued for the concept of a third space, "which constitutes the discursive conditions of enunciation that ensures that the meaning and symbols of culture have no primordial unity or fixity; that even the small signs can be appropriated, translated, rehistoricized and read anew" (1994: 37). Inspired by Bhabha's notion of the constant modifications inherent in the meanings and symbols of culture, but convinced that changing symbolic meaning occurs within a specific sociohistoric framework of power relations, I concentrate on how people negotiate the social and cultural meanings of their various identifications.

54. See Karen Leonard's *Making Ethnic Choices* (1992).

Chapter 2: Being Vilayati, Becoming Asian

1. Hindi has a similar word that means outside: "*bahar.*" This literally refers to being just outside one's door, but it can also suggest being outside the nation. There is no precise Hindi equivalent term for the Punjabi word "Vilayati," which is based on being outside; rather, two terms — "*videshi*" and "*pardeshi*" — are the words that mark a person as being from the outside.

2. While the Baniya and Brahman statuses are generally well known, I need to provide some more details about the Punjab's Kshatriya Khatrīs. British administrators were the first to detail their caste position and customs (Ibbetson 1883: 1911). "Sir George Campbell's *Ethnography of India* admirably describes the position of the Khatri: — 'Trade is their main occupation [in Punjab and Afghanistan]. . . . They are in the Punjab the chief civil administrators, and have almost all literate work in their hand. . . . They are very generally well educated" (qtd. in Ibbetson 1911: 506).

3. See Raj 2000, on the silence surrounding Partition in the second generation.

4. Taken from Lord Paul's speech commemorating the Silver Jubilee of CAPARO. According to the 1997 *Sunday Times* "Britain's Richest 500 List," his worth is estimated at £500 million.

5. Robinson has criticized the paucity of research on middle-class Asians: "The almost total concentration of academics on this group of Indian migrants [the labor migrants] has obscured the existence of a sizeable group of Indian profes-

sional or white collar workers within the UK" (1988: 456). Aside from reviewing some "official statistics indicate that the Indian middle class is growing both in absolute numbers and in relative proportion within the Anglo-Indian population" (1988: 458), he points to the connection between achieving middle-class status and dispersal phenomenon using the term "counter urbanisation." The earlier literature noted this phenomenon in referring to the second-generation achievements of middle-class status and movement beyond their parent's working-class existence (Ballard and Ballard 1977). However, the London Hindu Punjabis with whom I worked had achieved comfortable middle-class status during the migrant's generation, a process reflected in their changing residential patterns, which are dependent on their changing status and means. A notable exception has been the keen interest of economists in self-employed Asians and Asian businessmen (Basu 1996; Srinivasan 1992; Lyon, Lyon, and West 1995).

6. Ali Rattansi makes the connection between class and ethnic identity clear: "Aspirations to middle classness are often seen as heralding a weakening commitment to 'blackness' " (Rattansi 2000: 124).

7. I join other anthropologists in this regard (with the exception of Eade) of not really looking at class as a modality of identity, but instead opting to think through ethnic identity. Although it is clear that I adopt the problematic Weberian notion that class and status are analytically distinct, I have problems with this approach and have begun work on a project that would provide a more nuanced reading of middle-class identity — "Globalization and the American Family: Work, Life and Class for Middle-Class America," Harvard University.

8. A support group for Black and Asian lawyers and a young Asian professional group exists in the United Kingdom, however at the time of my research my interlocutors were not involved in any of these organizations.

9. On the changing nature of the Docklands, see Eade 1996.

10. This sentiment is best captured in the quaint term "repatriation," a proposed procedure calling for the return of the colonial migrants to their colonies and thus, in effect, treating them akin to indentured laborers.

11. The immigration year was before the marriage year for ten men from my core of thirty families. Of those, three were married in the United Kingdom, and for the remainder, the average time in Britain before marriage was 4.28 years. For the four women whose marriage year was earlier than their immigration (that is, they were married before they immigrated), the average wait was 2.9 years after marriage.

12. A few of the direct migrants (both male and female) had come to further their educational qualifications (in teacher training, law, or business studies) after receiving a first degree in India. For these people, there was a sense that perhaps they would return to India after gaining British qualifications.

13. A few of the men had relations in East Africa and they arrived in Britain only after working in East Africa for approximately one to four years.

14. The year 1947 refers to the divide creating India and Pakistan; I review the full details of the Partition in Chapter 3.

15. For exceptions, see Bhachu 1993, 1995, 1999; and P. Werbner 1996b. For gender-informed work on South Asians in America, see Mohanty 1997; Bhattacharjee 1997; Mahmood and Brady 2000; and Maira 2002.

16. In the remainder of the book I use the terms "Uncle" and "Aunty" to refer to those of the parental generation (see below regarding fictive kin terms). At other times I use fictive names and change or omit identifying details.

17. Areas such as Newham (East and West Ham and part of North Woolwich joined to make the London borough of Newham in 1965) have a large West Indian population, Somalian and Bosnian refugees, as well as South Asian migrants from diverse backgrounds. The cultural markers of previous migrations, for example, Jewish cemeteries and synagogues, or remains of synagogues that are found near temples and mosques are reminders that this was an area where immigrants have been settling for many generations.

18. The fact of their work on the factory floor does not immediately contradict the claims for these people to be middle class. Before migration they were from the middle classes and took the job out of necessity, because those in the United Kingdom did not recognize their Indian educational qualifications.

19. Religious education researcher Eleanor Nesbitt (1991, 1995a, 1995b) has conducted the most detailed studies of Hindu Punjabis in Britain to date. Moreover, Hindu Punjabis have been included in other studies, such as Baumann (1996) and Gillespie (1995).

20. See Nesbitt 1991, 1994, 1998a, 1998b, and 1998c. Also see Robinson 1988.

21. There were, however, many studies, beginning in the late 1970s, which included Britain and India or Pakistan as their field sites. These were concerned with cultural change and will be addressed below.

22. On the connections between the army and migration, see Anwar 1979: 21; and Tatla 1995. For a historical account, see Visram 1986.

23. Language is one example, and below I review the historical changes of religion for Hindu Punjabis.

24. For example, Hindustani spoken by Punjabi Hindu Delhi-ites today is a mixture of Punjabi, English, Urdu, and Hindi.

25. For a review of the specific challenges, see Tabili 1994.

26. This is not a call to deny the connections (particularly familial) that individuals may have with India. It is a call to sever the research connection with South Asia that views migrants from South Asia as complicated cultural outposts from the Asian Subcontinent, a position that renders India as the "motherland" and source of all things Asian, denying the ways that Asian identifications occur without reference to a cultural connection to India.

Chapter 3: "I Am from Nowhere"

1. An earlier version of this chapter was published in Raj 1997.

2. My Punjabi teacher and her husband were two of "the few" migrants I met during fieldwork who were young adults at the time of the Partition (I detail her specific concerns in the section on language below).

3. Merging Halbwachs's "collective memory" (1980) with Paul Connerton's ideas of social memory as inscribed in bodily practice (1995) and with Werbner's notion of "postcolonial memory problematics" (R. Werbner 1998), I am interested here in how memory creates a specific notion of an ethnic self. Part of this alludes to the role of forgetting as silence (see Lambek and Antze 1996; Gershon and Raj 2000)

4. The five rivers of the Punjab are the Indus, Jhelum, Chenab, Ravi, and Sutlej.

5. This quotation of Punjab as an "administrative dream" is taken from one of my informants.

6. "Koh-i-Noor" means mountain of light. This diamond is one of the most famous of the Crown Jewels of Great Britain. "On the annexation of the Punjab in 1849 this diamond was claimed by the British" (Howarth 1980: 11); it is now on display at the Tower of London, presented as the main piece in the State Crown of Queen Elizabeth the Queen Mother.

7. On the negotiations of the actual boundary line, see Yong 1997.

8. It should be made clear that none of the references or memories were at first solicited, but once iterated and released during conversations, they were encouraged (for an example, see the reference to Kohat below).

9. The sense and place of homeland for Hindu Punjabis as being forever lost is a repeated theme and will be reviewed below.

10. The silences of the complexity of the past and the "clear" division of the present have already affected young people in Britain, especially regarding Hindu-Muslim tensions. For example, one young Hindu student organization has been speaking to Hindu and Sikh organizations (of the parental generation) around the county about putative acts of religious conversion to Islam by young Hindu and Sikh women. Fear mongering is encouraged by the terms being used, such as "forced conversions," a heated topic reminiscent of 1920s pre-Partition Punjab.

11. While there has been some research on intrareligious tensions (for example, see Nye 1993; Knott 1987; Vertovec 1992), there is a growing need to examine the interreligious tensions of British Asians (see Kundu [1994], who explores tensions between Hindus and Muslims post-Ayodhya). Most work on interreligious factionalization and difference is from CRE research (for example, see R. Singh 1992).

12. The attempts to distance oneself from the racist label "Paki" by the British-born generation include quick replies needed to counter the illogical and ill-informed racists. Being called "Paki," although hurtful, could be countered by claiming one was not a "Paki," and indeed could not be if one was not from Pakistan.

13. On the significance of this date, see Das 1985.

14. Two such advertisements are quoted in full below in Chapter 5, "The Search for a Suitable Boy." I give further ethnographic evidence of this in the next chapter.

15. A *kara* is one of the "five Ks" of Sikhism. Oberoi defines them as "the five external symbols which must be worn by all members of the Khalsa, so called because all five begin with the initial letter 'K.' The five symbols are: *kes* (uncut

hair), *kangha* (comb), *kirpan* (dagger), *kara* (steel bangle) and *kachh* (a pair of breeches)" (1994: xxi).

16. Some of my interlocutors, including but not limited to my core families, would vehemently disagree with this statement. This is especially true for the people who migrated directly from the Punjab. However, for those who are from Partition families, or who experienced the Partition themselves, such as my language teacher, the preference for Hindi and the claim of Hindi as "our" language was not uncommon.

17. According to Oberoi, "[*Mon*] . . . is at present used for those Sikhs who choose to cut their hair" (1994: xxi).

18. Brass writes, "Gurumukhi and Devanagri both have been and can be used to write either Hindi or Punjabi. Since the Sikh scriptures are written in Gurumukhi Sikhs favour the use of that script to write Punjabi. For the same reason, even those Hindus who acknowledge Punjabi as their mother tongue refuse to acknowledge Gurumukhi as its proper script and prefer to use Devanagri instead" (1974: 291). Sachdev states, "There is little doubt that its [Gurmukhi script's] current status as *the* script for writing Punjabi has developed as direct consequence of its association with Sikh identity" (1995: 177).

19. Oberoi explores the importance of Gurmukhi as the Punjabi script of the Sikhs, which resonates with religious meaning as a Gurmuk(i) person is "a follower of the Sikh Gurus and their doctrines" (1994: 51). He also indicates the fluidity of the meaning of the term "Gurmukh."

20. The irony is that this is already the case in India, where the same generation of those who were born in Britain (that is, those who are outside of the Punjab, such as Delhi) understand but do not speak Punjabi.

21. This is parallel with the Muslim Punjabis who might speak Punjabi at home but who are sent to Urdu classes after school or on weekends.

22. Indeed the resources of Hindi popular culture are immense (compared to *regional* languages as Punjabi or Tamil) and the range of Hindi popular culture in England vastly overwhelms what is available in Punjabi. In this the Bombay film industry, Bollywood, is central. However, as Sachdev points out, "Punjabi is the only language in North India which has succeeded in establishing its distinctiveness and vitality vis-à-vis Hindi to the extent of recognition at both nation and state levels in India" (Sachdev 1995: 176).

23. See K. Hall (2002) for details on Sikh youths being taught Punjabi language and the Gurmukhi script through informal classes at the Gurdwara.

24. A raggabhangra pop star whose hit "Arranged Marriage" topped the UK charts in 1992, he is often seen as the epitome of many recent trends and has been used as an example or researched by a few academics (see, for example, Back 1993; Gillespie 1995; Sharma, Hutnyk, and Sharma 1996; Jackson and Nesbitt 1992).

25. In Chapter 7, I seek to carry these ideas farther by exploring the issues of homeland and belonging with respect to the parental generation.

26. This is a reference to the former Conservative minister Norman Tebbit's infamous "test" of allegiance for Britain's ethnic minorities. In 1985 he suggested that an Asian's allegiance could be ascertained by which cricket team he or she supported during a match between England and Pakistan or India.

Chapter 4: Becoming a Hindu Community

1. Although I do not pursue the discussion here, the sense of a minority religion is interconnected in part to the activism and "rebellion" of young Asians in different places (Southall, Bradford, and so forth), and in part because of the ways that Muslims and Sikhs are thought to be much more visible in the public sphere in Britain.

2. See, for instance, the text of the Hansard debate of Tuesday, June 20, 2000, or Lord Hansard's text for Thursday, February 3, 2000.

3. For a discussion of difference as the construct of the state, see Gershon 2001.

4. As discussed in the Introduction, the last census does not ask about religious affiliation. However, the importance of boosting the Hindu population can be seen by the various estimates offered by "community leaders" (these range between 450,000 and 1 million).

5. *Sahajdhari* is defined as "those who practiced Guru Nanak's inward practise of *nam simeran* [repeating the name of God] as opposed to the exterior practises of khalsa identity" (McLeod 1989: 45). By contrast, *keshdharis* display the five Ks of Sikhism (*kangee, kesh, kacha, kara, kirpan*, respectively, comb, hair, undergarment, steel bangle, and small sword). These attributes are related to the anti-Islam cause of the 10th Sikh guru, Guru Gobind Singh. Those who follow these teachings are known variously as Singh, Khalsa, or Keshdhari Sikhs.

6. I am using the categories of "Sikh" and "Hindu" discretely (an unfamiliar usage for that period). However, a language that can only indicate syncretism in the terms of modern-day categories binds me to this reference.

7. See, for example, Cohn's exegesis on the census (1990) and his *Colonialism and its Forms of Knowledge* for how the colonial state governed by using "objectification" and the "documentation" project (1996: xv).

8. For the effects of the creation of boundaries in the Punjab, see K. Jones 1976; Juergensmeyer 1982; and Fox 1985, who all recount various competitions for limited resources. Accounts of census taking and the politics of enumeration are reviewed by Cohn (1990).

9. I do not see the creation of distinct "religions" and the competition of limited resources as an explicit divide-and-rule policy; the British used their own worldview to understand India and to administer it cheaply. For example, after the Mutiny Rebellion of 1857 soldiers were kept in mixed caste and regional units within the ranks.

10. See Chapter 3 on how language boundaries also separated along community fractures.

11. Similarly, problems arose for classifying Hindus. For example, in the 1881 census Ibbetson states that classification as "Hindu" was done residually as "he who is not a Muslim, Christian, Sikh, Jain or Buddhist" (Ibbetson 1883). Max Weber also reviews the various definitions of "Hindu" found in the British India census (1958: 4).

12. For a different interpretation of how Singh identity came to be solidified, see Oberoi 1994.

13. In some respects, Arya reforms instituted in the nineteenth century still resemble early Protestantism: for example, they do not practice idol worship, and

religious lectures are the focus of communal gatherings. Moreover, the Vedas are seen as the supreme text of Hinduism (the only text), forcing single text and belief system onto the heterodox. As K. Jones (1976) and others have argued, the movement began with urban middle-class Hindus who thought they were being discriminated against in terms of the allotment of government posts.

14. For details on the "to be or not to be" vegetarian debates, see K. Jones 1976: 170. Furthermore, for many Hindu Punjabis meat eating is neither forbidden nor surrounded by proscriptions (in fact, vegetarianism for Punjabi Hindus has only become more common since the Partition).

15. These policies have continued as revealed by the Mandal Commission report (1980) submitted by B. P. Mandal on December 31, 1980, to the President of India. In 1991, the first attempts to introduce the Mandal Commission reforms resulted in self-immolation and widespread protests. The reforms were implemented in September 1993 and they guaranteed the reservation of approximately 50 percent of the places in employment in government services and education for "scheduled castes, tribes, backward castes and other backward castes (OBC)."

16. See Chapter 3 for more details of the historic changes in Punjab's boundaries and the implications for Hindu Punjabi identity.

17. For the importance of food purity, see Khan 1994; for the political significance of food in a South Asian context, see Appadurai 1981. On the changing nature of the status of vegetarian and nonvegetarian; see K. Jones 1976: 170. On the relationship between food and socioeconomic structure, see Goody 1982.

18. The domestic temple is where pictures, statues of deities, and holy books are kept in the home. It may also be a place where regular worship occurs in the home.

19. There has been an immense and long-standing focus on changed ritual practice in the Hindu diaspora. For an example of the emphasis on contrasting Subcontinental South Asians and those overseas found in earlier accounts, see the articles by Morris and Firth and others in the special issue of the *British Journal of Sociology* (H. S. Morris 1957; R. Firth 1957). The perspective of comparing and contrasting Indians overseas with the "home culture" is condemned by Khan (1994). For a more recent example, see Burghart (1987) and S. Firth (1996), who separately write on death and dying rituals and the submersion of ashes in the Thames.

20. Thus, the historically documented cultural experiences outlined above do not indicate an "original cultural practice" (albeit syncretic), which has become polluted by migration.

21. For instance, the Department of Environment hearings regarding public worship at Bhaktivedanta Manor in Letchmore Heath became a debate with two opposing sides: the right to worship versus the right to protect the environment.

22. As mentioned above, I also met people through the temple. The ironic thing is that without first going to each temple, I couldn't locate the temple where these people went. I had to find the people to first take me to the temple and then meet people through the temple.

23. The statue of Baba Balak Nath is a recent addition with which many of the families of my research were not familiar, or they knew him only by name. Baba Balak Nath is a male hermit guru followed in rural Punjab by lower castes; in Britain he is associated with working-class migrants.

24. The Swaminaryan movement is a neo-Hindu Vaishnavite reformist movement that began in the eighteenth century in Western India (mainly in Gujarat). For details on its rising popularity among overseas Gujaratis, see Dwyer 1994: 175–78.

25. The Satya Sai Baba guru movement "centers on the figure of Satya Sai Baba, who was born in 1926 and claims to be the reincarnation of the Sai Baba of Shirdi who died in 1918" (R. Williams 1988: 51). He claims to be the incarnation of Shiva and has gained a large following among middle-class Hindus in India (J. Kelly 1995: 44, passim) as well as a large number of "Westerners" (R. Williams 1988: 50). He is a transnational guru with a large global following.

26. The poster in support of the Manor found in this temple (and indeed in other places, such as businesses) further supports the connections between ISKON and the Hinduism of migrants.

27. Whereas Friday is sacred for Muslims, Saturday is for Jews, and Sunday is for Christians, in Hindu practice there are no prescriptions such as a day of Sabbath. However, specific days of the week are associated with specific deities, for instance, Tuesday is associated with Hanuman.

28. I was told that weddings and wedding receptions are often on Sunday for these reasons as well, since "it is a well known fact that if you have a wedding on a Saturday, less people will turn up."

29. R. Ballard (1989) has documented the factionalization of Sikh "community" in spaces of public worship. The divisions of Jain community in belief and practice are established in Banks (1991).

30. In fact, it is not only in the visit to the temple that the checking out of potential marriage partners is done, but often temples have publications that list and advertise eligible potentials who are "looking" (see the extensive related discussion below in Chapter 5).

31. I explore the concept of community and fixity of religious identity further in Chapter 6.

32. The rituals of the temple, such as puja and seva, which are done six times a day at ISKON temples, or where deities' outfits are changed twice daily, is not a requirement of home temples because most of the murtis in the home temples have not undergone *pran pratishtha*, the giving of "life" to the murti, when the deity enters and inhabits the stone.

33. In general, the regular worship is a woman's domain. They are seen and see themselves as the keepers and bearers of tradition. This role can be seen in the practices of women who on behalf of their husbands or children can perform certain rituals for well-being and success. What is interesting is not women's roles as bearers of tradition (McDonald 1987: passim; Burghart 1987: 9), but rather how this has changed because of the diaspora. Many families have only remote extended families (sometimes not in the same city), if their families are in the U.K. at all. The implications for home worship are clear. Because there is no elderly mother-in-law guiding what is done, the women often continue with their natal home practices. However, in their natal families, they were familiar with but not (as daughters) responsible for the family worship (this was their mother's role). For this reason, many rituals and practices put into use after migration and marriage are often gleaned from friends or others performing ceremonies. This pat-

tern of worship stands in sharp contrast to India, where virilocal residence requires that certain family traditions of the husband's family be followed.

34. In two cases I observed, the men were responsible for home worship. One man (himself born in India and married to a British-born Hindu Punjabi woman whom he met while studying in London) said that since she "didn't know" the traditions, he was responsible for them. Eventually she would take over this duty. He was also concerned that their son be raised in a Hindu home. "She doesn't know anything, I have had to teach her. . . . Unless you know about the religion then what can you do? I have had to teach her. . . . I light a jot at home and here at work every morning [he owns his own business]." The other was a male who did puja, lighting the jot and performing arti together with his wife every morning and night. On Sunday, they performed a longer reading from the *Ramayana*. These men are exceptions. Men, if they worshipped at home, usually did so not in connection to their wife's activities. For men who owned their own business they might have had a temple in their office, at work, or in a corner of their shop, or they lit an incense sick in front of a picture of a deity mounted on a wall. At home they prayed in front of the mandir, and often they recited mantras (not necessarily in front of the mandir).

35. By this I do not mean to imply that commodification of Hinduism is a novel practice, but rather that the forms that this commodification takes are specific to the late twentieth century. The *Mahabharat* and the *Ramayan* are performative epics, and for centuries their media have been tale-telling, traveling performers, and regular recitals. Television and video have replaced these forms.

36. See Nesbitt 1991, who examines the role of video for young children. Gillespie has called this "devotional viewing," but I did not observe anyone who linked orthodox practice with their viewing in the manner that Gillespie describes "at the start of a religious film, incense is lit and when a favourite god such as Krishna appears, the mother will encourage her children to sit up straight and make a devout salutation. An extra *puja* . . . may be performed before or after viewing" (1995: 89). When I asked people if they did anything even slightly religious, or if they had seen anyone do anything religious in connection with watching religious TV, the responses were all negative.

37. The Gayatri Mantra, translated in the Glossary, is often seen as a defining and easily learned core to Vedic knowledge.

38. The lack of child-focused activities is perhaps due to recent political problems; there were classes being held in the temple previously. Other temples, the Vishwa Hindu Parishad temple most significantly (the group connected to Hindu activism in India), have regular classes for children in Hindi, as well as music instruction, while followers of Sai Baba hold Bal Vikas classes to teach about religion. (On Hinduism and children, see Pocock's 1976 work with the Swaminarayan in London; and Jackson and Nesbitt 1992).

39. With the rise in second-generation Hindu activism and awareness, and a general change in the ethnic nature of Hinduism in diaspora (see Bhatt and Mukta 2000), the HP youth sense of their Hinduism has changed dramatically since my initial fieldwork.

40. For story, see Kripalani, "Virtual Virtue," *Business Week*, February 26, 2001, 10.

Chapter 5: The Search for a Suitable Boy

1. The assumptions of cultural clash and marriage can also be found in many media portrayals of marriage. For example, see two articles: "Wedding Values of East and West," *International Herald Tribune*, July 21, 1998, 2; and "Slaying, Trial of Clashing Cultures," *The Washington Post*, August 29, 2000, B7.

2. These time spans are based on the periods between first introductions and marriage, not including the time from which the topic of marriage is first raised, which could in fact be as long as ten years.

3. This chapter repeatedly highlights the importance of caste for deeming the suitability of marriage partners; however, the social phenomenon of caste is not debated in this book. As this chapter reflects, my fieldwork allows me only to speak of caste as part of the marriage process and as only one criterion among many for vetting potential partners. Caste plays a less crucial role among those I researched because of their relatively small population and the acceptance of inter-marriage between Brahmans, Khattris, and Banias (for a full exploration of caste in India, see S. Bayly 1999; for an overview of caste and other concepts related to studying Asians in Britain, see P. Werbner 1987).

4. Chanana (1993) indicates a more relaxed attitude to regional exogamy among post-Partition Hindu Punjabis.

5. Westwood (1984) explores these claims of arranged marriage, as does Vatuk (1972) in her work in urban India.

6. "Coconut" is a derogatory term used by the British-born generation, but now also by their parents. It was explained to me thus: "It's brown on the outside and white on the inside," an image of those who despite having "brown" skin are culturally "white."

7. See P. Werbner 1996b, on the effervescence of social relationships among British Pakistanis.

8. North India ethnographies often record parental obligations; for example, Lewis states, "It is a vital obligation for a man to get his daughters married. His salvation in the other world and his peace of mind in this one depend on it" (O. Lewis 1958: 158).

9. Many Gujarati communities have adapted the process of arranged marriage in a particularly British way. Caste-based community centers hold a function approximately six to twelve times a year where young males and females meet. Some of these are highly organized and individuals are given colored name tags indicating their age range. Older women and men in the room can be asked for an introduction to a particular person. Often the rooms deliberately do not have any chairs, thus ensuring circulation. Parents are sometimes present at these functions. I have not heard of any Punjabi Hindus who have organized such events and suspect that this is because of the relatively small population.

10. Ballard documents this out-migration using census numbers. He states, "Out-migration, not so much back to India itself, but rather onwards to the United States and Canada [occurred for Asians]. The majority of such migrants were young adults, usually with advanced educational and professional qualifications, but who had grown frustrated by the forces of racial exclusionism they so routinely encountered in Britain; as word began to circulate that those constraints were far less intense on the other side of the Atlantic, and ever increasing number of young British Indians appear — given the results of the 1991 Census — to have taken the opportunity to move on yet further to take advantage of the better opportunities elsewhere" (R. Ballard 1999).

11. "Uncle's cousin" was in fact Uncle's second cousin: Uncle's mother and this man's mother are cousins.

12. This is an enduring American dream for the migrants, which they are attempting to realize through their children. The migration possibilities of America and Canada (not only through marriage) were often a topic of discussion for British-born Asians. During field research my husband and I were often asked about migration to America and Canada, that is, about the "possibilities" (economic climate), the general temperament of the people, as well as the legal aspects involved in green-card status.

13. Other existing sources "for looking" that a few people I knew would consider using included marriage bureaus, advertisements in Asian newspapers, as well as the Sunday afternoon show on Sunrise Radio to which people would call in their son's, daughter's, or friend's details to be broadcast around London and via satellite to Europe, Mauritius, and other places.

14. Bhachu identifies the others as caste endogamy, cognate exogamy, and village exogamy. She also indicates preferences for marriage alliance, such as regional endogamy, that have arisen because of living in Britain (Bhachu 1985: esp. chap. 5).

15. The phrase "clean shaven" indicates a preference for not marrying an observant Sikh or a Khalsa Sikh, because long hair signals the man's "traditional outlook." It is not an aesthetic judgment.

16. Similarly, "a marriage advertisement placed by an Indian immigrant [to America] provides a fascinating mix of self-portrait and image of a future spouse" (Menon 1989: 180).

17. Westwood refers to the opportunities for "flirting" at Gujarati weddings (1984: 153); and Gillespie indicates that the Sikh temple in Southall is also one such space: "Young people are encouraged to attend regularly and many do so not only for religious reasons but also because it is an opportunity for socialising. The Gurdwara is a good place to 'spot' and 'check out' potential boy- and girl friends, many young people claim; their parents turn a blind eye to surreptitious, silent flirtation in this context, because it poses no threat to the norm of caste endogamy" (Gillespie 1995: 31).

18. Pointing to the "claim" does not call into question the nature of the alliance, but rather reiterates that marriages that claim to be arranged sometimes are not. Of course, this is only possible in cases where both male and female are Hindu Punjabi. In fact, before one wedding I attended the groom's mother had told me that the couple had known each other at university. She boasted, "I don't

get involved in that for any of my sons, that is their life." Yet, at the wedding itself, she said that she had found the girl through friends who knew her mother's brother "up north."

19. This is an unstated but valued concern related to the guest-host relationship and to entertaining guests in a specific way.

20. The pundits may be connected with a temple, or may be "part-time," that is, from Brahmin families and who already have other full-time employment, but they practice some religious ceremonies and functions.

21. "Registry wedding" refers to the registration of the wedding at the local authority in England, a process of state recognition of a marriage. Aside from the official questions and responses with the official, the family attend and there are ceremonies surrounding this state wedding ceremony.

Chapter 6: Becoming British Asian

1. On a "new European racism," see Balibar 1991a; on the move from an "ethnocentric to a Eurocentric racism," see Sivanandan 1988.

2. A very interesting proposition about the significance of race for global capitalism has been advanced by Brodkin as the conundrum of making "nations at once multiracial and racist (or otherwise xenophobic)" (2000: 250). This framing speaks directly to the experiences I document.

3. On the entanglements of cultural difference, racism, and the nation-state in Britain, see Gilroy 1987; on the European turn to culture, race, and immigration in Europe, see Cole 1997; and Stolcke 1995. For a review of research on race in Britain, see Malik 1996; for race and the connections between Europe and South Asia, see Robb 1995.

4. The term "visible ethnic minorities" is modified from the Canadian phrase "visible minority," the opposite of "invisible minority." Basically the two terms differentiate by color: invisible minorities are "white" migrants from Ukraine, Italy, and so on, while the "visible minorities" are South Asian, Chinese, and Afro-Caribbean migrants.

5. There are, however, some who have been concerned with class and discrimination research, such as the Commission for Racial Equality (CRE).

6. Quudas Ali was a young Bangladeshi man from Tower Hamlets whose head was "smashed around like a football" by twenty National Front young men. One of those who did the beating was charged, because his girlfriend turned him in after he had bragged to her and her mother about "killing a Paki." The story made national headlines during my fieldwork.

7. For a comparative understanding of parental strategies toward race as articulated in the United States, see Lessinger 1995.

8. This relates to many men's and women's pursuit of further schooling and qualifications in Britain while working full time.

9. By "Guru Nanak," this woman meant Gurpurb, celebrated as the day of Guru Nanak's birth.

10. For a scholarly challenge to ideas of "Asian" success, see Modood 1992,

who provides figures on educational achievements among Pakistanis and Bangladeshis. The 1991 census also contains detailed information.

11. He is not alone. Recently it was revealed that "the CRE is 'concerned' that doctors from ethnic minority backgrounds are less likely to be given consultant or other senior posts in the health service than white doctors (Guardian 26/4/96)" (from the ASACACHIB newsletter, September 16, 1996).

12. Thanks to Ilana Gershon for this helpful way to think about how people interpret racism.

13. See Banks 1996: 101, for a review of Asian versus Black; see Baumann 1996: 161–72, for an ethnographic discussion of "Black" and "Asian" political communities in Southall.

14. The "Newham Seven" trials exposed the racist policing of Newham when seven young Asian men were put on trial because they had started a fight with "scruffily dressed" men who were verbally abusing them. The "scruffy" men were in fact plainclothes police officers who "in defense" had attacked the youths involved (see Newham Monitoring Project 1991, "The Forging of a Black Community," for more details)

15. By "misunderstandings and perceptions" I am glossing the general comments made by the women after the meetings; they asked me how my family had arranged my marriage.

16. I tape-recorded with their permission.

17. The young man helped young Hindus to organize around a category of identity despite regional differences; HPs in this audience were moved enough to form a group.

18. To claim that the documentaries have a liberal multicultural ethic in their programming gives the producers full benefit of any doubt about their intentions. However, the multiculturalism they espouse is in fact "illiberal," partially because the buzzwords such as "diversity" and "difference" in fact become explorations of cultural gaps in experience. This reification of cultural difference is no less likely to lead to misunderstanding and conflict than the premulticulturalism approaches because it shares the same understanding about what constitutes "culture."

19. This figure is found in the introduction to Clarke, Peach, and Vertovec 1990.

20. This, I believe, relates to the eclecticism and minimal religious practice of some of my younger informants. They do not assert any identity overtly and instead negotiate the categorical labels by constantly shifting their identifications and the meanings that they attach to them (see, for instance, the examples given in Chapter 4 regarding eating practices).

Chapter 7: Becoming a Person of Indian Origin

1. *India Abroad*, November 3, 2000, 28.

2. See Rouse 1991, who sets up this distinction with respect to his work in Mexico.

3. I take issue with this research and the assumptions that allow a researcher

to go to India to understand British Asians (whose individual members may have migrated as many as forty years ago). Present-day South Asia, where rapid economic, social, and political changes have occurred so radically as to alter the society from which the migrants came, is not a repository of information shedding light on British Asians. The fact of change is perhaps best noted by the children of migrants who travel to India only to discover that their values and customs are of an India of twenty-odd years ago. Youth have spoken about their cousins or relatives' musings about the "traditionalism" of their Vilayati kin, or the British-born youth recount the shock experienced when they see girls wearing miniskirts or shorts when visiting Delhi or Bombay. Yet even today there is an understanding that migrants can be understood by looking to South Asia.

4. As it is typically used, "diaspora" has no social scientific analytical power; of course it has enormous folk and NGO symbolic value/power. It could perhaps be made into a more useful social science category with careful delimitation and use. For example, one way (and there are many others) might be to restrict it definitionally to apply to the domain of folk speech and talk about being displaced from "home." However, like the symbolically potent cousin word "refugee" (ditto "racism"), the folk and NGO meaning load of "diaspora" is so strong that in practice just about everyone doing studies of "diasporas" uses the word more or less like the people being researched. The result is often a kind of vacuous circularity; at the heart of explanation, it seems to me, is an effort to explain one thing by establishing its connections to other things. One can't easily do this—get outside the box—if one's analytical concepts are identical with the folk domains you are studying. My thanks to Norman Buchignani for this additional insight.

5. "East Indian" in both instances differentiates the migrant population from the "Indian," or Native American indigenous population. In Canada, "East Indians" are sometimes also referred to as "Canadians of South Asian descent."

6. Radhakrishnan's Moebius strip reference is reminiscent of Zizek, who writes, "The frontier that separates us from them is explored in all its arbitrariness. . . . We are forces to renounce the safe distance of external observers: as in a Moebius strip, the part and the whole coincide, so that it is not longer possible to draw a clear and unambiguous line" (qtd. in Bhabha 1998a: 124).

7. The "myth of return" is an example of an early attempt to move beyond a simple there/here phenomenon and reject the ideas of connections between the migrant and a homeland, hence the reference as "myth."

8. For a brilliant exegesis on the complexities of the connections and the imagination of homeland, see Khan 1994.

9. See Ballard and Ballard 1977, who separate the experiences of Sikhs and Muslims regarding the myth of return.

10. Part of the sense of "being from nowhere" felt by the Hindu Punjabis is related to the fact that their families are scattered around the world. For many, they may have one sibling in India and another in Canada, or perhaps, cousins in America. For the core group of families, only one had immediate relatives in London (Nishma's father's brother lived nearby). The location of close relatives

allowed them to travel a lot, for weddings and other ceremonies. While I was conducting fieldwork, only Arti's sisters came to visit from America; afterward however, there were visits from various aunts and uncles from India.

11. Of course the purchase of NRI flats is also related to citizenship, taxation, and legalities of property ownership (foreign-passport holders cannot own land in India).

12. This is a somewhat ironic stance, given the response of India to the East African refugee situation.

13. For a history of the changed meaning of overseas Indian, see Axel 2002.

14. See Lessinger 1992, for details of NRI investments.

15. See Indian Foreign Exchange Regulation Act of 1973, for official interest in developing relations with India's' émigrés. Ong (1999) and Louie (2000) outline comparative examples of homeland building, from China. Ong refers to "*hai-wai huaren*" (1999: 43), which is "an ambiguous label that removed the old stigma of huaquio [overseas Chinese] but retains the master symbol of irrefutable racial/cultural links to the motherland" (1999: 43).

16. A high commissioner is the equivalent of an ambassador for emissaries between Commonwealth countries.

17. From http://www.indianembassy.org/special/cabinet/president/addressto theparliament.html.

18. From http://www.indianembassy.org/inews/April99/PIO.html.

19. Ibid.

20. Ibid.

21. The full text of the PIO card application form states: "Expression 'India' as given in sub-section (1) of the section 311 of the Government of India act, 1935 means British India together with all territories of any Indian ruler under the suzerainty of His Majesty, all territories under the suzerainty of such an Indian ruler, the tribal areas, and any other territories which His Majesty in council may, from time to time, after ascertaining the views of the federal Government and the Federal legislature, declare to be part of India."

22. One man I met in a temple asked if I was from Delhi and, on finding I was from Canada, told me of his plans to establish a "Delhi wala" club. Unfortunately, this club, which would have supported the reformulated homeland proposition, has not yet been instituted.

23. *The Observer Magazine,* September 19, 1999, 17.

24. In a way, this process could be taken for further evidence for Axel's assertion that the "*diaspora* has produced the homeland" (2001: 199).

Chapter 8: "Where Are You *Originally* From?"

1. September 29, 2000, at FT.com. The full article is found on: http://news.ft. com/ft/gx.cgi/ftc?pagename = View&c = Article&cid = FT3VU40TODC&live = true&tagid = ZZZU2IUKJoC. My thanks to Tara Arden Smith, of the Radcliffe Institute for Advanced Study, for this information and for providing the Web address.

2. Andrew Marr, *The Observer Review,* January 30, 2000, Culture Section 5.

3. On the challenge to posed by European Integration, see Darian-Smith 1999.

4. The report discusses, among other issues, the conflation of British with English.

5. In Britain, governing ethnic minorities has never been a hot topic, excepting when those seeking elected office conflate immigration with issues of existing minorities for political gain.

6. On the differences between the United States and Spain, see Greenhouse with Roshanak Kheshti 1998.

7. Britain's long-standing colonial encounters with the "other" partially challenge the very self that created the notion of an absolute other.

8. In 1985 Norman Tebbit suggested that Asians' allegiances could be ascertained by which cricket team they supported during a match between England and Pakistan or India. "Tebbit's 'cricket test' was understood as a measure whereby fans from minority ethnic communities . . . revealed their ultimate lack of willingness to join mainstream *English* society by cheering on teams from their ancestral homes when that team played England in international cricket matches" (Kundu 2002, personal communication).

9. During this period "Black" identity was promoted for all people of color, a topic of much debate among academics.

10. This organization has successfully established Hindu societies across UK institutions of higher education and is involved in actively promoting a Hindu identity, which is separate from an Asian identity.

11. From *Figure One, Final Report of the Advisory Group on Citizenship,* September 22, 1998, 44.

12. I borrow here from Strathern's (1997) ideas of accountability and "audit culture" for organizations, in which performance is monitored and complexity is leveled by the act of making institutions monitor and describe themselves. "Audit culture is audit enhanced" (Strathern 1997: 5); it includes a management consultancy view of the world in which measurements, targets, and improvements are emphasized. I am emphasizing the former sense in which individuals are accountable for their own difference.

13. Nira Yuval-Davis and F. Anthias (1989) explore how categories were discussed, thought about, and refined with feedback from representatives of those communities.

14. These categories are regional ethnic differences that are used by Asians to distinguish themselves. Thus, young people meeting each other for the first time might ask, "Are you Punjabi or Gujurati?" as I was asked by one young man.

15. One way people in the field wanted to respond to the inaccurate use of the term "Indian" was to add a religious category (particularly during the political activism incited by the controversy surrounding Bhaktivedanta Manor, the Hindu temple that had an injunction to close its doors to public worship). The 2001 census, for the first time in British census-taking history, included a question of religion: subsumed in the box "Christian" are Church of England, Catholic, Protestants, and all other Christian denominations. The coalescence of ethnicity

to nation to religion may have very politically charged long-term social consequences. In particular, it will change the ways that the British/non-British divide is fragmenting.

16. The first category for ethnic group identification, is after all, white, a racial category then broken down into British and Irish.

17. This does not imply that the replacement of one categorical identification for another (that is, Hindu Punjabi for Indian) is more precise and therefore always more desirable. For example, the verification of exclusion and disadvantage (discrimination based on ethnicity) constitute one such moment and would be a case when nominal identification with a larger category is necessary.

18. Greenhouse and Greenwood write, "Official discourses of difference are competitive, given their implied access to entitlements and resources, and ambivalence is potentially costly. It is that zero-sum (i.e., the pressure to choose an identity) prefigured in official discourse that constitutes the hegemonic aspect of liberalism" (1998: 15).

19. This question is distressing for the children of migrants. They are strangers in their parent's putative homelands, because like their parents, they are Vilayati, from the outside. Yet, by virtue of being asked where they are from, they are also receiving the message that they do not belong in Britain either.

20. Thanks to Purnima Mankekar for this insight.

21. For an official exegesis of the conflation of English and British, see British Council Report, *Looking into England* (2000).

22. The English once thought of the Irish as nonwhite.

23. *India Abroad,* November 3, 2000, 28.

24. *Express India,* January 9, 2001.

25. *India Abroad,* November 3, 2000, 28.

26. Debates on the utility of "culture" and identity as analytical concepts include: Geertz (1973); Strathern (1995b); Kelly and Kaplan (2001); and Handler (1994).

27. This is Geertz's term used to critique E. B. Tylor's idea of culture as "'most complex whole,' which, its originative power not denied, seems to me to have reached the point where it obscures a good deal more than it reveals" (Geertz 1973: 4).

28. For example, see Elliston 2000.

29. See, for example, Shukla 1997: 304.

Bibliography

Abu-Lughod, L. 1988. Fieldwork of a dutiful daughter. In *Arab women in the field: Studying your own society*, ed. S. Altorki and C. F. El-Solh. New York: Syracuse University Press.

Ahmed, S. 1978. Asian girls in culture conflict. *Social Work Today* 9: 14–16.

Alexander, Claire. 2000. *The Asian gang*. Oxford: Berg.

Altorki, S. 1988. At home in the field. In *Arab women in the field: Studying your own society*, ed. S. Altorki and C. F. El-Solh. New York: Syracuse University Press.

Altorki, S., and C. F. El-Solh, eds. 1988. *Arab women in the field: Studying your own society*. New York: Syracuse University Press.

Anderson, Benedict. 1983. *Imagined communities*. London: Verso.

Andrews, A. 1996. Social deprivation and South Asian religions in the UK. Paper presented to the Comparative Study of the South Asian Diaspora Religious Experience in Britain, Canada and USA, SOAS, November 4–6, 1996.

Anthias, F. 1998. Evaluating "diaspora" beyond ethnicity. *Sociology* 32: 557–80.

Anwar, M. 1995. "New Commonwealth" migration to the UK. In *The Cambridge survey of world migration*, ed. R. Cohen. Cambridge: Cambridge University Press.

———. 1979. *The myth of return: Pakistanis in Britain*. London: Heinemann.

———. 1976. Young Asians between two cultures. *New Society* 38: 563–65.

Appadurai, A. 1998. Dead certainty: Ethnic violence in the era of globalization. *Public Culture* 10: 225–47.

———. 1996. *Modernity at large. Cultural dimensions of globalization*. Minneapolis and London: University of Minnesota Press.

———. 1991. Global ethnoscapes: Notes and queries for a transnational anthropology. In *Recapturing anthropology*, ed. R. G. Fox. Santa Fe, N.M.: School of American Research Press.

——. 1990. Disjuncture and difference in the global cultural economy. *Theory, Culture and Society* 6: 295–310.

——. 1981. Gastropolitics in Hindu South Asia. *American Ethnologist* 8: 494–511.

Appiah, K. A. 1994. Identity, authenticity, survival: Multicultural societies and social reproduction. In *Multiculturalism: Examining the politics of recognition,* ed. Charles Taylor and Amy Gutmann, 149–63. Princeton, N.J.: Princeton University Press.

Axel, Brian Keith. 2002. The diasporic imaginary. *Public Culture* 14.

——. 1996. Time and threat: Questioning the production of the diaspora as an object of study. *History and Anthropology* 9: 415–43.

——. 2001. *The nation's tortured body.* Durham, N.C.: Duke University Press.

Back, L. 1993. X amount of Sat Siri Akal — Apache Indian, Reggae music and intermezzo culture. Unpublished paper.

Balibar, Etienne. 1996. Is European Citizenship possible? *Public Culture* 8, no. 2: 355–76.

——. 1991a. Es Gibt Keinen Staat in Europa: Racism and politics in Europe today. *New Left Review,* no. 186: 5–19.

——. 1991b. The nation form: History and ideology. In *Race, nation, class: Ambiguous identities,* ed. E. Balibar and I. Wallerstein. London: Verso.

Ballard, C. 1979. Conflict, continuity and change: Second generation South Asians. In *Minority families in Britain: Support and stress,* ed. V. Saifullah-Khan. London: Macmillan.

Ballard, Roger. 1999. Polyethnic Britain: A comparative and historical perspective. http://www.art.man.ac.uk/CASAS/Publicat.htm.

——. 1997. The construction of a conceptual vision: "Ethnic groups" and the 1991 UK Census. *Ethnic and Racial Studies* 20: 182–94.

——, ed. 1994a. *Desh Pardesh: The South Asian presence in Britain.* London: C. Hurst and Company.

——. 1994b. Introduction: The emergence of Desh Pardesh. In *Desh Pardesh: The South Asian presence in Britain,* ed. R. Ballard. London: C. Hurst and Company.

——. 1992. New clothes for the Emperor?: The conceptual nakedness of the race relations industry in Britain. *New Community* 18: 481–92.

——. 1989. Differentiation and disjunction amongst the Sikhs in Britain. In *The Sikh diaspora,* ed. N. G. Barrier and V. A. Dusenbery. Delhi: Chanakya Publications.

Ballard, R., and C. Ballard. 1977. The Sikhs: The development of South Asian settlement in Britain. In *Between two cultures,* ed. J. Watson. Oxford: Blackwell.

Ballard, R., and V. S. Kalra. 1994. *The ethnic dimensions of the 1991 census: A preliminary report.* Manchester: Manchester Census Group.

Ballard, R. et al. 2000. Letter response to Nigel Rapport's commentary on the state of British Anthropology. *Anthropology Today* 16, no. 4: 25

Banks, M. 1996. *Ethnicity: Anthropological constructions.* London: Routledge.

——. 1991. Orthodoxy and dissent: Varieties of religious belief among immigrant Gujarati Jains in Britain. In *The assembly of listeners: Jains in society,* ed. M. Carrithers and C. Humphrey. Cambridge: Cambridge University Press.

Barker, M. 1981. *The new racism.* London: Junction Books.

Barrier, N. G. 1989. Sikh emigrants and their homeland: The transmission of information, resources and values in the early twentieth century. In *The Sikh diaspora,* ed. N. G. Barrier and V. A. Dusenbery. Delhi: Chanakya Publications.

Barrier, N. G., and V. A. Dusenbery, eds. 1989. *The Sikh diaspora.* Delhi: Chanakya Publications.

Barth, F., ed. 1969. *Ethnic groups and boundaries: The social organization of cultural difference.* London: Allen and Unwin.

Bashram, R. 1978. *Urban anthropology: The cross cultural study of complex societies.* Palo Alto, Calif.: Mayfield Publishing Company.

Basu, A. 1996. Migration and entrepreneurship: South Asian businesses in Britain. Paper presented to the 14th European Modern South Asia Conference, Copenhagen.

Baumann, G. 1996. *Contesting culture: Discourses of identity in multi-ethnic London.* Cambridge: Cambridge University Press.

Bayly, C. A. 1985. The pre-history of communalism. In *Modern Asian Studies* 19: 177–203.

Bayly, S. 1999. *Caste, society and politics in India.* Cambridge: Cambridge University Press.

Bell, C., and H. Newby. 1972. *Community studies.* New York: Praeger Publishers.

Benson, S. 1996. Asians have culture, West Indians have problems: Discourses of race and ethnicity in and out of anthropology. In *Culture, identity and politics: Ethnic minorities in Britain,* ed. T. Ranger, Y. Samad, and O. Stuart. Aldershot, UK: Avebury.

———. 1981. *Ambiguous ethnicity: Interracial families in London.* Cambridge: Cambridge University Press.

Bhabha, Homi K. 1998a. Anxiety in the midst of difference. *Political and Anthropology Review* 21, no. 1: 123–37.

———. 1998b. Culture's in-between. In *Multicultural states: Rethinking difference and identity,* ed. David Bennett. London and New York: Routledge.

———. 1994. *The location of culture.* London: Routledge.

———. 1990a. The third space: Interview with Homi Bhabha. In *Identity: Community, culture, difference,* ed. J. Rutherford. London: Lawrence and Wishart.

———, ed. 1990b. *Nation and narration.* London: Routledge.

Bhachu, Parminder. 1999. Multiple-migrants and multiple diasporas: Cultural reproduction and transformations among British South Asian women in 1990s Britain. In *The expanding landscape: South Asians in the diaspora,* ed. Carla Peteivich. Ann Arbor: Association of Asian Studies Monograph Series, University of Michigan Press.

———. 1995. New cultural forms and transnational South Asian women: Culture, class and consumption among British Asian women in the diaspora. In *Nation and migration,* ed. P. van der Veer. Philadelphia: University of Pennsylvania Press.

———. 1993. Identities constructed and reconstructed: Representations of Asian women in Britain. In *Migrant women: Crossing boundaries and changing identities,* ed. Gina Buijs, 96–114. New York: Berg.

———. 1989. The East African Sikh diaspora: The British case. In *The Sikh diaspora,* ed. N. G. Barrier and V. A. Dusenbery. Delhi: Chanakya Publications.

———. 1985. *Twice migrants: East African Sikh settlers in Britain.* London: Tavistock.

Bhatt, Chetan, and Parita Mukta (guest coeditors). 2000. Hindutva movements in the West: Resurgent Hinduism and the politics of diaspora." *Ethnic and Racial Studies* 23.

Bhattacharjee, Anannya. 1997. The public and private mirage: Mapping homes and undomesticating violence work in the South Asian immigrant community. In *Feminist genealogies, colonial legacies, democratic futures,* ed. M. Jacqui Alexander and Chandra Talpade Mohanty, 308–29. New York: Routledge.

Boddy, J. 1994. Spirit possession revisited: Beyond instrumentality. *Annual Review of Anthropology* 23: 407–34.

Bott, E. 1971 [1957]. *Family and social networks.* London: Tavistock.

Bowen, D. 1981a. The Hindu community in Bradford. In *Hinduism in England,* ed. D. Bowen. Bradford, UK: Bradford College.

———, ed. 1981b. *Hinduism in England.* Bradford, UK: Bradford College.

Brah, A. 1996. *Cartographies of diaspora: Contesting identities.* London: Routledge.

———. 1992. Difference, diversity and differentiation. In "*Race," culture and difference,* ed. A. Rattansi and J. Donald. London: Sage.

Brass, P. 1974. *Language, religion and politics in north India.* Cambridge: Cambridge University Press.

British Council Report. 2000. Looking into England. *British Studies* 13. Also found online http://www.britishcouncil.org/studies/england/report.htm.

Brodkin, K. 2000. Global capitalism: What's race got to do with it? *American Ethnologist* 27: 237–56.

Brubaker, Roger, and Frederick Cooper. 2000. Beyond "Identity." *Theory and Society* 29: 1–47.

Burghart, R., ed. 1987. *Hinduism in Great Britain.* London: Tavistock.

Caglar, A. S. 1997. Hyphenated identities and the limits of "culture." In *The politics of multiculturalism in the New Europe,* ed. Tariq Modood and Pnina Werbner, 169–85. London: Zed Books.

Calhoun, C. J. 1978. History, anthropology and the study of communities: Some problems in Macfarlane's proposal. *Social History* 3: 363–73.

Cannadine, David. 1990. The decline and fall of the British aristocracy. New Haven, Conn.: Yale University Press.

Carey, S. 1987. The Indianization of the Hare Krishna movement in Britain. In *Hinduism in Great Britain,* ed. Richard Burghart. London: Tavistock.

Carrithers, M., and C. Humphrey. 1991. Jains as a community: A position paper. In *The assembly of listeners: Jains in society,* ed. M. Carrithers and C. Humphrey. Cambridge: Cambridge University Press.

Centre for Contemporary Cultural Studies, ed. 1982. *The empire strikes back.* London: Hutchinson.

Chanana, K. 1993. Partition and family strategies gender education linkages among Punjabi women in Delhi. *Economic and Political Weekly* (April): ws25–ws34.

Clarke, C., C. Peach, and S. Vertovec, eds. 1990. *South Asians overseas: Migration and ethnicity.* Cambridge: Cambridge University Press.

Clifford, J. 1997. *Routes.* Cambridge, Mass.: Harvard University Press.

———. 1994. Diasporas. *Cultural Anthropology* 9: 302–38.

———. 1983. On ethnographic authority. *Representations* 1: 118–46.

Cohen, Abner, ed. 1974. *Urban ethnicity.* London: Tavistock.

Cohen, Anthony. 1985. *The symbolic construction of community.* London: Tavistock.

Cohn, B. 1996. *Colonialism and its forms of knowledge.* Princeton, N.J.: Princeton University Press.

———. 1990. *An anthropologist amongst the historians and other essays.* Delhi: Oxford University Press.

Cole, Jefferey. 1997. *The new racism in Europe.* Cambridge: Cambridge University Press.

Collins, Patricia Hill. 1990. *Black feminist thought: Knowledge, consciousness and the politics of empowerment.* London: Unwin Hyman.

Connerton, P. 1995 [1989]. *How societies remember.* Cambridge: Cambridge University Press.

Dahya, B. 1974. The nature of Pakistani ethnicity in industrial cities in Britain. In *Urban ethnicity,* ed. A. Cohen. London: Tavistock.

Danforth, Loring M. 2001. Is the "world game" an "ethnic game" or an "Aussie game"? Narrating the nation in Australian soccer. *American Ethnologist* 28: 363–87.

Darian-Smith, Eve. 1999. *The Channel tunnel and English legal identity in the new Europe.* Berkeley: University of California Press.

Das, Veena. 1995. *Critical events: An athropological perspective on contemporary India.* Delhi: Oxford University Press.

———. 1985. Anthropological knowledge and collective violence: The riots in Delhi, November 1984. *Anthropology Today:* 4–6.

Davis, J. 1994. Marriage and trade in Libya, 1830–1979. Paper presented to the Friday Seminar, University of Cambridge, February 25.

Daye, S. J. 1994. *Middle class blacks in Britain.* London: MacMillan Press.

Desai, R. 1963. *Indian immigrants in Britain.* London: Oxford University Press.

Duffield, M. 1984. New racism, new realism: Two sides of the same coin. *Radical Philosophy* 37.

Dusenberry, V. A. 1995. A Sikh diaspora? Contested identities and constructed realities. In *Nation and migration,* ed. P. van der Veer. Philadelphia: University of Pennsylvania Press.

Dwyer, R. 1994. Caste, religion and sect in Gujarat: Followers of Vallabhacharya and Swaminaryan. In *Desh Pardesh,* ed. R. Ballard. London: C. Hurst and Company.

Eade, John. 2000. *Placing London: From Imperial Capital to Global City.* Oxford: Berghahn Press.

———. 1997. Reconstructing places. In *Living the Global City,* ed. John Eade, 127–45. London: Routledge.

———. 1996. Ethnicity and the politics of cultural difference: An agenda for the 1990s? In *Culture, identity and politics: Ethnic minorities in Britain,* ed. T. Ranger, Y. Samad, and O. Stuart. Aldershot, UK: Avebury.

———. 1994. Identity, nation and religion: Educated young Bangladeshi Muslims in London's "East End." *International Sociology* 9: 377–94.

———. 1989. *The politics of community: The Bangladeshi community in East London.* Aldershot, UK: Avebury.

Eagleton, Terry. 2000. *The idea of culture.* Oxford: Blackwell.

Eberstadt, Nicholas. 2001. The population implosion. *Foreign Policy:* 42–53.

Eck, Diana L. 2000. Negotiating Hindu identities in America. In *The South Asian religious diaspora in Britain, Canada, and the United States,* ed. John R. Hinnells, Harold Coward, and Raymond Brady Williams. Albany: State University of New York Press.

Elliston, Deborah A. 2000. Geographies of gender and politics: The place of difference in polynesian nationalism. *Cultural Anthropology* 15, no. 2: 171–216.

El-Solh, C. F. 1988. Gender, class and origin — Aspects of role during fieldwork in Arab society. In *Arab women in the field: Studying your own society,* ed. S. Altorki and C. F. El-Solh. New York: Syracuse University Press.

Erndl, K. 1993. *Victory to the mother: The Hindu goddess of north west India in myth, ritual and symbol.* New York: Oxford University Press.

Fabian, J. 1983. *Time and the other: How anthropology makes its object.* New York: Columbia University Press.

Ferguson, James. 1999. *Expectations of modernity.* Berkeley: University of California Press.

Ferguson, James, and Akhil Gupta. 1992. Beyond "culture": Space, identity, and the politics of difference. *Cultural Anthropology* 7, no. 1: 6–23.

Firth, Raymond. 1957. Factions in Indian and overseas Indian societies. *British Journal of Sociology* 7: 291–94.

Firth, Shirley. 1996. *Death and bereavement in British South Asian communities.* Unpublished paper.

Fisher, Tracy L. 2001. Shifting ideologies, social transformations: Black women's grassroots organization, Thatcherism, and the flattening of the left in London. In *Anthropology.* New York: City University of New York.

Fox, R. 1985. *Lions of the Punjab: Culture in the making.* Berkeley: University of California Press.

Frankenberg, Ruth, and Lata Mani. 1996. Crosscurrents, crosstalk: race, "postcoloniality" and the politics of location. In *Contemporary postcolonial theory: A reader,* ed. Padmini Mongia. London: Arnold.

Freeman, L. 1968. Marriage without love: Mate selection in non-Western societies. In *Selected studies in marriage and the family*, ed. R. F. Winch and L. W. Goodman. London: Holt, Rinehart and Winston.

Friedman, J. 1994. *Cultural identity and global processes*. London: Sage.

Fryer, P. 1984. *Staying power: The history of black people in Britain*. London: Pluto Press.

Ganguly, Keya. 2001. *States of exception: Everyday life and postcolonial identity*. Minneapolis: University of Minnesota Press.

———. 1992. Migrant identities: Personal memory and the construction of self-hood. *Cultural Studies* 6: 27–50.

Gardner, K., and A. Shukur. 1994. "I'm Bengali, I'm Asian, and I'm living Here": The changing identity of British Bengalis. In *Desh Pardesh: The South Asian presence in Britain*, ed. R. Ballard. London: C. Hurst and Company.

Geertz, C. 1973. Thick description: Toward an interpretive theory of culture. In *The interpretation of cultures*. New York: Harper Collins.

Gell, S. M. S. 1996. The gatekeepers of multiculturalism. *Critique of Anthropology* 16, 325–35.

———. 1994. Legality and ethnicity in marriage among the South Asians of Bedford. *Critique of Anthropology* 14: 355–92.

Gershon, Ilana. 2001. *Making differences cultural: Samoan migrants encounter New Zealand and US governments and families*. Unpublished Ph.D. dissertation. University of Chicago.

Gershon, Ilana, and Dhooleka S. Raj. 2000. Introduction: The symbolic capital of ignorance. *Social Analysis* 44: 3–14.

Ghosh, A. 1992. *In an antique land*. London: Granta Books.

———. 1989. The diaspora in Indian culture. *Public Culture* 2: 73–78.

Gillespie, Marie. 2000. Media culture and economy in the Indian diaspora. In *Culture and economy in the Indian diaspora*. New Delhi: India International Centre. Also http://www.transcomm.ox.ac.uk.

———. 1995. *Television, ethnicity and cultural change*. London: Routledge.

Gilroy, P. 1993. *The black Atlantic*. London: Verso.

———. 1987. *"There ain't no black in the Union Jack": The cultural politics of race and nation*. Chicago: University of Chicago Press.

Glick-Schiller, Nina, Linda Basch, and Cristina Szanton Blanc. 1996. From immigrant to transmigrant: Theorizing transnational migration. *Anthropological Quarterly* 68: 48–63.

Goody, Jack. 1982. *Cooking, cuisine, and class: A study in comparative sociology*. Cambridge: Cambridge University Press.

Gordon, Avery, and Christopher Newfield. 1996. *Mapping multiculturalism*. Minneapolis: University of Minnesota Press.

Green, Sarah F. 1997. *Urban amazons: Lesbian feminism and beyond in the gender, sexuality, and identity battles of London*. New York: St. Martin's Press.

Greenhouse, Carol, and Davyyd Greenwood. 1998. Introduction: the enthography of democracy and difference. In *Democracy and ethnography*, eds. Carol Greenhouse and Roshanak Kheshti. Albany, N.Y.: University of New York Press.

Greenhouse, Carol, with Roshanak Kheshti. 1998. *Democracy and ethnography : Constructing identities in multicultural liberal states.* Albany: State University of New York Press.

Gregory, Steven. 1999. *Black corona.* Princeton, N.J.: Princeton University Press.

Grewal, J. S. 1990. *The Sikhs of the Punjab.* The New Cambridge History of India, vol. 2. Cambridge: Cambridge University Press.

Grillo, R. D. 1985. *Ideologies and institutions in urban France: The representation of immigrants.* Cambridge: Cambridge University Press.

Gupta, A., and J. Ferguson. 1997. *Culture, power, place: Explorations in critical anthropology.* Durham, N.C., and London: Duke University Press.

Habermas, Jurgen. 1994. Struggles for recognition in the democratic constitutional state J. In *Multiculturalism,* ed. Amy Gutmann. Princeton, N.J.: Princeton University Press.

Halbwachs, M. 1980 [1950]. *The collective memory.* Trans. Francis J. Ditter Jr. and Vid Yazdi Ditter. London: Harper and Row.

Hall, Kathleen D. 2002. *Lives in translation : Sikh youth as British citizens.* Philadelphia : University of Pennsylvania Press.

Hall, S. 1991a. The local and the global: Globalization and ethnicity. In *Culture, globalization and the world-system,* ed. A. D. King. Binghampton: Department of Art and Art History, State University of New York at Binghampton.

———. 1991b. Old and new identities, old and new ethnicities. In *Culture, globalization and the world-system,* ed. A. D. King. New York State at Binghamton: Department of Art and History.

———. 1990. Cultural identity and diaspora. In *Identity, community, culture, difference,* ed. J. Rutherford. London: Lawrence and Wishart.

Handler, Richard. 1994. Is "Identity" a useful cross-cultural concept? In *Commemorations: The politics of national identity,* ed. John Gillis, 28–40. Princeton, N.J.: Princeton University Press.

———. 1985. On dialogue and destructive analysis: Problems in narrating nationalism and ethnicity. *Journal of Anthropological Research* 41: 171–82.

Hannerz, Ulf. 1996. *Transnational connections: Culture, people, places.* London: Routledge.

———. 1989. Culture between centre and periphery. *Ethnos* 54: 200–16.

———. 1987. The world in creolization. *Africa* 57: 546–59.

———. 1980. *Exploring the city: Inquiries towards an urban anthropology.* New York: Columbia University Press.

Harding, P., and R. Jenkins. 1989. *The myth of the hidden economy.* Milton Keynes, UK: Open University Press.

Harris, Clive. 2001. Beyond multiculturalism? Difference, recognition and social justice. *Patterns of Prejudice* 35, no. 1.

Harrison, Faye V. 1995. The persistent power of "race" in the cultural and political economy of racism. *Annual Review of Anthropology* 24: 47–74.

Hazareesingh, S. 1986. Racism and cultural identity: An Indian perspective. *Dragon's Teeth* 24.

Helweg, Arthur. 1989 [1978]. *Sikhs in England.* Delhi: Oxford University Press.

Helweg, Arthur, and Usha Helweg. 1990. *An immigrant success story: East Indians in America*. Philadelphia: University of Pennsylvania Press.

Hershmann, P. 1981. *Punjabi kinship and marriage*. Delhi: Hindustan Publishing Corporation.

Hinnells, J. R. 1994. Parsi Zoroastrians in London. In *Desh Pardesh: The South Asian presence in Britain*, ed. R. Ballard. London: C. Hurst and Company.

Hiro, D. 1991. *Black British, white British: A history of race relations in Britain*. London: Grafton Books.

Hitchens, Peter. 2000. *The abolition of Britain*. San Francisco: Encounter Books.

Holland, Dorothy, William Lachicotte, Debra Skinner, and Carole Cain. 1998. *Identity and agency in cultural worlds*. Cambridge, Mass.: Harvard University Press.

Holmes, C. 1988. *John Bull's island*. London: Macmillan.

Howarth, S. 1980. *The Koh-i-Noor diamond*. London: Quartet Books.

Humphery, Caroline, and J. Laidlaw. 1994. *The archetypal actions of ritual*. Oxford: Clarendon Press.

Hutnyk, John. 2000. *Critique of exotica*. London: Pluto Press.

Hutnyk, John, and Sanjay Sharma. 2000. Music and politics–Introduction to special issue. *Theory, Culture and Society* 17: 55–63.

Ibbetson, D. 1911. *A glossary of the tribes and castes of the Punjab and north-west frontier province*. Lahore: Punjab Government Publications (Civil and Military Gazette Press).

———. 1883. *Outlines of Punjab ethnography being extracts from Punjab census report of 1881. Treating of religion, language and caste*. Calcutta: Government of India.

Jackson, R. 1987. Changing conceptions of Hinduism in "timetabled religion." In *Hinduism in Great Britain*, ed. R. Burghart. London: Tavistock.

Jackson, R., and Eleanor Nesbitt. 1992. *Hindu children in Britain*. London: Trentham.

James, A. 1974. *Sikh children in Britain*. Oxford: Oxford University Press.

Jeffrey, P. 1976. *Migrants and refugees: Muslim and Christian Pakistani families in Bristol*. Cambridge: Cambridge University Press.

Jones, D. J. 1970. Towards a native anthropology. *Human Organisation* 29: 251–59.

Jones, K. 1976. *Arya dharm Hindu consciousness in 19th-century Punjab*. London: University of California Press.

Jones, T. 1993. *Britain's ethnic minorities*. London: Policy Studies Institute.

Juergensmeyer, M. 1982. *Religion as social vision: The movement against untouchability in the 20th century*. London: University of California Press.

———. 1979. The Ghadar syndrome: Nationalism in an immigrant community. *Punjab Journal of Politics* 1: 1–22.

Kahlon, Raminder, and Virinder Singh Kalra. 1994. *From Br-Asian to Transl-Asian: Rearticulation global and local identities in relation to musical cultural production*. Paper presented to Punjab Research Group Meeting.

Kalra, Virinder S. 2000. *From textile mills to taxi ranks: Experiences of migration, labour and social change*. Aldershot, UK: Ashgate.

Kelly, E. 1990. Transcontinental families-Gujarat and Lancashire: A comparative study. In *South Asians Overseas,* ed. C. Clark, C. Peach, and S. Vertovec. Cambridge: Cambridge University Press.

Kelly, John D. 1995. Bhakti and postcolonial politics: Hindu missions to Fiji. In *Nation and migration,* ed. P. van der Veer. Philadelphia: University of Pennsylvania Press.

Kelly, John D., and Martha Kaplan. 2001. *Represented communities: Fiji and world decolonization.* Chicago: University of Chicago Press.

Khan, A. 1994. *Juthaa* in Trinidad: Food, pollution and hierarchy in a Caribbean diaspora community. *American Ethnologist* 21: 245–69.

Khosla, G. D. 1989 [1949]. *Stern reckoning: A survey of the events leading up to and following the partition of India.* Delhi: Oxford University Press.

King, Deborah K. 1988. Multiple jeopardy, multiple consciousness: The context of a black feminist ideology. *Signs: Journal of Women in Culture and Society* 14: 42–72.

Kirshenblatt-Gimblett, B. 1994. Spaces of dispersal. *Cultural Anthropology* 9: 339–44.

Knott, K. 1987. Hindu temple rituals in Britain: The reinterpretation of tradition. In *Hinduism in Great Britain,* ed. R. Burghart. London: Tavistock.

Kukathas, Chandran. 1997. Liberalism, multiculturalism and oppression. In *Political theory: Tradition and diversity,* ed. Andrew Vincent, 132–53. Cambridge: Cambridge University Press.

Kumar, N. 1992. *Friends, brothers and informants: Fieldwork memoirs of Banaras.* Berkeley: University of California Press.

Kundu, A. 2002. Personal communication via e-mail, August 15. Full reference with author.

———. 1994. The Ayodhya aftermath: Hindu versus Muslim violence in Britain. *Immigrants and Minorities* 13: 26–47.

Lal, Vinay. 1999. Establishing roots, engendering awareness: A political history of Asian Indians in the United States. In *Live like the banyan tree: Images of the Indian American experience,* ed. Leela Prasad, 42–48. Philadelphia: Balch Institute for Ethnic Studies.

Lambek, M., and P. Antze. 1996. *Tense past: Cultural essays in trauma and memory.* New York: Routledge.

Lavie, Smadar, and Ted Swedenburg, eds. 1996. *Displacement, diaspora, and geographies of identity.* Durham, N.C., and London: Duke University Press.

Lawrence, E. 1982a. In the abundance of water the fool is thirsty: Sociology and black "pathology." In *The empire strikes back,* ed. CCCS. London: Hutchinson.

———. 1982b. Just plain common sense: The "roots" of racism. In *The empire strikes back,* ed. CCCS. London: Hutchinson.

Leonard, Karen Isaksen. 1997. *The South Asian Americans.* Westport, Conn.: Greenwood Press.

———. 1992. *Making ethnic choices: California's Punjabi Mexican Americans.* Philadelphia: Temple University Press.

Lessinger, Johanna. 1995. From the Ganges to the Hudson: Indian immigrants in New York City. Boston: Allyn and Bacon.

———. 1992. Nonresident-Indian investment and India's drive for industrial modernization. In *Anthropology and the global factory: Studies of the new industrialization in the late twentieth century,* ed. F. A. Rothstein and M. L. Blimm. New York: Bergin ands Garvey.

Levine, N., and T. Nayar. 1975. Modes of adaptation by Asian immigrants in Slough. *New Community* 4: 356–65.

Lewis, I. 1991. *Sahibs, Nabobs and Boxwallahs — Dictionary of the words of Anglo-India.* Bombay: Oxford University Press.

Lewis, O. 1958. *Village life in northern India.* Urbana: University of Illinois Press.

Little, K. 1974. *Urbanization as a social process.* London: Routledge, Kegan, Paul.

Louie, Andrea. 2000. Re-territorializing transnationalism: Chinese Americans and the Chinese motherland. *American Ethnologist* 27, no. 3:645–69.

Lowe, Lisa. 1996. *Immigrant acts: On Asian American cultural politics.* Durham, N.C., and London: Duke University Press.

Lyon, M., B. Lyon, and J. West. 1995. London patels: Caste and commerce. *New Community* 21: 399–420.

Macdonald, Sharon, ed. 1993. *Inside European identities: Ethnography in Western Europe.* Oxford: Berg.

Macfarlane, A. 1977. History, anthropology and the study of communities. *Social History* 2: 631–52.

Mahmood, C. K. 1996. *Fighting for faith and nation: Dialogues with Sikh militants.* Philadelphia: University of Pennsylvania Press

Mahmood, Cynthia, and Stacy Brady. 2000. *The guru's gift: An ethnography exploring gender and equality with North American Sikh women.* Mountain View, Calif.: Mayfield Publishing Company.

Maira, Sunaina Marr. 2002. *Desis in the house: Indian American youth culture in New York City.* Philadelphia, Pa.: Temple University Press.

———. 1999. Identity dub: The paradoxes of an Indian American youth subculture. *Cultural Anthropology* 14: 29–60.

Malik, K. 1996. *The meaning of race: Race, history and culture in western society.* London: Macmillan.

Mankekar, Purnima. 1999. *Screening culture, viewing politics: An ethnography of television, womanhood, and nation in postcolonial India.* Durham, N.C.: Duke University Press.

———. 1994. Reflections on diasporic identities: A prolegomenon to an analysis of political bifocality. *Diaspora* 3: 349–71.

Mann, Gurinder Singh. 2000. Sikhism in the United States of America. In *The South Asian Religious Diaspora in Britain, Canada, and the United States,* ed. Harold Coward, John R. Hinnells, and Raymond Brady Williams. Albany: State University of New York Press.

Marcus, G. 1989. Imagining the whole: Ethnography's contemporary efforts to situate itself. *Critique of Anthropology* 9: 7–30.

Marcus, G., and J. Clifford, eds. 1986. *Writing culture*. Berkeley: University of California Press.

Marr, A. 2000. *The day Britain died*. London: Profile Books.

McDonald, Merryle. 1987. Rituals of motherhood among Gujarati women in East London. *Hinduism in Great Britain*, ed. R. Burghart. London: Tavistock.

McLeod, W. H. 1989. *Is a Sikh the problem of Sikh identity?* Oxford: Oxford University Press.

Memon, M. U. 1980. Partition literature: A study of Intizar Husain. *Modern Asian Studies* 14: 377–410.

Menon, Ramdas. 1989. Arranged marriages among South Asian immigrants. *Sociology and Social Research* 73, no. 4: 180–81.

Menon, Ramdas, and K. Bhasin. 1993. Recovery, rupture, resistance in the Indian state and abduction of women during partition. *Economic and Political Weekly* (April): ws2 – ws11.

Menski, W. 1987. Legal pluralism and the Hindu marriage. In *Hinduism in Great Britain*, ed. R. Burghart. London: Tavistock.

Merleau-Ponty, Maurice. 1973. *Adventures of the dialectic*. Trans. Joseph Bien. Evanston, Ill.: Northwestern University Press.

Messerchmidt, D., ed. 1981. *Anthropologists at home in North America*. Cambridge: Cambridge University Press.

Minow, Martha. 1990. *Making all the difference: Inclusion, exclusion, and American law*. Ithaca, N.Y.: Cornell University Press.

Modood, Tariq. 1992. *Not easy being British*. London: Trentham.

———. 1988. "Black," racial equality and Asian identity. *New Community* 14: 397–404.

Modood, Tariq, and Pnina Werbner, eds. 1997. *The politics of multiculturalism in the new Europe: Racism, identity and community*. London: Zed Books.

Mohanty, Chandra Talpade. 1998. Feminist encounters: Locating the politics of experience. In *Feminism and politics*, ed. Anne Phillips. Oxford: Oxford University Press.

———. 1997. Defining genealogies: Feminist reflections on being South Asian in North America. In *Making more waves*, ed. Elaine H. Kim, Lilia V. Villanueva, and the Asian Women United of California, 119–27. Boston: Beacon Press.

Mohapatra, Prabhu. 1996. Longing and belonging: The dilemma of return among Indian emigrants to the West Indies 1880–1940. In *South Asian studies seminar*. Centre of South Asian Studies, University of Cambridge.

Morgan, Kenneth O. 1999. The twentieth century (1914–1918). In *The Oxford history of Britain*. Oxford: Oxford University Press.

Morley, D., and K.-H. Chen, eds. 1996. *Stuart Hall: Critical dialogues in cultural studies*. London: Routledge.

Morris, H. S. 1957. Communal rivalry among Indians in Uganda. *British Journal of Sociology* 7: 301–7.

Morsy, S. 1988. Fieldwork in my Egyptian homeland: Toward the demise of anthropology's distinctive-other hegemonic tradition. In *Arab women in the field: Studying your own society,* ed. S. Altorki and C. F. El-Solh. New York: Syracuse University Press.

Nakhleh, K. 1979. On being a native anthropologist. In *The politics of anthropology from colonialism and sexism toward a view from below,* ed. G. Huizer and B. Mannheim. The Hague: Mouton.

Narayan, K. 1989. *Storytellers, saints and scoundrels.* Philadelphia: University of Pennsylvania Press.

Nash, J. 1979. *We eat the mines and the mines eat us: Dependency and exploitation in Bolivian tin mines.* New York: Columbia University Press.

Nesbitt, Eleanor. 1998a. Being religious shows in your food: Young British Hindus and vegetarianism. In *International conference on Hindu diaspora,* ed. T. S. Rukmani. Montreal, Canada: Concordia University Press.

——. 1998b. British, Asian and Hindu: Identity, self-narration and the ethnographic interview. *Journal of Beliefs and Values.*

——. 1998c. The impact of Morari Bapu's Kathas on Britain's Young Hindus. In *Youth and youthfulness in the Hindu tradition,* ed. J. Lipner. Calgary, Canada: Bayeux Arts.

——. 1995a. Celebrating and learning: The perpetuation of values and practices among Hindu Punjabi children in Coventry, UK. *Indo-British Review* 20: 221–40.

——. 1995b. Punjabis in Britain: Cultural history and cultural choices. *South Asia Research* 15: 221–40.

——. 1994. Celebrating and learning in community: The perpetuation of values and practices among Hindu Punjabi children in Coventry, UK. *Indo-British Review* 20: 119–31.

——. 1991. *"My dad's Hindu, my mum's side are Sikhs": Issues in religious identity.* University of Warwick Paper published by NFAS and University of Warwick.

Newham Monitoring Project. 1991. *The forging of a black community.* London: Institute of Race Relations.

Nye, M. 1996. The Iskonisation of British Hinduisms. Unpublished paper.

——. 1993. A place for our gods: Tradition and change among Hindus in Edinburgh. In *Religion and ethnicity: Minorities and social change in the metropolis,* ed. R. Barot. Kamper, The Netherlands: Pharos.

Oberoi, H. 1994. *The construction of religious boundaries.* Delhi: Oxford University Press.

Ong, Aiwa. 1999. *Flexible citizenship.* Durham, N.C.: Duke University Press.

——. 1996. Cultural citizenship as subject making. *Current Anthropology* 37, no. 5: 737–62.

Pandey, G. 1992. In defence of the fragment: Writing about Hindu Muslim riots in India today. *Representations* 37: 27–55.

——. 1990. *The construction of communalism in colonial North India.* Delhi: Oxford University Press.

Parekh, Bhikhu. 1996. The Indian diaspora and its conception of home. In *The longing for home,* ed. Leroy S. Rouner, 230–42. Notre Dame: University of Notre Dame Press.

———. 1992. India: A million mutinies now (book review). *Contemporary South Asia* 1: 147–59.

Parmar, P. 1982. Gender, race and class: Asian women in resistance. In *The empire strikes back,* ed. Centre for Contemporary Cultural Studies. London: Hutchinson.

Pocock, D. 1976. Preservation of the religious life: Hindu immigrants in England. *Contributions to Indian Sociology* 10: 342–65.

Poulter, S. 1990. *Asian traditions and English law.* Stoke-on Trent, UK: Trentham Books.

Prashad, Vijay. 2000. *The karma of brown folk.* Minnesota: University of Minnesota Press.

Pratt, M. L. 1986. Fieldwork in common places. In *Writing culture,* ed. G. Marcus and J. Clifford. Berkeley and Los Angeles: University of California Press.

Puri, H. K. 1993. *Ghadar movement: Ideology, organisation and strategy.* Amritsar, India: Guru Nanak Dev University Press.

Raban, J. 1974. *Soft city.* London: Hamish Hamilton.

Radhakrishnan, Rajagopalan. 1996. *Diasporic mediations.* Minneapolis: University of Minnesota Press.

Raj, Dhooleka S. 2000. "Who the hell do you think you are?" Promoting religious identity among young Hindus in Britain. *Ethnic and Racial Studies* 23: 135–58.

———. 1997. Partition and diaspora: Memories and identities of Punjabi Hindus in London. *International Journal of Punjab Studies* 4: 101–27.

Rangaswamy, Padma. 2000. *Namaste America: Indian immigrants in an American metropolis.* University Park: Pennsylvania State University Press.

Rapport, Nigel. 2000. COMMENT–on the new anthropology of Britain. *Anthropology Today* 16.

Rattansi, A. 2000. On being and not being brown/black-British: Racism, class, sexuality and ethnicity in post-imperial Britain. *Interventions: International Journal of Postcolonial Studies* 2: 118–34.

Robb, P., ed. 1995. *The concept of race in South Asia.* Oxford: Oxford University Press.

Robinson, V. 1988. The new Indian middle class in Britain. *Ethnic and Racial Studies* 11: 456–73.

———. 1981. The development of south Asian settlement in Britain and the myth of return. *In Ethnic segregation in cities,* eds., C. Peach, V. Robinson, and S. Smith. London: Croon Helm.

Rodman, Margaret C. 1992. Empowering place: Multilocality and multivocality. *American Anthropologist* 94: 640–56.

Rosaldo, Renato. 1999. Cultural citizenship, inequality and multiculturalism. In *Race, identity and citizenship,* ed. Louis Miron Rodolfo Torres and Jonathan Xavier Inda, 253–61. Malden, Mass.: Blackwell.

Rouse, R. 1991. Mexican migration and the social space of postmodernism. *Diaspora* 1: 8–23.

Runnymede Trust–Commission on the Future of Multi-Ethnic Britain. 2000. *"The future of multi-ethnic Britain": Report of the Commission on the Future of Multi-Ethnic Britain / chair, Bhikhu Parekh.* London: Profile Books.

Rushdie, Salman. 1991. Imaginary homelands. In *Imaginary homelands: Essays and criticism,* 9–21. London: Granta Books.

Sachdev, I. 1995. Predicting Punjabi linguistic identity. *International Journal of Punjab Studies* 2.

Safran, W. 1991. Diasporas in modern societies: Myths of homeland and return. *Diaspora* 1: 83–99.

Saifullah-Khan, V. 1977. The Pakistanis: Mirpuri villages at home and in Bradford. In *Between two cultures,* ed. J. L.Watson. Oxford: Blackwell.

Samad, Yunas. 1997. The plural guises of multiculturalism: Conceptualizing a fragmented paradigm. In *Politics of multiculturalism,* ed. Tariq Modood and Pnina Werbner. London: Zed Books.

Samuel, R., and P. Thompson, eds. 1990. *The myths we live by.* London: Routledge.

Sassen, Saskia. 1999. Spatialities and temporalities of the global: Elements for a theorization. *Public Culture: Society for Transnational Cultural Studies* 12: 215–32.

Schlesinger, Arthur. 1992. *The disuniting of America: Reflections on a multicultural society.* New York: W. W. Norton.

Schuster, Liza, and John Solomos. 2001. New perspectives on multiculturalism and citizenship: Citizenship, multiculturalism, identity. *Patterns of Prejudice* 35, no. 1: 3–12.

Shami, S. 1988. Studying your own — The complexities of a shared culture. In *Arab women in the field: Studying your own society,* ed. S. Altorki and C. F. El-Solh. New York: Syracuse University Press.

Sharma, S., J. Hutnyk, and A. Sharma, eds. 1996. *Dis-orienting rhythms : The politics of the new Asian dance music.* London: Zed Books.

Shaw, A. 1988. *A Pakistani community in Britain.* London: Blackwell Books.\

Shukla, Sandhya. 2001. Locations for South Asian diasporas. *Annual Review of Anthropology* 30: 551–72.

———. 1997. Building diaspora and nation: The 1991 "cultural festival of India." *Cultural Studies* 11: 296–315.

Singh, Madanjeet. 1989. *This, My people.* New York: Rizzoli International.

Singh, Raminder. 1992. *Immigrants to citizens: The Sikh community in Bradford.* Bradford, UK: The Race Relations Research Unit, Ilkley Community College.

Siu, Lok. 2001. Diasporic cultural citizenship: Chineseness and belonging in Central America and Panama. *Social Text* 69: 7–28.

———. Forthcoming. *Memories of a future home: Transnational belonging for Chinese in Panama.*

Sivanandan, A. 1990. *Communities of resistance.* London: Verso.

———. 1988. The new racism. *New Statesman and Society* 1, no. 22: 8–9.

Smith, Michael Peter, and Luis Eduardo Guarnizo. 1998. *Transnationalism from below*. New Brunswick, N.J.: Transaction.

Sokefeld, M. 1999. Debating self, identity, and culture in anthropology (in debating identity). *Current Anthropology* 40, no. 4: 417–47.

Solomos, J. 1991. Political language and racial discourse. *European Journal of Intercultural Studies* 2: 21–34.

Srikanth, Rajni, and Sunaina Maira, eds. 1996. *Contours of the heart: South Asians map North America*. New York: Asian American Workshop.

Srinivasan, S. 1992. The class position of the Asian petty bourgeoisie. *New Community* 19: 61–74.

Stolcke, V. 1995. Talking culture: New boundaries, new rhetorics of exclusion in Europe. *Current Anthropology* 36: 1–13.

Strathern, Marilyn. 1997. From improvement to enhancement. *Cambridge Anthropology* 9: 1–21.

Strathern, Marilyn, ed. 1995a. *Shifting contexts: Transformations in anthropological knowledge*. London: Routledge.

———. 1995b. The nice thing about culture is that everyone has it. In *Shifting contexts: Transformations in anthropological knowledge,* ed. Marilyn Strathern. London: Routledge.

———. 1987. The limits of auto-anthropology. In *Anthropology at home,* ed. A. Jackson. London: Tavistock.

Tabili, L. 1994. The construction of racial difference in twentieth-century Britain: The special restriction (coloured alien seamen) order, 1925. *Journal of British Studies* 33: 54–98.

Talai, V. 1986. Social boundaries within and between ethnic groups: Armenians in London. *Man, New Series* 21: 251–70.

Tambs-Lyche, H. 1980. *London Patidars: A case study in urban ethnicity*. London: Routledge and Kegan Paul.

Tatla, D. S. 1995. Sikh free and military migration during the colonial period. *Cambridge Survey of World Migration,* ed. R. Cohen. Cambridge: Cambridge University Press.

Taussig, M. 1980. *The devil and commodity fetishism in South America*. Chapel Hill: University of North Carolina Press.

Taylor, Charles. 1994. The politics of recognition. In *Multiculturalism,* ed. Amy Gutmann. Princeton, N.J.: Princeton University Press.

Taylor, J. H. 1976. *The half way generation*. Newcastle, UK: NFER.

Thapar, R. 2000. On historical scholarship and the uses of the past. *Ethnic and Racial Studies* 23: 594–616.

———. 1989. Imagined religious communities? Ancient history and the modern search for a Hindu identity. *Modern Asian Studies* 23: 209–31.

Tinker, Hugh. 1977. *The banyan tree: Overseas emigrants from India, Pakistan, and Bangladesh*. New York: Oxford University Press.

Tölölyan, K. 1991. The nation-state and its others: In lieu of a preface. *Diaspora* 1: 3–7.

Toren, C. 1994. Cannibalism and compassion: Transformation in Fijian concepts of the person. Paper presented to the Friday Seminar, University of Cambridge.

Toulis, N. 1994. Belief and identity: Pentecostalism among first generation Jamaican women in England. Unpublished Ph.D. dissertation, University of Cambridge.

Van der Veer, P., ed. 1995. *Nation and migration*. Philadelphia: University of Pennsylvania Press.

Vansittart, Peter. 1998. *In memory of England*. London: John Murray.

Vatuk, S. 1972. *Kinship and urbanization*. London: University of California Press.

Vertovec, Steven. 2000. *The Hindu diaspora*. London: Routledge.

——. 1999. Conceiving and researching transnationalism. *Ethnic and Racial Studies* 22 (2): 447–62.

——. 1996. On the reproduction and representation of Hinduism in Britain. In *Culture, identity and politics: Ethnic minorities in Britain*, ed. T. Ranger, Y. Samad, and O. Stuart. Aldershot, UK: Avebury.

——. 1992. Community and congregation in London Hindu temples: Divergent trends. *New Community* 18: 251–64.

——. 1990. Religion and ethnic ideology: the Hindu youth movement in Trinidad. *Ethnic and racial studies* 13: 225{-}49.

Visram, R. 1986. *Ayahs, lascars, and princes: The story of Indians in Britain 1700–1947*. London: Pluto Press.

Wallerstein, Immanuel. 1990. Culture as the ideological battleground of the modern world-system. *Theory, Culture and Society* 7: 31–55.

Wallman, S. 1979. Introduction: The scope for ethnicity. In *Ethnicity at work*, ed. S. Wallman. London: Macmillan.

——. 1978. The boundaries of "race": Processes of ethnicity in England. *Man, New Series* 13: 200–17.

Watson, J., ed. 1977. *Between two cultures*. Oxford: Blackwell.

Weber, Max. 1958. *The religion of India*. Trans. Hans H. Gerth Don Martindale. Glencoe, Ill.: Free Press.

Weller, P. 1993. *Religions in the UK*. Derby, UK: University of Derby.

Werbner, Pnina. 1997. Afterword: Writing multiculturalism and politics in the new Europe. In *The politics of multiculturalism in the new Europe: Racism, identity and community*, ed. Tariq Modood and Pnina Werbner. London: Zed.

——. 1996a. Essentialising the other: A critical response. In *Culture, identity and politics: Ethnic minorities in Britain*, ed. T. Ranger, Y. Samad, and O. Stuart. Aldershot, UK: Avebury.

——. 1996b. Fun spaces: On identity and social empowerment among British Pakistanis. *Theory, Culture and Society* 13, no. 4: 53–79.

——. 1995. Critique or caricature? A response to Wilcken and Gell. *Critique of Anthropology* 15: 425–32.

—— 1990a. Manchester Pakistanis: Division and unity. In *South Asians overseas*, ed. C. Clark, C. Peach, and S. Vertovec. Cambridge: Cambridge University Press.

———. 1990b. *The migration process: Capital, gifts, and offerings among British Pakistanis.* New York: St. Martin's Press.

———. 1987. Barefoot in Britain: Anthropological research on Asian immigrants. *New Community* XIV: 176–81.

Werbner, Pnina, and M. Anwar, eds. 1991. *Black and ethnic leadership in Britain.* London: Routledge.

Werbner, Pnina, and Tariq Modood, eds. 1997. *Debating cultural hybridity.* London: Zed Books.

Werbner, Richard. 1998. Beyond oblivion: Confronting memory crisis. In *Memory and the postcolony,* ed. Richard Werbner, 1–20. London: Zed Books.

Westwood, S. 1984. *All day, every day: Factory and family in the making of women's lives.* London: Pluto Press.

Williams, Brackette. 1989. A class act: Anthropology and the race to nation across ethnic terrain. *Annual Review Anthropology* 18: 401–44.

Williams, Raymond. 1988. *Religions of immigrants from India and Pakistan.* Cambridge: Cambridge University Press.

Yong, T. 1997. "Sir Cyril goes to India": Partition, boundary-making and disruption in the Punjab. *International Journal of Punjab Studies* 4: 1–20.

Young, C. 1983. The temple of ethnicity. *World Politics* 35: 652–62.

Young, Iris Marion. 1990. *Justice and the politics of difference.* Princeton, N.J.: Princeton University Press.

Yuval-Davis, Nira, and Floya Anthias. 1992. *Racialized boundaries.* London: Routledge.

———, eds. 1989. *Woman, nation, state.* New York: St. Martin's Press.

Index

Compositor: BookMatters
Text: 10/13 Galliard
Display: Galliard
Printer: Edwards Brothers
Binder: Edwards Brothers